# BETRAYAL

The shattering sex discrimination case of
Silver vs Pacific Press Publishing Association

Merikay McLeod

MARS HILL PUBLICATIONS, INC.

Dedicated to
my friend Joan Kurt Bradford —
a women who not only believes in justice
but sacrifices to see it accomplished.

Library of Congress Cataloging in Publication Data

McLeod, Merikay, 1946-
  Betrayal: the shattering sex discrimination case of Silver vs.
Pacific Press Publishing Association.

  Includes index.
    1. McLeod, Merikay, 1946-      . 2. Pacific Press Publishing
Association.    3. Sex discrimination in employment —
California. 4. Equal pay for equal work — California. 5.
Employee fringe benefits — California.
I. Title.
HD6060.5.U52C26    1985          331.4′133          84-62638
ISBN 0-9614230-0-5

Printed in the United States of America
Library of Congress Catalog Card Number: 84-62638
ISBN: 0-9614230-0-5


MARS HILL PUBLICATIONS, INC.
P.O. Box 362
Loma Linda, California 92354

10 9 8 7 6 5 4 3 2 1

# Contents

## Before

## During

## After

# Before

*The willingness to surrender one's independence,
to barter the evidence of one's senses
for the comfortable but reality-distorting satisfaction
of feeling in harmony with a group
is, of course, the stuff on which
demagogues and dictators thrive.*

Paul Watzlawick
*How Real is Real?*

# 1971

EVERY NOW AND THEN SOMEBODY GETS A CHANCE TO MAKE a difference. Those who face the opportunity aren't necessarily any better or more gifted than anyone else. They just happen to be in the right place at a crucial moment.

Pacific Press Publishing Association in Mountain View, California, gave me the opportunity to make a significant difference.

Owned and operated by Seventh-day Adventists, Pacific Press publishes books, magazines, and pamphlets on religious and health topics for adults and many storybooks for children as well.

Until I went to work at the Press, my life within the church community had been rich, comforting, full of love and acceptance. But I asked a question which was to change everything.

In 1972, after nearly a year as an assistant book editor at Pacific Press, I asked my employer for equal pay. It was an honest request, made in the simplicity of trust. I truly believed my fair petition would be granted. I had a lot to learn.

My request shattered the peaceful world I'd known. The years between 1972 and 1975 were dizzying, exhilarating, and exhausting. They brought out the best and the worst in the people I knew. And they accelerated and intensified my own growth. They propelled me to the extremes of all my emotions. There is no way those years could have done more to me and still have left me breathing.

This is my story of those years — my experience gleaned

from diaries, letters, documents, memory. It is the story of change — and the incredible resistance people and institutions will mount to fight change.

In the mid-1800s when eager young idealists formed the Seventh-day Adventist church, it might have been called a cult or sect. By the 1970s, however — with more than two million members world wide — the Adventist church had become a full-grown fundamentalist Christian denomination persuaded that its precepts are central to world history.

Adventists worship on Saturday.

Adventists believe that the literal second coming of Jesus Christ is very near, and that just prior to His return the world will suffer a "time of trouble" worse than any other ever known.

Adventists believe that the spiritual crisis of this time of trouble will force every person to choose between worshiping on the seventh-day Bible Sabbath (Saturday) or the pagan and papal Sabbath (Sunday).

Many Adventists believe that the U.S. government will support the Sunday-worship movement by enacting a national Sunday law, that will exact a death penalty for those who worship on Saturday. A deeply ingrained fear of government persecution is part of the Adventist mindset.

The person most responsible for founding Adventism is Ellen G. White. Ellen established schools and hospitals and, with her husband James, expanded the church's publishing work. But more important, Ellen White is revered by many Adventists as a genuine prophet. Her visions helped solidify Adventist doctrine and give firm, authoritative direction to the fledgling church. Through approximately seventy-five bound volumes and hundreds of articles, Ellen White wrote detailed instructions for the members of her denomination.

Although church leaders in her day sometimes ignored her words, once she died they quoted her writings selectively throughout the world field to ensure conformity to church doctrines and traditions. Adventists refer to her writings as "the Spirit of Prophecy."

When I attended church-sponsored high school (Grand Ledge Academy in Michigan) in the mid-1960s, Ellen White's word was law. "Mrs. White says" preceded demands, requests, and threats. "Mrs. White says" was often the only explanation needed for a belief or opinion.

While I was a junior at Grand Ledge Academy, my classmates and I studied Ellen White's *The Great Controversy*. This book is about the struggle between good and evil. It begins with the war in heaven when Satan was cast out, proceeds through the spiritually tumultuous history of the human race, and projects the violent end of this world — complete with Sunday law and death decree. The book culminates in the victorious second advent and the reward of eternal life for those who worship on the Bible Sabbath.

For one semester we studied *The Great Controversy*. The drama, action, courage, and the victory inherent in the time of trouble scenario captured my imagination. Near the end of the semester when our teacher asked us to write a story about the time of trouble, I was thrilled. I hurried back to my dorm room and began writing. Within two days I had completed the forty-five page story *NOW!*

Basing it on Ellen White's descriptions and Daniel 12:1 -"... and there shall be a time of trouble such as never was since there was a nation, even to that same time; and at that time thy people shall be delivered ...," I wrote an imaginative, personalized account of the period.

My story took a teenage sister and brother through the terror-filled time, up to the second coming. In one of the jail scenes, I wrote:

> The hours passed. The guard came by and gave us all some watery vegetable soup. After dishing us all a bowl, he sneered, "Just four more hours."
> All of us knew what he meant. It was 8:00, just four hours from the time when the Death Law went into effect.
> "Don't you guys care about your families?" he went on in a derogatory tone. "Can't you see that they are going to be persecuted because of you? I never could understand how people could break the law. It's the ones back home who suffer."

The words hurt. I wondered if people were being mean to Mom and Dad because of me.

"And besides, what gives you the idea you're so almighty holy? Look, everybody else goes along with this law. Just who do you think you are to say no to God?" he shook his head in disgust. "People like you are crazy. When an animal is crazy it is shot." He walked away, leaving the unspoken words hanging thick before the bars of our cell.

*NOW!* captured the imagination of my classmates. In personalizing the theory we'd been studying, I'd made it real to them. They retyped and mimeographed copies of *NOW!* Soon students at other academies also duplicated it. Thousands of Adventists all over the country read it, shared it, and used it for various religious gatherings.

Evangelist Fordyce Detamore published a condensed version. Within five years it sold more than 100,000 copies. The royalties he paid me helped with school expenses.

It was through *NOW!* that I met my husband, Kim Silver. Kim read it in Seattle, was deeply moved, and wrote to me. I'd received many letters because of the story, but Kim wrote back again and again and finally telephoned. Later, when I met him in person, we began a friendship which eventually led to marriage.

I believe *NOW!* also led to my employment at Pacific Press. While a freshman at Andrews University in Michigan, I read *NOW!* for a religious service. Following the service, Max Phillips, a columnist for the student newspaper, offered to let me write a guest column. That was the beginning of our friendship.

Later when Max was working at Pacific Press, he phoned to say there was an opening for an assistant book editor and he hoped I'd want the job. Asking if I'd be interested was like asking someone with an incurable sweet tooth if a job as taste tester in a candy factory sounded interesting.

The moment I knew such a position was available I wanted it more than I'd ever wanted anything. I felt that being a religious book editor would be the culmination of all my loves — my love of books, my love of writing, my love for God and Jesus and the church.

I dedicated my life to Christ when I was a teenager and

for years had longed to play a more active role in the great mission of the "remnant" church. The Pacific Press job seemed to offer me that possibility.

I'd already been freelancing for several years and had been published scores of times in newspapers and religious journals. But Max said it was my story *NOW!* that Press officials knew. *NOW!* impressed them with my writing ability and my spiritual earnestness.

Thirty-three candidates were being considerd for the position. Most of them were college graduates; one had a Ph.D. Yet none had been published as often as I.

For weeks I hoped and prayed that I would be chosen, although I suffered keen self-doubt. I had not yet completed my B.A. degree (a lack I was sure would deny me the position), and I felt that only the most spiritually advanced people were "called" to work for God's church. Although sincere and idealistic, I did not consider myself spiritually advanced.

When I finally received word that the position was mine, I was nearly ecstatic. At last I could really serve the Truth I loved.

When I timidly asked about wages, I was not answered with a firm dollar amount. I knew that people don't enter denominational employment expecting to be paid at the same rate they could earn in industry. There are other more idealistic magnets that draw one to "the work."

However, I assumed that I would receive a paycheck close to that received by the assistant editor whom I was replacing. The woman I was replacing had earned approximately $600 per month. I did not press the paycheck issue. Money was not vital to me. I was certain the Press would be more than fair in taking care of its own.

Although circumstances changed my attitude, in the beginning income was my last concern. I was simply thrilled at the chance to edit books for God; and I determined to be the best book editor, the most spiritually discerning employee, Pacific Press had ever hired.

In 1971 California was moving into the fast lane. The
Santa Clara Valley, which for years had stretched un-
endingly in prune and pear orchards, sprouted new
housing developments and business parks from San Jose
to San Francisco.

The term "Silicon Valley" was barely born; but the
booming, high-tech industry was hiring assemblers and
office personnel by the thousands, paying a little more
than the federal minimum wage of $1.60 per hour.

Salaries and the cost of living were higher in the San
Francisco Bay area than they were throughout the rest of
the nation.

One-bedroom apartments rented for $120 per month;
two-bedroom places ranged from $150 to $200 per
month. New three- and four-bedroom homes began selling at around $27,000.

During the summer of '71 musician Louis Armstrong
died, the Nixon Administration was negotiating peace
with the Viet Cong, scientists were studying moon rocks,
and newspapers such as the *San Francisco Chronicle* still
ran classified employment ads under sex-differentiated
headings. Employers advertised for typists for "two-girl"
or "four-girl" offices.

Clerk typists earned $300 to $400 per month; junior
bookkeepers started at $300; stenographers started at
around $500.

Californians as a group were ambitious and creative.
Life was faster in the Bay area than in the gentle Michigan countryside of my youth or on the rainy streets of
Seattle where Kim and I had lived during the last few
years. There was a feeling of excitement in California's
air, a feeling of great possibilities that echoed my own
optimistic outlook. I was going to do the kind of work I
loved, in a wholesome Christ-centered atmosphere, in
sunny California. Who could ask for more?

☙

In 1971 the Pacific Press was a model of consistent stability. Most of the workers were middle-aged or older. Many were former missionaries, returned to the U.S. to work their last few years at "home."

Pacific Press was a quiet, somewhat dignified establishment, filled with workers who held common beliefs and a similar world view. The fiery, trail blazing days of the early church and its institutions were history. When I joined the Press, no philosophical or theological upheavals were taking place; there were no explosions of corporate social conscience. The Press reflected a comfortable, middle-class, pleased-to-know-the-truth, status-quo existence.

There was a sameness about the Press and its workers; a comforting routine filled lives as well as offices. As in many established organizations, innovation was suspect, variation dangerous, alteration impossible, and change — especially transforming change — totally destructive.

Pacific Press and I were unprepared for each other — and for the cataclysmic changes we would work together.

## June 1971

The name on my office door says MERIKAY SILVER in big white letters. My supervisor, Richard Utt, smiles at my surprise and pleasure over the name. He made sure it would be here by the time I arrived — a courtesy extended to make me happy.

Richard unlocks the door and we walk in. The room holds a desk, two bookcases, a file cabinet, an electric typewriter, and a long oak table. Two chairs sit in front of my desk; a whole wall of windows behind the desk fills the room with light.

It's a big office, with tweedy-green carpeting and twelve-foot ceilings. It's old. It's seen a lot of book editors come and go. I sit in my executive chair and know I'm going to love it here.

Richard leaves me alone to get the "feel" of my office.

The excitement, the commitment, the sense of having arrived at the threshold of my "real work" — my "meaning" — is almost overwhelming. I want to be the best book editor Pacific Press has ever hired. I want to help create literary masterpieces, to develop the finest writers in the denomination, and to bring their work to the church.

Max Phillips, an old friend and the other assistant book editor, walks in. He has a tightly coiled step, his shoulders hunched, his whole slim body leaning forward, his dark brown curls tumbling around bright, intense blue eyes. He's walked that way ever since I've known him.

Back at Andrews University in Michigan in the mid-sixties he stalked around like that. In those days I was a freshman and he was a graduate seminary student, fiery and brash. We both wrote for Andrews' student newspaper. And we both admired each other's way with words.

Intensity. Idealism. Integrity. That's how I'd describe Max Phillips.

Now here we are, both working at Pacific Press.

"Richard's a good head," Max says, sitting down. "A lot more liberal than some. He and I have really been working hard to upgrade manuscripts. Our goal is to develop a line of books for non-Adventists and market them in special racks in supermarkets and in secular and religious bookstores."

I open the windows behind my desk and the fragrance of roses and jasmine floods in.

"Richard is a progressive, good guy," Max says.

I'm glad to be working with Christian men — men whose values I share, whose vision of a better world I, too, grasp. It will be so easy spending my workdays in an atmosphere of love and trust.

As Max and I talk, the flowers' sweet perfume filling my office, I know I've come home. This is where I'm supposed to be. I can feel it.

Richard Utt is a tall, thin man with walnut-brown hair and matching eyes. He wears glasses, sports a dark mustache, and has a somewhat nervous smile. As head editor of English language books, he supervises four of us: Ted Torkelson, the associate book editor; Max Phillips and me, the assistant book editors; and Arbie Kreye, the secretary.

Richard's office is paneled and carpeted. Windows open to palm trees and jasmine bushes. Behind his desk the wall of shelves is crammed with Pacific Press books. A photograph of his wife smiles from one shelf.

"We work with a lot of, shall I say, low-grade ore," he says as he kneels next to my chair with a stack of books. Flipping through the pages, he points out the weaknesses of writing style and content. He is enthusiastic. I like him.

"My goal is to improve the quality of manuscripts we publish. You can't do that by sitting here waiting. See these?" He drops several pamphlets in my hands with titles such as "Why God Allows Trials" and "Dealing with Discouragement."

"All of these manuscripts came in the mail. They have good messages, but they aren't dynamic. They're pretty typical preachers' sermons. To get the kind of books we need, we have to go out in the field and meet with the good writers and woo them. But some people around here just don't understand that. They can't seem to tell the difference between doggerel and sonnet. You know, some of them actually brag that they haven't read a book since they left school!" Richard's face registers disgust.

"If you don't read, if you're not aware of writing styles and reading trends, how can you make decisions on manuscripts?"

Richard has a story about every book in the pile. His face glows as he describes his research for the photographs illustrating the book on Creation. Suddenly he laughs, "I'd better get off this knee before people think I'm proposing to you." He stands up and walks back to his desk.

Like Max, Richard has an abundance of energy and enthusiasm and hope. I love hope.

He leans back in his chair. "You know, we Adventists are so privileged." His hands form a teepee as the

finger-tips touch, and then fly off like fireworks to make
his point. "The world is running scared about the
future, wondering what's going to happen. And *we
know*." His dark eyes shine behind his glasses. "We have
the answer to their questions." He brushes his dark hair
back off his forehead.

I nod, feeling comfortable in his presence, feeling a
wonderful sense of belonging. If everyone knew this joy
of purpose and unity, surely all problems would vanish.

"But we can't do anything about the questions if we
don't couch our answers in publications that the world
will read," he says. "Max and I've been working to get
the other men here used to the idea of marketing our
books to the public. That's the real goal."

My first week flies by in a rush of enthusiasm. I am part of "the work," part of the great Advent movement to convert the world and hasten the second coming of Jesus.

The feeling of belonging, of being in my own secluded and sacred world, has not been this strong since I graduated from church-sponsored boarding school. There is something magnetic and secure about belonging to a world in which everyone subscribes to the same Truth and works for the same ends.

However, the thrill of working "in the Lord's vineyard" is dulled somewhat by the poor quality manuscripts I edit. As Richard has warned me, the contents and style are often appalling.

And Kim is still in Seattle. That's a drag. He's finishing a project for his employer.

Each night after work I have searched for an apartment, and tonight I find one I love. It's beautiful, with a darling kitchen and two spacious bedrooms. The living room and dining room are big and airy. It's within walking distance of the Press.

It costs nearly $200 a month, and I still haven't found out for certain what I'm earning; but I'm sure we'll be able to afford $200 a month.

When I phone Kim to tell him about the apartment, he says he'll ship the furniture within a week. Then he asks what I'm being paid.

"Max says I'll earn about $600 because that's what the woman I'm replacing earned. But I don't know anything for sure yet."

I don't dare initiate a discussion of salary for fear of appearing too materialistic, too concerned with worldly things.

"I miss you," Kim says. And I miss him! I can't wait until we are together again.

❧

The first order of business every Monday is the half-hour chapel period. Chapel, which meets in an old Spanish-style auditorium with stucco exterior and red tile roof, is where all the Press employees — from the general manager to the bindery stitchers — gather for thirty minutes each week to listen to department heads tell about their projects, or to guest speakers from the community tell about their work.

Chapel periods bring us together, reminding us that each worker is part of the great Adventist family and that we're all striving for the same goal. Even though most chapel periods are designed to motivate us in our work-achievement, I feel inspired here.

I have a good "family" feeling when I walk into chapel each week. These people are my people, my family, since their God is already my own. It is truly a close-knit circle, and I feel privileged to be moving into it.

Today my office is filled with ice cream, root beer, and cupcakes — a very fattening "Welcome to Pacific Press" party. Everyone is here — Louis Schutter, editor of the children's Sabbath school papers; Juanita Tyson-Flyn, his assistant; Lawrence Maxwell, editor of *Signs of the Times* magazine; Richard, Ted, Max, and Arbie. Ted (who also helps Lawrence prepare *Signs*), is a returned missionary from India and always smiles and bows when he greets someone. The copy editors, people from the art and photography departments, and several secretaries join the party.

The person who most commands my attention is Lorna Tobler. Lorna is an attractive woman with large blue eyes. She seems younger than most of the others, perhaps because of her smiling eyes, sparkling with enthusiasm. Maybe it's her stylish dress, more attractive than the average Press attire.

Lorna is Lawrence Maxwell's secretary.

She grew up in Missouri. At seventeen years of age she moved to California to become a secretary in Los Angeles at one of the Adventist hospitals. Later she worked as a secretary in Switzerland, where she met and married Gustav Tobler, a minister.

Afterward she and Gus moved to the States, where they attended the Adventist college in Lincoln, Nebraska. She has been denominationally employed for nearly twenty years, the last twelve at Pacific Press.

After work, I spend the evening unpacking our things. How beautiful the apartment looks now. No more big, empty, echoing rooms. Now the living room has our sofa and love seat. And our bed is all set up in the bedroom, with fresh linen and a beautiful spread. I only wish Kim were here to share it with me.

Lorna loans me a book about the Press. I learn how important this publishing house is, and I am even more grateful to be working here.

Pacific Press began April 1, 1875, in Oakland, California. It was the west coast expansion of the Seventh-day Adventist publishing work.

Ellen and James White, launched the Adventist publishing work in the 1850s. Ellen's prophetic visions helped develop a sense of destiny within the fledgling religious movement. She viewed publishing as a way to unite the scattered believers and spread the truth to those who were not yet members of the flock.

During the 1870s James and Ellen left Battle Creek, Michigan, and headed west to start a publishing house in California for the Lord. They raised $20,000 and with it began Pacific Press.

In 1904 the Press moved from Oakland to Mountain View (about an hour's drive south of San Francisco).

Pacific Press now occupies twenty acres (eleven under roof). There are warehouses, a boarding house, an administration building, a 500-seat auditorium, and two editorial wings, along with printing, binding, and other production facilities. The editorial wings house English and international language editorial departments, two reference libraries, typesetting facilities, and photography and art departments. Chapel Records and various other buildings and departments complete the complex.

A gentle rap on my office door surprises me. "Come in," I say, noticing a small shadow against the opaque window.

A short white-haired man, wearing glasses and a gray suit, opens the door. "I'm Wes Siegenthaler," he says. "I work with the Book Department and just wanted to stop by and say hello."

He sits down.

"My family and I are fans of yours. Have been for years," his voice glows. I've "heard" the glow before. "We've been fans ever since we read your little booklet *NOW!*"

I smile, nod, feel the familiar pleasure of having someone appreciate my work — and the equally familiar knot of apprehension.

If you move people — if you write a story or deliver a stirring speech or, I suppose, sing an inspiring song or artfully photograph an event — and your work touches people's innermost souls, they seem to idolize you. They want to thank you for touching them, for making them feel a little more alive. They want to give back to you some of that very special experience your work gave them. Perhaps that's why there's so much screaming and crying at rock concerts, why applause is as necessary for the audience as for the performers.

In any event, I've been receiving a kind of applause ever since I wrote *NOW!*

*NOW!* caught the imagination and hearts of most Adventists who heard or read it. And for years people have wanted to tell me what the story meant to them. They wanted to express how it had changed their lives, made them more devout, more aware of spiritual issues. And as they have praised the story, I could see they were also praising me. They thought I was special. How could a seventeen-year-old write such a moving, almost prophetic story? Obviously she must be very special, very spiritual.

Not wanting to disappoint them, I tried to live up to their expectations. Now as Wes Siegenthaller sits telling me how much my writing has meant to him and his family, I can feel the "burden of perfection" settling once again on my shoulders.

Even here at Pacific Press Publishing Association (PPPA), where I feel *so grateful* to be, even here people expect me to be above the average. And I reluctantly accept the pressure of perfection. I want to be all that they think I am. I want to be noble and good and kind, filled with love and understanding. But the burden of being all those things, of meeting all those expectations when I'm merely a normal person with normal problems, creates stomach knots and a stabbing realization of how far from perfection I really am.

"You have a real gift, Merikay, a God-given talent," Wes Siegenthaler says. "The church needs more young people like you."

He speaks ponderously, his words emerging slowly and with great emphasis. His eyebrows rise and his head nods at those phrases he considers most important.

"You know the brethren here are well meaning. But sometimes they can be, how shall I say it," he leans forward and half whispers, "real sticks in the mud." Then speaking in a normal tone, "Why some of these guys haven't had an original idea this century."

Then, finished for the moment with criticism, Wes talks about his wife and son with pride. He discusses some of the ideas he has for marketing books and records. He wants me to get involved in his marketing projects. "I need new blood, fresh ideas just like everyone else," he says.

I feel flattered because he's asking my advice.

One by one people come to my office to tell me what my writing has meant to them, how it has changed their lives, how it has renewed their faith. I smile and thank them.

Being a spiritual celebrity is difficult. I never asked to be one. But years after I wrote *NOW!*, people still act as though I'm something very special.

Mrs. Wright, from proofreading, has asked me over to her house for Sabbath dinner. I'm to be the guest of honor. She has a whole group of people coming who want to meet "the girl who wrote the story *NOW!*" And she hopes I'll be what her daughter needs — "to see the light," to come back to "the ark of safety" before it is too late.

People come to my office to thank me for my writing. They come to ask my advice. They come to talk, to look at me, to smile.

I feel the uncomfortable burden of trying to be one of the church's exemplars. I do want to be a good example, a representative of Christ . . . but I am not perfect, and I am not any more special than anyone else.

Lorna Tobler is one of the most interesting women I've ever met. She seems so alive!

She is always reading theological books and talking about the different ideas they spark within her mind. She is always reading articles about women and the women's movement and women in the history of our church. She discusses issues intelligently.

I like to talk ideas with her because she has well-thought-out opinions and because she doesn't grow angry when I disagree. She makes me think. I like her.

She has a good sense of humor — which to me means, of course, that what strikes me as funny also strikes her as funny. She laughs at my jokes. I love people who laugh at my jokes.

After lunch I find Max in my office, his face alive with emotion.

"We've got a problem," he says with solemn excitement. "The hiring committee just found out you haven't got a college degree."

"Just found out? I told you the first time you called. And Richard knew. And you guys said it didn't matter." I stand over him, looking down, confused by his words. What do they mean?

"Well," he hesitates. "Sit down, sit down," he motions me to my desk.

I walk to my chair. "What's this 'just found out' stuff?" I ask, dropping my purse in the bottom drawer and sitting down.

"Well, Richard was trying to slip you in without anyone knowing you didn't have a degree," he says. "See, he's been griping for three years about hiring college graduates. He's been on everyone's case about hiring people educated in the field they're to work in. In the past they tended to hire unqualified returned missionaries or whoever knocked loudest on the door. Richard's been trying to upgrade the editorial department so that he could then upgrade the manuscripts."

"Yes, but . . ."

"Well, you were so well qualified — with all the articles and stories you've published, and with *NOW!* — he just wanted to hire you. So he never told the executive committee anything about your education. He just kept stressing your superior qualifications as a writer, hoping the question of your college degree would never come up. And he almost pulled it off."

Does this mean I'm *not* hired, that I'll have to move back to Seattle? My stomach tightens.

"So what happened today?"

"They were just getting ready to vote on hiring you, and Dr. Fernando Chaij asked about your education. I mean it was the very last question before the big vote. Well, Richard got all embarrassed and had to admit you hadn't graduated from college yet." Max shakes his head in disgust. "I *told* Richard not to try to do it that way," he says.

I could envision Richard blinking rapidly, grinning, brushing his dark hair off his forehead.

"It was pretty hard on Richard — pretty embarrassing after all the fuss he's made about hiring college graduates."

"What's going to happen now?"

Max shrugs. "I guess they'll have some more meetings, and you'll probably have to put together a portfolio of your writings or something."

A knock at my door interrupts. Richard glances in, then enters. "You've heard?" he asks me.

I nod, wondering if I'll lose the apartment. Has Kim already given his company notice? Should I phone him and tell him to wait? Questions and fears rumble through me.

"I told them you were completing your degree, that you would no doubt finish up very shortly," Richard says, sitting down in the chair beside Max's.

"I thought I made it clear that if I came here I wanted to continue going to college," I say. One of the reasons the Press position was so perfect is that PPPA is only twenty miles from San Jose State University, where I could continue the studies I was pursuing in Seattle.

"Well, I kind of stuck my neck out hiring you in the first place," Richard says. "You're the youngest book editor we've ever had. And you know I'm always doing controversial things, at least in some people's eyes; so they just automatically think you're another." He and Max laugh. I don't. I want to know what is going to happen next.

"Oh, there'll be some political skirmishing," Max says, his eyes snapping. "That's all."

"Well, am I hired or . . . ?"

"Oh yes, you're hired. I hired you, so you aren't going to be unhired," Richard assures me. "I'm glad to have you here. I think you're going to be a real boon to the department. We need fresh ideas. But we'll just have a little rough sailing for a while."

He lays a manuscript on my desk. "This will keep you busy."

"I'll write a letter about her qualifications," Max says.

"I was going to ask for that." Richard says nodding. "I'll need all the ammunition I can get."

When both men leave, my office feels very empty. I haven't been here two weeks and already there's trouble.

I walk to the windows and stare out at the fat bees droning from flower to flower. I hate controversy and confrontation. I want to work here in an atmosphere of peace and support. I don't want to start having to defend my position, to say, "Yes, I am well qualified; here, let me prove it."

"Please, Father, please let this work out right."

June 24, 1971

Memo to:   L.F. Bohner [General Manager]
From:      Max Phillips
Re:        Merikay Silver

The policy to hire individuals who have college degrees is, in my opinion, an excellent one. In general, and all else being equal, it is better to have a college degree than not. However, at the same time, we all recognize that there are individuals with degrees who are mediocre at best; and there are also individuals without degrees who have made outstanding successes.

Merikay Silver is a special case. She is not "a college dropout" in the ordinary sense of the word. After her freshman year at Andrews University, which she finished with good grades (she has always made high grades in school), she was forced to stay out and go to work for financial reasons. Subsequently she moved west and married. She had to continue working full-time so that her husband could finish with his B.A. degree. As soon as he finished, she immediately started school again, taking considerably more unit hours than the average. In the quarter she has just finished she took 28 unit hours (the average is about 17) of basic, solid subjects and maintained a 3.57 grade point average, which is close to an all-A average in all her subjects. She is now in her junior year. Merikay has tremendous drive and is well able to hold a job and at the same time to obtain her degree in journalism in a reasonably short length of time. In fact, she is willing and anxious to do this very thing.

I have known Merikay since her freshman year at Andrews University, where I was doing graduate work in the Seminary. I was impressed with her creative writing ability at that time, especially her story *NOW!*, which has sold tens of thousands of copies. Since then she has kept up a freelance writing program and has published widely. Her "Travels with Duffy" series for young children proves that she is especially talented in writing for young children. Of all the persons I have known who are trained in journalism, none is a better creative writer, in my opinion, than Merikay. Hers is the sort of talent, drive, and ability that we need to continue the successful work done by Barbara Herrera. In the area of editing creative narratives and books for children, as well as in books especially for women, Merikay is presently, in my opinion, the most qualified of any available. And when she does obtain her journalism degree in a reasonably short time, she will be even that much more valuable.

It is better to get a promising person who is going to get her degree soon than a mediocre person who already has a degree. If we let this one slip through our fingers, we may be forced to settle for someone who in the long run will not serve the Press nearly so well.

Richard's shadow fills the window of my office door, and then his smile peeks in. "Bohner wants to see you at 11:00."

My face panics.

"Don't worry. I'll go with you. He'll probably ask a few perfunctory questions about your schooling. You'll do fine."

He closes the door. I shiver. This is getting unpleasant.

Here I am full of excitement and enthusiasm, determined to be the best book editor they've ever had. I want to be an active part of the Lord's work, contributing something meaningful to the fulfillment of the gospel commission.

Nobody ever mentions what they'll pay me for my work. And I don't ask. I don't want them to think I'm more concerned with money than with the contribution I can make. But still you'd think they'd say something, or write a letter spelling out my duties and wages . . . something.

And now I'm being called into the top man's office to be questioned about my education. This situation is just too tense.

Leonard Bohner has an ample stomach, a shock of gray hair, buck teeth, and wears glasses. He and Richard exchange small talk while I sit waiting.

Bohner's office is larger than any other at the Press. Rich wood paneling, thick carpeting, and on two walls windows opening onto garden settings.

From his desk drawer he pulls out a copy of *Newsweek*, then lifts his eyes to meet mine. "There's quite a controversy brewing about whether Mrs. White is a true prophet or not," he says to me. He refers to an article reporting intra-church arguments over her inspiration.

Ellen White's visions formed the basis of many church traditions and beliefs. Since she and her husband, James, founded Pacific Press, any attack on her or her inspiration could be perceived as an attack on Pacific Press.

"I think it's important to know that all the people working here are good, strong Adventists," Bohner says, his eyes boring into me, "true to the original vision of the publishing work."

I nod, hoping I look good and strong and true to the vision.

"Do you believe that Mrs. White is the anointed prophet of the Lord, sent to instruct His last remnant people?"

His question slams into me. I thought he'd ask about my college work and how close to completing my undergraduate studies I am.

"I find her counsel most inspiring and important," I say. "It's certainly been a guiding influence in my life."

I wonder at this strange question. I'm being required to confess my faith in Ellen G. White? My very thoughts are up for review?

After a very long month, my first paycheck — what a shock! Less than $400 is typed on my blue slip of paper. It takes twice that to live (even modestly) in this area. There must be some mistake. I stare at the check for a few minutes, and then walk across the hall to Richard's office.

"Is this a mistake?" I ask, showing him the check.

He grins, blinking rapidly. "Well, no, not really. Here's how we worked out the hiring problem. Since you haven't finished college yet, the committee decided to title your position 'editorial assistant,' instead of 'assistant book editor.' The pay for an editorial assistant is less than that for an assistant book editor."

I slowly sink to a sitting position on the couch facing his desk. What will I tell Kim? How can we afford the apartment? Discouragement oozes through me.

## July 1971

I can't believe how people package manuscripts. Some come in wrinkled brown bags with nearly undiscernible, handwritten pages. Others come in photography paper boxes, with paper clips and return postage. Most come in manila envelopes.

Being a writer, I know that each arrives bearing the heart hopes of its author, a writer praying for an acceptance letter instead of a rejection slip.

I remember when I started writing at fifteen. I remember dropping manila envelopes into the big blue corner mailbox and praying that the editor would buy my offering.

Now here I am, sitting in the editor's chair, handing out rejection slips.

Most of the manuscripts crossing my desk are unacceptable. They have no discernible theme or structure. Once in a while I find one copied word-for-word from already-published material. Most are just plain boring. Even those manuscripts which were accepted before I came here, which I now edit, need to be rewritten. Max and I groan over the quality of manuscripts we have to edit.

"They should retitle us 'ghost writers,'" he laughs.

Kim arrived today and he loves the apartment! I thought he would, but it's always reassuring to know your husband loves the same things you do.

It's been exciting getting settled here, but I've missed him terribly.

We stay up all night. He tells me about the project he just completed in Seattle. I tell him about the Press. He's not happy with my salary.

At least we're together! It must be scary to just pick up from the city where you've always lived and move some place where you don't even have a job.

He's such a wonderful husband! Not many other men would do what he's doing because their wives had the opportunity of their lifetime handed to them. Kim is very special. I love him!

Kim and Max discuss my wages and decide that what I'm earning is disgraceful.

Four hundred dollars per month is less than some clerk-typists earn. According to the newspaper classifieds, industrial editing jobs range from $600 for beginners with no experience, all the way to $1,400 for those with much experience.

My meager paycheck doesn't even approach the bottom rung of the pay scale. Of course, we knew that I wouldn't earn top dollar, or even average dollar for my work. People choose denominational employment because they believe the message and want to have an active part in the Christian commission to spread the gospel.

In spite of that, Kim and Max believe that my wages are far too low for the work I'm performing. I agree. So tonight they both go to Richard's house to ask if an improvement can be made.

Kim returns discouraged. "Richard doesn't have any real power over wages," he says. "All he could do was suggest that we move to a cheaper apartment."

"Sure," I laugh, "and where will we get first and last month's rent, and a big cleaning deposit, and all that?"

He shakes his head. "I'll get a job soon and everything will be fine."

I'm concentrating my editorial efforts on the Uplook and STW (Stories That Win) series. These are little booklets that go in racks in Adventist physicians' and dentists' office waiting rooms, where patients can read them.

I want to develop these two series into something really good. My goal is to find good writers to author several new booklets, sort of "perk up" these series, make them relevant and interesting. So I've been writing and phoning professional writers, asking them to submit booklet ideas.

If I'm to make a contribution here, I've got to begin making a difference. I can't just sit working on poorly conceived, poorly written manuscripts. I've got to actively bring in better material.

Besides, I want Richard to be happy with me. He's always talking about how great the woman I replaced was, what an important contribution she made with the cookbook series, how sweet she was, and so on. I hope I can make a lasting impression on him and our department.

At Kim's urging, I decide to submit a collection of my own short stories. Maybe the book committee will publish them in STW form. It's slightly embarrassing because I'm on the committee, but I know my stories appeal. I know the Press can make money on my writing; so I'm going to submit a collection. I'll call it *The Church and Huckleberry Finn,* after the first story in the collection.

## August 1971

The most marvelous manuscript came in today — *WAR* by George Target. I've admired Target's writing for some time. He's an Irishman living in England who weaves words like a magician weaves spells. *WAR* will be one of the finest books we ever publish, if the book committee decides to accept it. I can't imagine they'll refuse.

*WAR* is beautifully crafted, with a strong antiwar message. A great book for Seventh-day Adventists, who traditionally are conscientious objectors. A perfect manuscript for any publishing house called "Pacific."

After finishing his manuscript, I can't help writing a letter to thank him for it and for all his other works, which have moved and inspired me. I also mention that I'm looking for authors for my Uplook and STW series. I hope he'll submit a manuscript.

Kim is hired as graphics artist by the College of San Mateo. He's so happy! I'm so proud! He's doing all the graphics and art work for the college TV station. It's a fun, creative job — just what he needs. Since he's working, I feel so much more relaxed.

How intimidating bills can be! They can ruin almost every aspect of life when you have too many of them. Not that we have so many — rent, car payments, school, the regular — but when you have no money or very little, any bills are too many.

Good manuscripts are coming in for the Uplook and STW series. They're well written, on relevant topics. Richard is pleased. So am I. It just proves that we can interest accomplished authors in writing for us. Once these books start turning a profit for the house, maybe we can persuade the management to allow us to go out on manuscript acquisition forays.

The Book Publishing Committee voted to publish my collection of stories. They're changing the title from *The Church and Huckleberry Finn* to *Huck Finn Goes to Church*. I like my title better — it flows, sounds melodious. But who's going to argue over a few words?

I'm thrilled. Not only can I be an effective editor, but I can also function as a writer here.

A wonderful surprise — a letter from George Target! My heart skips with joy. His writing is beautiful — a melody of words.

To tell you the truth, I was miserably ashamed when your exhilarating letter of high praise drifted in with the cornflakes this morning; because, so help me, I have been on the brink of writing to you ever since that anniversary *Insight*. It must sound intolerably conceited, but every time I read any of your work I would say, "Well, at least there are two of us trying to do something about the state of Seventh-day Adventist writing — making *some* attempt to drag the church into the twentieth century" — which made life seem that much less lonely . . . .

But here you are, having beaten me to it! And another good intention bites the dust of grovelling humility!

Word of warning from a middle-aged pro: Please don't allow your *writing* to be nibbled away by your editorial duties! Only too easy! I've worked five years in a publishing house and know what it can do to the Big Work which *ought* to be in progress! Writers are writers, and editors are editors — BUT THEY'RE DIFFERENT CRITTERS!

But isn't life marvellous! Isn't the church something worth being in when two total strangers can plunge straight into such an open relationship like this! And isn't it great that the love of Jesus is big enough to include us all! If heaven isn't like *this* . . . well, I don't want to be there! Just think of an eternity writing and communicating and . . . Wow!

George Target says he'll put together a collection of stories and submit them for my STW series.

I'm so happy working here!

Max and Richard fight their battle to get books out to the public. The power struggles here amaze and confuse me. But I don't spend much time thinking about them. I'm too busy trying to bring good writers to the Press, trying to mold exciting books out of dusty-dry memoirs.

I hope Max and Richard are successful. It seems terribly ingrown simply to write books for ourselves decade after decade.

But for now I'll concentrate my efforts on being the best possible book editor I can be.

Lorna and I have been talking about women's liberation. I'm not a women's libber, but I know women and men are equal. That seems too obvious to argue about.

I'm just not into boisterous demonstrations and I've never liked confrontation.

Equal pay for equal work is a fair and reasonable concept. Anyone who thinks about it would support it, I'm sure. It's simply common sense.

Of course, the Press is unique. The Press has a wage system based on need. That's what I've been told. The church's institutions take care of their workers. It's a family-centered concept.

## September 1971

It's fun to be back at school. There is something *so* exciting about books full of knowledge, class discussions of new ideas and perspectives. When I'm working at the Press I look forward to my classes. When I'm on campus, I look forward to getting back to the office and editing.

Now that Kim and I are together, this whole world of California/Pacific Press/school seems wonderful. I love it here!

Richard says I can take the time I need for school, and I needn't worry about "making up" the work hours I miss. I know that many other workers, including Richard himself, have been released from work in order to complete degree requirements.

However, I don't want to be considered a part-time student worker. So I go to work at 5:30 each morning and work until it's time to leave for class. Then I come back and work at the Press until I've put in a full eight hours, just like every other full-time worker here.

I like being able to work full time and still take the classes I need for my degree. It's a challenge and I'm glad I can meet it.

# January 1972

SOUTHERN PUBLISHING ASSOCIATION (THE SEVENTH-DAY Adventist publishing house in Tennessee) has accepted a collection of my short stories for publication. I'm thrilled.

Pacific Press will soon bring out *Huck Finn Goes to Church*, and now Southern Pub will publish *Luv Is Not Enough*. It feels *so* good to have my work accepted. Writing is my life. Nothing gives me greater pleasure. And now, to see my work accepted for publication in book form — well I can't express my joy, my gratitude. I know this is just the beginning.

Max takes me home from work tonight. On the way he asks why I haven't approached Bohner for a raise. I should be earning more, I know that. But the thought of asking for more frightens me. Kim and I are making enough to pay the bills, and I don't want to ask for anything "extra" until I've finished college.

"When I have my degree I'll ask," I say.

I think Max thinks I'm cowardly.

Today is W-2 forms day, which means income tax time; all the unpleasantness it brings is here. At the xerox machine Max is copying his W-2 form. I'm waiting to copy letters I'm sending to potential authors. The figures on his form catch my eye.

"May I look at that?" I pick up his W-2. Max's income is nearly double mine. Stunned, I stare at his form. "You earn almost twice as much as I do."

"Aw, come on," he scoffs.

We walk to my office to get my W-2. He examines the forms, does some quick figuring and says, "You earn 60 percent of what I earn."

We sit down, shocked. My desk is piled high with manuscripts. Here's my work load, mountains of mostly boring manuscripts over which I work and struggle, for 60 percent of what Max earns! Am I *that* bad at what I do? I feel dazed.

His searing blue eyes stare from under dark curls. "What are you going to do about it?"

I'm too weak to do anything right now. "I'll wait until I get my degree and then confront them," I say, wishing I hadn't seen his W-2 form.

I'm aware of the equal pay for equal work law. I know sex discrimination is illegal. I simply don't like confrontation. And I can't believe that the huge difference in our pay is based solely on sex. That's inconceivable.

My lack of a college degree is probably part of the difference. Until I earn my B.A. I won't be in a very good bargaining position. I feel sick. I don't want to talk about wages.

Our conversation turns to Target's *WAR* manuscript. Max thinks the other publishing committee members will deep-six it. "It's just too good. They'll feel intimidated. They always do. Besides, it's against war," he says.

"It doesn't matter that we're conscientious objectors. I think most Adventists are really for war. Just don't ask *us* to pull the triggers. We're too holy for that!" Max seems bitter.

When he goes back to his office, I sit feeling miserable. About Target's wonderful manuscript. About my paltry pay. I thought everyone "in the work" received sacrificial paychecks. Mentally I review the top administrators here. They're all quite old. And they're all men. They treat me like a daughter or granddaughter, with a warmth that has always made me happy. Right now it's doing nothing for me.

After about an hour of self-pity I walk across the hall to Richard's office.

"Am I doing acceptable work?" I ask.

"More than," he insists with his wide smile. "Why?"

I explain that I've just learned how much Max and I are earning. Richard motions for me to close the door and take a seat.

"Our system is called 'head-of-household,'" he explains, eyes smiling softly from behind his glasses. "You know, we all sacrifice to work for the Lord. But we believe that a family's main wage earner should receive more — because of his added burdens. So at the Press, the head-of-household receives certain benefits that other workers don't. For instance, he receives more insurance coverage so he can cover his wife and children. A single worker doesn't need that."

I nod. That sounds reasonable.

Richard is not known for brevity; so I listen as he describes how blessed the "head-of-household" system is, for it allows people with dependents to work for the Lord.

I return to my office, somewhat reassured that Max's and my pay difference does not indicate what Pacific Press thinks of my work.

## February 1972

In the past week I have received requests for articles from the *Review and Herald* and *Insight* (both Adventist publications). And then this morning Lawrence Maxwell comes to my office with a similar request.

Lawrence's father, Arthur Maxwell, wrote *The Bible Story*, a series of ten children's books which tell the Bible stories in simple language. *The Bible Story* and other books are sold door-to-door. *The Bible Story* has done well over the years, making Arthur Maxwell, during his lifetime, wealthy and (within the circle of Adventism) famous. To most Adventists he was, and is, "Uncle Arthur."

When I was nine, my mother bought *The Bible Story* books. It was from that purchase that our family began attending the Adventist church and finally became members through baptism by immersion.

In those days Lawrence edited *The Junior Guide*, the Sabbath school paper for kids ages ten through fifteen. I was very impressed by his letter in the front of every *Guide*, urging us to be good kids and to live for Jesus.

Later when I started selling stories and poems, the *Guide* was one of my regular buyers.

Now Lawrence Maxwell works right down the hall from me, editing *The Signs of the Times*. He walks stiff, straight, and unsmiling. He talks with a slightly British accent, a leftover from his first few years as a child in England. His serious gray eyes match his suits.

He's Lorna's boss.

Today he askes me to write for the *Signs*. He wants an article on avoiding worldly music and one on tithing (paying ten percent of your income to the church). I know the kind of material he wants. I don't know if I can write it, but I agree to try.

I consider Lawrence Maxwell an ultraconservative. I, on the other hand, am not. I think if God leaned one way or the other, in human terms, he'd be "liberal." To have created humans at all, to have created us with the freedom of choice, is a lavishly liberal thing to do. For God to allow us to act out our choices freely is so creatively gracious it couldn't possibly be termed "conservative." Of course, that's just my opinion.

However, I haven't kept my opinions to myself. And if, after all my "liberal" speeches on committees and in the halls and offices of Pacific Press, Lawrence Maxwell still wants me to write for the *Signs*, I feel it must be because of the quality of my work.

His visit and the other writing requests I've received lately reinforce my desire to be the best writer possible.

Since coming to the Press I've been filled with book and article ideas. I can feel my creativity expanding. I long to become a valuable and inspiring voice within the denomination.

"Thank you, Jesus, for the talent you've given me."

Max was right about Target's *WAR* manuscript. There's all sorts of resistance to it on the Book Publishing Committee. Some think it's antipatriotic, if not seditious. Others argue against it because Target writes novels. (Adventists aren't supposed to read fiction.) Some say that he puts swear words in his novels.

Richard and Max and I groan.

If you write a story, if you create characters and plot and setting, and weave a tale in which a character must swear to be real, you allow him (or her) to swear.

Most Book Publishing Committee members know very little about writing books, almost nothing about the creative process. I don't know why they're committee members. Most of them don't like to read, don't care about books, and don't want to hear about what makes the difference between a good book and a pile of yawns.

Richard withdrew the Target manuscript, suggesting that we have a few "leaders" review it and give their recommendations. So now he has to ship the manuscript off to several ministers, and maybe some official from the General Conference, and wait weeks or months before those people read and evaluate it; and then (if their comments are favorable) he'll bring it back to committee.

## March 1972

The biggest monkey wrench in the world has just been dropped into our life. Kim has lost his job. He's really discouraged. Strange how important a job is to a person's self-image. Probably more so for a man than a woman.

At least when I first came to the Press he was working in Seattle and able to help with the bills. Now he's home and depressed. He's not sure what he wants to do. We've talked about his returning to school to get a master's degree.

I only want him to be happy, to feel good about himself, to feel as though he's doing something with his life. We both have a strong need to contribute, to feel as though we're doing something significant.

I'm sure that if he decides to enter school, I can ask for head-of-household allowance since I would be the financial "head" of our household. That extra money could cover all our bills plus Kim's college expenses.

I talk to Max about my requesting head-of-household allowance. He thinks it is a good idea. He's just finished putting Jeanette through her bachelor's degree. If I support Kim through his master's, I'll be in a similar position to Max's — sole wage earner in our family.

## April 1972

I talk with Richard about asking Bohner for head-of-household allowance. He laughs, blinks rather nervously, then says it might not be a bad idea. He asks me to give him some time so he can write a letter to Bohner first and pave the way.

He asks if I want him to go along. I decline. It seems I should ask on my own. I should act like a head of household.

I tell Lorna. She just stares at me. Then she smiles a funny little smile as though she doesn't believe I'll go through with it. But later in the day she stops by, full of enthusiasm.

"You just might get head-of-household," she waves a small pamphlet toward me. "Here are the new wage scale guidelines from the General Conference. They go into effect July 1. And listen to this." She reads aloud: "'The wage scale provides one basic salary scale for each job classification based on education and experience to all employees without discrimination on the basis of race, religion, sex, age, national origin or color, with minimums and maximums expressed in percentages as well as in dollar amounts per month.

"'While no recognition of the difference in financial responsibilities between those who are heads of families and those who are not is given in the basic wage scale, it is recognized that the differences are to be provided in the living allowance granted.'"

She looks at me. "Now here's the good part. 'On the basis of need determined by marital status, dependents and financial responsibility, an additional amount of money may be paid to employees without discrimination on the basis of race, religion, sex, age, national origin or color.'"

We laugh, then giggle.

"Well, the government and the General Conference agree that I qualify," I say.

∾

Kim registers for summer classes at San Jose State University this morning. He wants a master's degree in educational technology. In that course he can make films, and he's always wanted to be a film maker.

As excited as he is about school, he thinks my asking Bohner for head-of-household allowance is risky.

"I want you to take Max with you when you see Bohner," he insists. "If for no other reason, it will illustrate the similarities between you. Max just put Jeanette through school. You'll be putting me through. Max does the same kind of work you do. The two of you together should make a strong statement. And it will probably keep Bohner from eating you alive."

I don't think Len Bohner will eat me alive, but I'll ask Max. At least he'll make a good visual aid.

May 10, 1972

Elder L.F. Bohner, Manager
Pacific Press

Dear Len:

Merikay tells me she wants to talk with you about her personal financial affairs. She says her husband, Kim, is being laid off very soon, or has already been laid off, and without a job, plans to go back to school. She wonders if she could not receive some of the fringe benefits as the head of household, supporting the family.

I realize this is somewhat irregular and not according to the long traditions of church institutional policy.

I also realize that Merikay does not have the pleasing appearance or personality of Barbara. But I hope this will not influence you unduly. The important thing is that she is doing superb work in writing and editing for us. I don't know where we would go to get a replacement. She is doing as good work as any man could do, and better than any young man we might have brought in, that I know of.

I know that younger people today do not take the attitude that you or I might have taken 25 or 30 or 40 years ago — that we will gratefully accept whatever the church pays us and get along on it the best we can. We are living in a prosperous country; and young people have much higher expectations, even from the beginning of their employment, than we used to in earlier days. But I do hope that we will take a liberal, conciliatory attitude and not respond in such a way that it will create a situation which will discourage Merikay, who is certainly one of the outstanding writers of the denomination.

I realize that she is young, a bit controversial, and has not quite finished her college work. But on the other hand, she is far beyond most college graduates in her ability to do excellent writing and editing. So I hope this fact will balance out the other considerations.

Thank you for giving consideration to this viewpoint.

Cordially,

Richard H. Utt
Book Editor

Although I'm sure Bohner will give me head-of-household allowance, Kim is worried. He insists we meet with an attorney he heard lecture a few months ago. Her name is Joan Bradford.

It's a bright, sunny spring day when we meet her for the first time.

Joan Kurt Bradford is a tiny, fragile-looking woman with short black hair and snapping eyes. She's fifty-two years old, the same age as my mother.

She listens while I explain Pacific Press' head-of-household system. Then she says the system is illegal. She asks if I want to sue.

"Of course not," I laugh. "I just want to know if what I'm asking for — head-of-household allowance — is legal. Am I within my rights?"

She says, "The Press' head-of-household system is illegal; under the law you are entitled to equal pay for equal work. And since it seems you have a clear-cut male counterpart, asking for equal pay is certainly legal —and fair."

I feel better. Kim is still sure there's going to be trouble.

I think there'll be some shock, some confusion perhaps, but not much more. My request is too practical, too fair, too just.

Max is all excited, thinking we're going to have a fight when I ask for head-of-household pay.

Lorna just smiles, making me feel like a really stupid kid going in for the slaughter. She's encouraging, but I don't think she believes I'm going to get what I'm asking for.

Kim thinks I'm right.

I'm plain scared. I've never done anything like this in my life. I never even asked how much I'd earn when I was being interviewed for the job. And now I'm going to go in and ask a man old enough to be my grandfather for head-of-household allowance!

I stand in Lorna's office smiling confidently and saying, "Of course I'll get head-of-household. You just watch. It's only fair. I qualify — the General Conference and the U.S. Government agree on that. You know the old axiom: 'Ask and ye shall receive.'"

I hope I don't look as scared as I feel. I hope my voice doesn't quaver when I ask Bohner. I hope I don't throw up.

Why is it so hard to ask for things you really deserve — especially when your request concerns money? I always feel like a groveling beggar when it comes to money.

"Ready?" Max pokes his head in Lorna's office, where I'm confidently telling her there'll be no problem persuading Bohner. I nod, and off we go.

Bohner's secretary ushers us in. When I was here last, almost a year ago, Bohner quizzed me about my faith in Ellen G. White.

Now I'm in for another uncomfortable session with the big boss.

Leonard Bohner enters. I'm struck with how large he is. He seems to tower over us both. He shakes hands with Max, smiles and nods toward me, and takes his seat.

For a moment there is silence. I try to breathe deeply, to relax. He looks at me expectantly.

"Did you get Richard's letter?" I ask. The words sound louder, more confident than I feel.

He nods. "Basically, didn't it say Silver is no longer working and so you want some fringe benefits?"

"Uh huh."

The phone rings; he picks it up quickly and talks for several minutes.

Max sits near the door, back straight, eyes first on mine,

then on Bohner's. I sit close to Bohner's desk. I wish I were prettier. I wish I didn't have so many butterflies in my stomach.

He sets the receiver on its cradle, then turns to me.

"Since you got Richard's letter, you know my need," I say. Bohner seems to straighten papers on his desk.

I continue, "The reason I asked Max to come with me is that I thought it would help you see the fairness of my request." Bohner seems to brush dust or crumbs off his desk. "Because we are both doing the same work," I continue, "and we both have spouses who are in college. Yet he is receiving much higher wages."

"Yes, but Max has an advanced degree, Merikay. And about six years of editing experience. You don't even have one year's experience yet."

"But I have ten years' professional writer's experience, plus my experience as assistant editor on the largest insurance trade magazine in the Northwest," I say quickly, surprised at my strength. "That might not be equal to a degree, but it is something. I'm not just a rank beginner."

"Well, I don't know. There are other women working here, four or five, who have children in school. And we help them out with their tuition." He is quiet for several seconds, as if considering my request. My hopes begin to rise. I'm sure he'll do what's fair. I begin to smile.

"If we do something for you, and those women in the bindery come in expecting the same thing, then where will we be?"

I'm confused. Am I understanding him?

"I really don't think a woman can do the same work as a man in everything. Like Max here, he goes out to the churches and preaches. He stands in the pulpit, representing us and *The Signs*. If we sent you, the churches would look down their noses at us."

My face begins to burn.

"Besides, I don't think the base salaries are that different. When Barbara was here, she and Max were making almost the same. I think he made $2 more a week."

"But when I got married," Max speaks up, "my check took a big jump. I got all sorts of benefits added on."

"Just the rent subsidy," Bohner snorts. "That's the only thing you got increased. And it wasn't that much. Maybe $15."

Max leans forward. "Well, it was so big I called the Treasury Department to see if the computer had made a mistake. And I got other benefits. For example, I can cover Jeanette with insurance."

"I'd like to get life and health insurance for Kim," I say.

Bohner sputters, his face turning pink. "Now do you really think we could do that?" His voice condescends. "Times may be changing, but the husband is still the head of the house. *He* should be supporting you. You should be the one going to college. You need a degree worse than he does."

My face burns again.

Max jumps in, "But we have men in the Book Department who haven't even finished high school. And they're making big salaries."

Bohner says, "Well, now, that's something different. A salesman doesn't need a B.A. to sell books. But an editor, an editor really needs a degree."

I try to steer the conversation back to the original point.

"I'm merely asking for the same pay and benefits you would give a married man with my qualifications."

"Well, we've never had anyone working in that department without a degree before; so there's no precedent," Bohner says. "I don't know what we can do."

"You could have hired a man," I say. "And if you had, you'd be paying him more and giving him more benefits than I'm receiving. I'd simply like equal pay for equal work. I do the same work Max does; I'd like the same benefits. I'm a married person with a dependent."

I couldn't believe my mouth. My fear had all but disappeared. I was actually talking with Bohner now, actually asking for what I wanted. And I wasn't groveling or apologizing.

"Merikay, your having a dependent is really not the Press' concern, is it? I mean, we can't be held accountable for a decision you and your husband came to," Bohner says. "Kim is supposed to be bringing home the bread. If you two decide that he'll return to school, why should we then have to raise your salary?"

"Because I'm doing the same work a married man is doing, and am getting paid so much less." I can't understand why he doesn't understand. It's so plain and simple.

Max speaks softly from his chair, "You know, the law

states that equal pay should be paid for equal work, regardless of sex."

"I don't know about that," Bohner says.

"It could be very embarrassing for us," Max says.

Bohner doesn't seem to hear. He's looking at me. "Well, what if we give you 'head-of-household' and next week Kim goes out and gets a $20,000 a year job. Are we supposed to cut you back?"

"You have men working here as heads of household whose wives work at jobs earning $500 or $800 a month," I say, "and you don't cut back those men's salaries."

Bohner turns red and nearly shouts, "Let's not throw a red herring on the table. We're talking about you and Kim."

I think it's amusing that he turns red just when he's shouting about red herrings. I don't like his question but I answer it.

"I don't think Kim's going to get a $20,000-a-year job next week." Bohner doesn't respond but stares at me with a shocked and angry face. "Basically, I'm just asking for the same pay and benefits that a married man in my position would receive. I think that's a fair request."

Bohner's voice is cold. "This could very well be our parting of the ways."

"Yes it could," I say, surprised at how calm I am, how confident my voice sounds. "Because I can't live on the money I'm earning now."

Bohner mumbles, "We usually tell women what they'll be getting and they can take it or leave it at the time of employment."

"I wish you'd told me."

"Well, it never came up. By the way, when are you going to finish your degree program?"

"I'm taking classes at San Jose State, and I'm doing correspondence classes."

"Good."

"You know," Max says, "the law states equal pay should be paid for equal work, not taking title into account. I really think we should think about that."

"Well, we'd really have a problem if those women out in the bindery asked for what Merikay wants. I don't know what we can do."

His words hit me like a freight train. *Those women in*

*the bindery.* I had automatically assumed those who headed households were receiving head-of-household pay. Those bindery women are widows and divorcees, raising children alone, doing the Press' grimiest, hardest work. Suddenly I realize that no woman in the entire institution receives head-of-household pay. My mouth drops open. It's as if someone just poured a bucket of ice water on me.

Bohner's secretary opens his door to say that his next appointment is waiting.

Bohner stands and walks us to the door. "We'll see what can be done. There's more than one way to skin a cat."

"Well, if you fire Merikay we're going to be in a horrible mess," Max says. "We need another editor right now; and if she goes, well, we're just swamped."

Bohner shakes hands with Max, then me. "Don't lose the faith," he says to me. "We'll see what we can do."

I can't believe what I've just been through. I went in there scared to death, did the best reasoning job I could, and came out with absolutely nothing. Not one indication that the man understood what I was saying. Not a word about anything except that the women who are the sole breadwinners and work in the bindery would really cause a problem if they wanted head-of-household pay.

We enter Max's office. "Well, what are you going to do?" he asks. He's always asking that.

"I'll write a follow-up letter, and then wait to see what happens." I sound so mature, as if this is the kind of thing I do every day.

"I'll tell you something," Max speaks slowly, seriously. "If you take on the big boys, you've got to be hard as diamonds, because they will be."

I walk back to my office.

As the excitement — the adrenalin — drains away, depression sets in.

Not only did Bohner miss my point, not only did he give nothing — not a word of understanding, not a word of sympathy, not a promise of change, not a hint that the Press would offer me something more than I'm already earning — but I learned that no women, not even those who are struggling to raise families and put children through church school, receive head-of-household pay.

In other words, head-of-household really means "male."

I compose a letter to Leonard Bohner.

22 May 1972

Dear Elder Bohner:

To summarize our discussion this afternoon, I am requesting the same compensation and monthly benefits a married man, doing the work I'm doing, would receive. Below is a list of the benefits I've been able to get information on:

*Per-Month Figures*

Rent Allowance — $170 now; up to $185 in July 1972.

Local Mileage Allowance — (750 miles) . . . 8¢ per mile, or $60 per month.

Automobile Depreciation — $60 per month.

Telephone Allowance — $7.50 per month.

Medical Allowance for Family Members (which in my case would be Kim and myself) — 75% up to $500 every six months; beyond $500, Press allows 90%.

Automobile Insurance, first car — 100%.

Since I need these benefits (as well as the others I was unable to get information about) as much as anyone working here, and since I'm delivering the same amount and quality of work that people receiving these benefits are delivering, and since it is only fair that I receive them, I don't feel apologetic in asking for them.

I know you understand my position and will help me in this matter. Thank you so much for your time this afternoon and for your consideration of my request.

I hope to hear from you soon concerning this. It is very important to me.

Cordially,

Merikay Silver

"I'm just glad you took Max," Kim says over supper. "No telling what Bohner would have said, how he would have treated you, if you'd been there alone. Some of those old codgers think they're gods."

"Can you imagine looking at yourself in the mirror every morning knowing that widows were struggling desperately to make ends meet because of your policies?" I ask.

"How many women work at the Press?" Kim wants to know.

Maybe 100, maybe 150.

"But a lot of them are supporting children or invalid husbands or parents. And not one of them receives head-of-household benefits. All this time I just assumed that whoever was financial head-of-household earned the head-of-household allowance.

"I may be the highest paid female in the company," I say. "Can you believe a family existing on my salary?"

We eat in silence.

My mind reels. Something is very wrong at Pacific Press.

## May 23, 1972

Richard stands in the doorway to my office, grinning nervously. "You shook Bohner up yesterday," he says. Then he laughs a little, as if he likes the idea of my doing that.

"But remember his age and his generation. Give him a little time to absorb it all."

I nod.

I wonder if Richard knows that no woman at Pacific Press receives head-of-household allowance.

Later in the day Max enters my office. It is warm from the afternoon sun. The sweet scent of jasmine and roses floats through my open windows.

"I was just with Bohner," he says, sitting down. "He raked me over the coals because of your letter. He wanted to know if I helped you write it."

I grimace. Isn't that typical — thinking I'm too young or too innocent to be able to write my own letter.

"He's *really* upset," Max continues. "He thinks you're making a bunch of demands. He thinks, considering your genetic heritage and all ...."

"What's that supposed to mean?"

"Well, you're Scottish — and didn't you say you have some Jewish blood?"

"Maybe, so?"

"Well, he thinks you're a natural moneygrubber."

I laugh. I'm being grossly underpaid, and *I'm* the moneygrubber.

"I have a message for you from him," Max says. "Here it is: if you'll humble yourself and say to him, 'Let's just forget everything that's happened between us; I need more money' — then he'll get you some more money."

"Head-of-household?"

Max shakes his head no. "They'll probably give you another title and add a few benefits, things like that."

"No thanks."

A week ago any money would have been welcome. Since yesterday's meeting, since realizing that absolutely no woman receives head-of-household, something has changed. Something is settling, solid and firm, inside me.

"I want to be paid for the work I perform at the same rate as a married man with a dependent."

Max continues, "If you decide to take the 'hard line,' as Bohner calls it, you'll get nothing, nothing at all."

We stare at each other, Max's mouth a straight thin line.

"Bohner thinks you'll have to quit and he'll gladly let you go," he continues. "He's already told Richard to start looking for a new editor. Bohner feels it's the company's right to give some employees more benefits than others, since benefits are not salary but bonuses from the company."

"Will Richard look for a new editor?" Fear claws me.

Max shrugs. "Richard loves your work, but he doesn't need trouble."

When Max leaves, I think about what he's said. If I did go to Bohner and tell him to forget my request, if I threw myself on his mercy, what would I gain? Whatever was given would be handed me as a "favor," an "exception." It wouldn't be given because I earned it honestly with my hard labor.

And what about the other women, those I thought received it all along? If head-of-household is for the economic head of a household, if ours is a need-based system (as I've been taught), why aren't those women who need it receiving it? Why isn't equal and fair pay an everyday practice here?

And why was it not just automatically granted to me when I became head of our household? Why did I have to ask for it, only to be told I could not have it? And why should I now apologize for asking for something which should automatically be mine?

No, Bohner's offer is wrong. There's something rotten here; and I won't be a part of it, even if that means foregoing whatever merciful scraps Bohner might toss my way. No, I need and deserve head-of-household allowance. Anything less is unacceptable.

❧

## May 24, 1972

I heard that at today's Executive Committee meeting, Bohner read aloud the letter I'd sent him. I guess he got so upset that committee members had to help calm him down. They were afraid he'd have a heart attack.

No one on the committee was familiar with the 1964 Civil Rights Act or the section of that act dealing with equal pay. (It's only been eight years since that law was passed.) They appointed a committee to study it.

Richard stops by my office after the meeting to assure me that he is happy with my work.

Later in the day Lorna drops by. "I spoke with Brother Bohner this afternoon about Title VII," she says. (Title VII is that portion of the Civil Rights Act of 1964 dealing with equal pay for equal work.)

Seeing that Lorna wants to talk about her visit, I motion for her to have a seat.

"He was certain that a company can pay its employees whatever it wants, and they can either take it or leave it." She laughs. "I informed him that those days are gone forever."

We both chuckle.

It's not that the men here are evil. They're just out of touch. They've always lived in an isolated, church-centered world.

"He began talking about your lack of a degree, and I told him he could stack up all the degrees in this department and you'd still be the best-qualified book editor the Press has. And he agreed."

"He did?" I feel a rush of affection for Len Bohner. He's emotional, and he's somewhat removed from the realities of life today; but he's basically a good guy. I'm certain this whole thing will work out well.

∾

## May 25, 1972

Today there was another Executive Committee meeting.

I had hoped they'd discuss my request and perhaps grant me head-of-household pay. But the agenda did not include my request. Instead the committee voted to have all hourly employees punch a time clock from now on.

Until now only factory workers punched clocks. Now *all* women will have to punch, since *all* women are hourly employees. I am the *only* editor who must punch a time clock.

Ross Wollard's secretary complained to him about the new rule.

"There's going to be a lot more cracking down than this," he told her, "after that Executive Committee meeting the other day, the one where Merikay's letter was read."

I can't believe it! I ask for head-of-household, and suddenly every woman in the company gets punished.

May 26, 1972

Elder Len F. Bohner, Manager
Pacific Press

Dear Len:

Regarding our conversation the other afternoon: I have
been thinking about how our organization might avoid
possible embarrassment regarding sex discrimination and
to what degree it might or might not affect us according to
the laws passed in recent years.

I have discovered that the federal government has set up a
Committee for Urban Affairs as a branch of the Equal
Employment Opportunities Commission to advise employers of their rights and responsibilities under the law
in this matter. This committee has the best and latest
information available.

The director of this committee for the San Francisco
branch:

> Oscar Williams
> Attorney-at-Law
> 1105 Bush St.
> San Francisco, Calif.
> Telephone: 398-5354

Also, the EEOC itself is available for purposes of giving
out information to employers:

> Equal Employment Opportunities Commission
> 1095 Market St.
> San Francisco
> Telephone: 556-0360

> General Counsel:
> Chester Relyea
> Attorney-at-Law
> 1095 Market St.
> San Francisco
> Telephone: 556-7466

I'm sure that as Christians we want to do the right thing in
this matter. But we have to be properly informed before we
are able to make right decisions.

Sincerely your friend,

Max Gordon Phillips
Assistant Book Editor
cc: Bill Muir

30 May 1972

Dear Elder Bohner:

Just a little note: Could you let me know fairly soon about my request? Perhaps before the end of the week in a letter?

I would also like to ask if you considered my letter a demand? I heard that you did. If so, I'd like to emphasize that it was not a demand, but a request.

Thanks for your understanding.

Cordially,

Merikay Silver

May 31

Brethren L.F. Bohner, Manager
and W.L. Muir, Treasurer
Pacific Press Publishing Association

Dear Brethren:

Following our conversation last week, I thought it might
be well for me to describe for you some of the ways in
which I feel the Press might make improved use of its
women employees.

Here are some possibilities:

In the bindery, mailing, treasury, editorial, book, and
periodical departments there are women of many years'
experience and/or extensive training. Some of them have
leadership talent. These could be considered for upgrading in responsibility, title, and salary. In cases where they
are already bearing considerable responsibility, their title
and salary should be made commensurate with their real
services.

When new talent is sought from the field or colleges for
such work as art, advertising, promotion, editorial, or
treasury, women should receive equal consideration with
men. True, fewer of them receive training for this work
because they are led to believe their talents are unwel-
comed by the denomination. But more and more young
Adventist women are training anyway — to offer their
services to the world, if the church does not want them.
We should seek them out and make them welcome. We
need them.

In our apprenticeship program we could start desegre-
gating opportunities. There is one gifted woman employee at the Press who has had a lifelong desire to be a
printer. There are no logical reasons preventing it. But
one very illogical one. Women are excluded from ap-
prenticeships.

Students accepted for summer work as well as appren-
ticeships could be used in every department, regardless of
sex. Objective qualifications should be the sole criteria.
Young men as well as young women could be used in the
periodical department, for example, and young women

in the typeroom and pressroom. If this idea seems radical to you, just recall the days of World War II when Rosie the Riveter ran the factories. No problem!

Moreover, women, upon whom the Press depends heavily for its operation, should share the responsibilities of the Executive Committee, Foremen's Committee, and other decision-making groups, as they have begun to do in the book committees.

By following such a course we not only would be raising the standards of efficiency, morale, and economy, but we would also be voluntarily complying with the requirements of law. Still more important, when such a program of expanded vision and openness to every worker's potential contribution to the cause gets underway, the Press could well become the inspiration of the denomination — a dynamo of energy, production, and imagination in meeting the ever-increasing challenges of the literature ministry.

I don't mind telling you that I love all the leading brethren at the Press. Someday I hope to love all the leading sisters as well!

Sincerely,

Lorna Tobler

## June 1972

I'm afraid that Bohner will call me into his office and yell at me, like he did Max. I can't stand being yelled at. I phone Joan Bradford to talk about my fears.

She says she'll write Bohner a letter explaining the law, offering to help the Press legalize its employment practices, and asking that he deal with her office instead of directly with me.

The next day when Kim and I go to her office to talk about the letter, she suggests that I file suit.

"These men aren't evil, just uninformed," I say. "I know things will change once they understand the law."

Her smile says, "Boy, are you innocent-ignorant-stupid."

"How long will it take?" Kim wants to know.

"Believe me, once they get my letter, they'll be on the phone to this office," she says.

I feel relieved. I'll be glad to have everything straightened out so we can get back to normal again.

Driving home we talk and laugh about how good it will be to receive head-of-household. "It'll be a first for the Press," Kim says, as though that's a huge accomplishment, something akin to scaling Mount Everest.

"And after more than a century I think it's time for that first," I laugh.

Kim helps ease the pressure. His support and understanding mean everything to me.

June 1, 1972

Mr. L.F. Bohner, Manager
Pacific Press Publishing Assoc.
1350 Villa St.
Mt. View, CA 94040

RE: MERIKAY SILVER-PACIFIC PRESS

Dear Mr. Bohner:

Please be advised that this office represents Merikay Silver in regard to problems involving sex discrimination in her employment with Pacific Press. Mrs. Silver is desirous of settling this matter amicably, rather that resorting to formal charges with appropriate government agencies.

To the end of assisting you in bringing your employment practices in line with current law, both federal and state, I draw your attention to Title VII of the 1964 Civil Rights Act (as amended by the Equal Employment Opportunity Act of 1972); the Equal Pay Act of 1963; the California Fair Employment Practices Act, Sections 1410 et seq of the California Labor Code.

A photo copy of applicable sections of Title VII is enclosed for your reference. Please note that Section 703 of Title VII provides that:

(a) It shall be an unlawful employment practice for an employer —

    (1) to fail or refuse to hire or to discharge any individual, or otherwise to discriminate against any individual with respect to his compensation, terms, conditions, or privileges of employment, because of such individual's race, color, religion, sex, or national origin; or

    (2) to limit, segregate, or classify his employees or applicants for employment in any way which would deprive or tend to deprive any individual of employment opportunities or otherwide adversely affect his status as an employee because of such individual's race, color, religion, sex, or national origin.

Our records show that Pacific Press provides considerable benefits to married male employees while denying the same to married female employees, of which group Mrs. Silver is a member, (rent allowance, telephone allowance, local mileage allowance, automobile insurance, automobile depreciation, medical allowance for family members). Such practices are, of course, discriminatory with respect to compensation, terms, conditions and privileges of employment within the prohibited practices covered by Title VII.

Our records further indicate that, subsequent to the date of Mrs. Silver's complaint to you regarding discriminatory employment practices, Pacific Press initiated a practice of requiring female employees to punch a time clock while limiting such requirement of male employees to factory workers only. Such a practice is not only discriminatory with respect to conditions of employment under Section 703 of Title VII, but may also be a violation of Section 704 (a) as a method of retaliation against an employee who has opposed an unlawful employment practice.

In the event that you have some question regarding the applicability of Title VII to religious organizations, please note that Section 702 of the Act exempts religious associations and institutions only insofar as the employment of persons of a certain religious belief is concerned. Religious organizations remain subject to the provisions of Title VII with regard to race, color, sex, and national origin. The language of Section 702 reads:

> This title shall not apply ... to a religious corporation, association, educational institution, or society *with respect to the employment of individuals of a particular religion* ....
>
>                                             (emphasis added)

Explanatory reports from the Congressional Record clarify the position of religious associations in the matter of discrimination by sex:

> This Amendment would ... exempt religious corporations, associations, and societies from the application of this Act insofar as the right to employ people of any religion they see fit is concerned. This is the only effect of this Amendment.
>
>                         (Cong. Rec. (S 2061), Feb. 17, 1972)

Such organizations remain subject to the provisions of Title VII with regard to race, color, sex or national origin.

(Section-Analysis, Cong. Rec.
(H 1862), March 8, 1972)

If you have any questions regarding Mrs. Silver's rights to equal compensation, terms, conditions, and privileges of employment, please feel free to contact me.

If you should wish to make independent inquiry regarding these matters, I suggest that you contact an attorney of your own choosing or direct any inquiry to the following agencies:

Equal Employment Opportunities Commission
1095 Market Street
San Francisco, California
Telephone 556-0260

General Counsel for the Equal Employment
Opportunities Commission
Elihu Hurwitz
1095 Market Street
San Francisco, California
Telephone 556-7466

Office of the Regional Counsel of the Equal
Employment Opportunities Commission
Chester Relyea
620 Central
Alameda, California
Telephone 273-7177

Mrs. Silver is anxious to resolve her problems immediately in view of the personal needs that have arisen as a result of her husband's loss of employment and her resulting position as the sole wage earner of the family. I draw your attention, however, to the fact that Mrs. Silver's rights under the law would be no different even if she were not involved in circumstances of special need; by law she is entitled to equal benefits of employment as those accorded to male employees in a like position.

It has now been ten days since Mrs. Silver's conference with you, at which time she pointed out the problems set forth above. In view of the fact that you have so far failed to make any responsive communication to Mrs. Silver in regard to these matters, we are now notifying you that all future communication to Mrs. Silver regarding her rights to equal employment benefits are to be made through this office.

We are looking forward to hearing from you.

Thank you for your cooperation and attention.

Very truly yours,

Joan K. Bradford

Richard is in my doorway — bouncing up and down, puffing mad.

I sit at my desk feeling frightened, wordless before his fury.

"You just couldn't wait!" he yells. "Now you've brought a lawyer in on this. The next thing I know we'll all be marching to court."

I shake my head no, saying "We aren't going to court."

"I love my church," he continues, brushing back his hair. "I don't want to drag my brothers and sisters through that. Change takes time. Bohner is an old man. If you'd taken me with you, I could have gotten you extra money."

He yells. I listen. He paces in the hall in front of my door, spewing out his anger, his shock. After all he's done for me, stuck out his neck to get me this job, and now this.

My mind whirls with confusion and fear, but I can't get a word in.

"Did you show that . . . that lawyer," he spits the word, "the letter I wrote Bohner on your behalf?"

"Yes."

He spins around, his back to me, his face looking at the ceiling, his whole body rigid. Then he turns back and glares.

"You aren't loyal to anything. Not to the church, not to me, not to anything!"

He storms across the hall and into his office.

The tears come slowly, then in a torrent. I run to the bathroom where I can hide my hurt.

Richard hates me.

I walk a tight rope whenever I cross the hall to talk
with Richard about a manuscript. He blows hot and
cold. One day he says he understands what I'm trying to
do but that I should not push so hard. The next day he
won't speak to me. I know he's frustrated because he
wants people to concentrate on his goal of getting our
books out to the public.

But the problem of sex discrimination won't wait any
longer. Max describes the activity in Bohner's office. He
and Lorna and Gus have all visited PPPA's general
manager. They've all written him letters outlining the
problem and suggesting solutions.

Bohner told Lorna, "Merikay will never, never, never
get equal pay." He told Max that women are not worth
the same as men.

Gus and Max have both visited PPPA treasurer, Bill
Muir, to discuss the equal employment problems here.

"We're educating them," Max says. "Once they understand how serious this is, they'll come around."

I'm glad there are good people like Max and Lorna
and Gus to help urge the Press to do the right thing. Yet
it's been more than a week since Joan's letter was mailed,
and her office hasn't heard anything from the Press. She
is surprised at the silence. So am I. If Bohner would
respond — to Joan Bradford's or Lorna's letters, to Max's
and Gus' appeals . . . .

What can you do with silence?

## July 1972

Kim phones this morning to say he's found an apartment in San Jose that's about half as expensive as our apartment here. Of course it's also less than half the size. And it will mean a forty-mile commute for me every day; but I'll borrow the money from the Press credit union, and we'll make the move. Anything to economize.

It's so expensive in California. You have to pay first and last months' rent plus a cleaning deposit — just to get in somewhere. However, a lower monthly rental will certainly ease our pressures.

Then this afternoon Joan Bradford calls to say there's been a response. The Press has hired an attorney, one Don McNeil. McNeil contacted Joan to say that the Press is not breaking any laws, that there is no sex discrimination going on here and never has been.

I'm amazed. I sit stunned, the receiver to my ear as Joan tells me everything and urges me to file official complaints against the Press.

After hanging up I stare at my closed door, my only protection against a growingly hostile world. They've hired a lawyer. They're denying the truth.

I feel helpless and confused. Don't they want to do what is right? Don't they want to obey the law? Don't they want to be fair to the workers here? The questions tumble over each other in my head.

## July 20, 1972

(nearly 2 months since my visit to Bohner's office)

excerpt from Joan Bradford's letter to Don McNeil, attorney for PPPA

> "Not only has the Pacific Press failed to grant Mrs. Silver the benefits of head-of-household, but [it] has [also] disregarded the new guidelines of the Adventist church in so doing. In the guidelines effective July 1, 1972, the church added provisions for head-of-household status for persons of either sex. Thus, the Press' failure to correct its discriminatory practices can hardly be viewed as a mere reflecting of church philosophy."

Silence.

Letters fly back and forth between Joan Bradford's and McNeil's offices. Letters go from Lorna's typewriter to Bohner, and to the PPPA Board chairman, Elder R.R. Bietz. Gus Tobler and Max write letters to Bohner and Bietz. But there is no response.

I have had no word on my request. No one has contacted Joan saying, "Let's get together and talk this thing out."

I edit manuscripts, trying to act as if nothing's wrong — as if Kim and I are doing well, as if I don't know the horrible truth about the lies and injustice here. I feel sick every time I think about what is happening, what has been happening for decades.

Lorna has worked here for years and knows everyone. Most of the people with access to PPPA files and records are women who know and like her. So Lorna has photocopied all the pay scale records. She's busy analyzing them, putting the facts and figures in easy-to-recognize form for close comparison.

"There are two components to each workers' salary," she explains, "the basic wage amount and rent allowance. Now the basic wage is job related. Of course, all those jobs performed by men get a higher basic wage than all the jobs performed by women. But just the same, if women could move into those "men's jobs," they would receive the current basic wage for that job.

"The real clinker is the rent allowance." She shows me figures and columns and names. "The rent allowance is sex-related. All married men earn $1.00 per hour rent allowance. Single men earn 70 cents an hour, and all women earn roughly 30 cents an hour rent allowance."

What Joan Bradford can do with this information!

I wonder what Don McNeil will say when Joan shows him all these figures.

I am continually dazed by the revelations here. Has this been going on forever, and no one ever felt guilty about it? Don't people's consciences ever bother them?

My first collection of stories rolled off the press today: *Huck Finn Goes to Church*. My first book. It's really a booklet, but it's still my first collection of stories.

It looks beautiful! I turn each page, examining every sentence, each comma and period. I love it! I want to send copies to everyone I know. I want it to say, "See, I can do more than just complain about head-of-household."

At home Kim and I examine it, ooohing and ahhhing over every page as we talk about my writing future.

I'm at the threshold. I've been working at my craft for ten years, and the demand is beginning to build. Already I have the three major SDA publishing houses working on manuscripts of mine and asking for more, and most of the Adventist publications are requesting articles. The momentum is definitely building.

"It's good that you have something to give," Kim says. "And it's good that you have a following, a reputation, because that helps cushion your Press demands, I'm sure."

I wonder if my writing future will be affected by the Press problems. I can't imagine how a disagreement with my employer can spread beyond the Press.

We decide my smartest move is to establish good relationships with Southern Publishing Association in Tennessee and the Review and Herald Publishing Association in Washington, D.C. That way if PPPA decides to be vindictive and refuses to publish my work, I'll still have outlets for my writing.

After many meetings and letters to Bohner, Lorna writes to board chairman R.R. Bietz again. Her letter is logical and consistent, pointing out that despite General Conference policy that head-of-household should go to any employee with one or more dependents, the Press excludes all women from this benefit, regardless of their family responsibilities.

Her letter gives specific examples, quotes Len Bohner's belief that head-of-household should be reserved for men only, and asks for an opportunity to talk with Bietz.

His reply, dated July 26, says:

Dear Sister Tobler:

In your letter of July 21 you state that women employees who are chief supporters of their families are, according to denominational policy, entitled to head-of-household allowance but this is being denied them. This matter is under study at the present time and will be resolved. I trust that those involved will be patient and not contact the law as has been done. If the Pacific Press is not in full harmony with the policy this will be carefully considered and a solution will be found.

According to your letter you have talked to Elder Bohner several times but you evidently feel that he is not in the mood to solve the problem. You are within your rights to contact the chairman of the board. It is reported, however, that you have created considerable disturbance at the Press because of this situation. It is insinuated that you have counseled younger workers to contact attorneys. If this is true, I believe it is most unfortunate and unethical. As Christians I believe we should solve our problems without going to the courts of the land. We are now in a most embarrassing situation because an appeal has been made to the law. Before we are through we may be spending thousands of dollars which could have been used to solve some of the financial problems referred to.

According to my schedule I expect to be in Mt. View on Wednesday, August 9. As per your request I shall be happy to see you at that time and discuss the matter further.

Your brother in Christ,

R.R. Bietz

Richard wants to see me in his office. When I enter he motions for me to sit down.

"I've been thinking about your situation," he says, "and there's at least one more step you can try if you don't get satisfaction from Len Bohner."

I wait for his suggestion.

"You really should write to Elder Bietz. He's above Bohner in authority and he's a good Christian man. I'm not implying that Brother Bohner isn't — but Bietz is a man of action."

I wonder if writing to Bietz will do any good. Lorna's letter elicited a reprimand. What would a letter from me do?

"Think about it," Richard says. "I'm sure you'll feel better once you contact Bietz."

Maybe if I send him a copy of *Huck Finn Goes to Church* . . . if I come "bearing gifts," so to speak, perhaps he'll listen and help.

I go back to my office and write to Bietz, sending a copy of my letter to Elder Robert Pierson (president of the General Conference of Seventh-day Adventists).

There are so many rumors. Even here in Mountain View people think I'm suing the Press. Perhaps my letter will correct misconceptions. I try to explain to Bietz what I'm asking for. I support my requests/expectations with the following quotes from Mrs. White:

> If a woman is appointed by the Lord to do a certain work, her work is to be estimated according to its value. Every laborer is to receive his or her just due.

> It may be thought to be a good plan to allow persons to give talent and earnest labor to the work of God, while they draw nothing from the treasury. But this is making a difference, and selfishly withholding from such workers their due. God will not put His sanction on any such plan. Those who invented this method may have thought that they were doing God service by not drawing from the treasury to pay these God-fearing, soul-loving laborers. But there will be an account to settle by and by, and then those who now think this exaction, this partiality in dealing, a wise scheme, will be ashamed of their selfishness . . . .

> Those who work earnestly and unselfishly, be they men or

women, bring sheaves to the Master; and the souls converted by their labor will bring their tithes to the treasury. When self-denial is required because of a dearth of means, do not let a few hard-working women do all the sacrificing. Let all share in making the sacrifice. God declares, I hate robbery for burnt offering.

*Manuscript 47, 1898.*

If women do the work that is not the most agreeable to many of those who labor in word and doctrine, and if their works testify that they are accomplishing a work that has been manifestly neglected, shouldn't such labor be looked upon as being as rich in results as the work of the ordained ministers? Should it not command the hire of the laborer? . . .

You are to do your duty to the women who labor in the gospel . . . .

*Manuscript 142, 1903.*

Injustice has sometimes been done to women who labor just as devotedly as their husbands, and who are recognized by God as being necessary to the work of the ministry. The method of paying men laborers, and not paying their wives who share their labors with them, is a plan not according to the Lord's order. . . . God is a God of justice, and if the ministers receive a salary for their work, their wives who devote themselves just as disinterestedly to the work, should be paid in addition to the wages their husbands receive, even though they may not ask for this.

Seventh-day Adventists are not in any way to belittle woman's work.

*Gospel Workers,* pp. 452-53 (1915)

In my letter I try to explain that I have not filed any legal actions against Pacific Press, that I love the Lord's work, and that my only desire is to help the Press obey the law.

I enclose a copy of *Huck Finn Goes To Church*, hoping that both Elder Bietz and Elder Pierson will read and enjoy the booklet and will realize that I have a deep desire to serve the Lord. Now I wait for their reply.

## August 1972

The car breaks today. Max drives to San Jose to pick me up so I wouldn't miss work. How I'd love to miss work, but I can't afford it. I must be there every day so that people will know I am sincere in my desire to work for the Lord — and so that the leaders will see that I am not going to quit insisting on equal pay.

How much will car repairs cost?

At noon I go to the credit union and borrow more money. I comfort myself with the assurance that as soon as I receive head-of-household, I'll be able to pay off all the loans.

At supper Kim says, "I'm going to find a job."

"Don't you like school?" I fill our dishes with tacos and rice.

"I love it; you know that. But how can we survive?"

"I got a loan from the credit union."

"And how are we going to pay for that?"

"When I get head-of-household I'll pay it back."

Kim is such a good man, honest and kind. My heart fills with resentment toward the Press. Why should he have to sacrifice his education because the Press discriminates against me? Why should he have to quit school and get a job when the wives of PPPA employees don't have to stop their various pursuits and go to work?

"Don't quit," I say. "We'll manage. If you get a job, it will just give Bohner another excuse for not paying me head-of-household. In fact, I'll probably *never* get it if you go to work."

"You won't need it."

"Yes, but I've started the fuss. If I drop it now because you go to work, then should I ever, ever need it again — it will be impossible to start over once I've stopped the momentum."

We eat in silence. And what about all the other women who deserve it, I wonder. If I don't speak for them, who will? No one else ever has. No one else is in as strong a position to speak out.

I resent having to move to a smaller apartment in San Jose, having to borrow money to fix our car, having next-to-nothing to eat. I resent putting my husband under such stress.

I resent the tension at work, tension based on the fact that I'm female and therefore automatically undeserving of head-of-household allowance. Most of all I resent feeling "out of place" in asking for something I'm entitled to.

Yesterday I received a letter from Elder Bietz. In it he bawled me out for going to Joan Bradford before coming to him. He did not comment on my personal situation, on the fact that I qualify for and need head-of-household allowance. Instead he wrote:

> I appreciate hearing your side of the story and shall make no further comment at this time. Brother Bohner and I are keeping in close contact in regard to the matter.
>
> I trust that you will be patient and keep on praying about it. We certainly are also making it a matter of prayer.
>
> I shall pray most earnestly that the problem can be resolved without further embarrassment to the church we love and respect.

I never felt quite so directly put off, set aside, ignored, as I did with his letter yesterday. So he's talking with Elder Bohner but he won't talk to me. Thanks a lot, mister.

Today a second letter arrived from Elder Bietz. In it he referred to all the Mrs. White quotes which I sent him:

> I don't think there is a single statement on that sheet which would give anyone the impression that women should have the same wages as the men, although I am not opposed to that idea. We should be careful that we don't make the Spirit of Prophecy say something that was not intended.

Lorna continues writing letters to the brethren. They are beautiful letters — well conceived, perfectly worded, very educational. If education is what the brethren need, they certainly have a wealth of it in Lorna's letters. I don't know if her words do any good. But I suppose they can't do any harm. At least they're keeping up the flow of communication.

I can't write letters by the dozen. I can't ask for meetings as she and Max and Gus can do. I just can't. I will see this thing through to the end, and I hope that will be soon. But I can't do more than that. Not now, anyway. I feel too raw from the truth I've learned, too afraid, to do more than I'm doing.

To maintain my resolve, to stand true to my integrity, I must have other things to concentrate on. My studies help.

I've decided to do a special senior project. I'm putting together a one-time, special-issue magazine aimed at Adventist women. It will be all about SDA women, and I think it'll be exciting. Kim will design it and do all the paste-up and production work. I'll edit it and write articles. It'll be a fun project, something the two of us can work on together — something to keep the creative juices flowing.

My writing is another "escape from the Press." Just this week the Review and Herald Publishing Association accepted my manuscript on boarding academy and sent me an advanced royalties check. Thanks to that money, Kim and I are breathing a little easier this month.

Arbie knocks timidly at my door, then peeks in. "Richard wants to see you," she says shyly. Her eyes look sad, as always. I wonder what great burden she carries.

"Have a seat," Richard motions to the couch as I enter.

"You know, you're acting as if you know all the truth and no one else around here knows anything," he says. His face is pale beneath his dark brown hair.

As usual, I'm wordless. What can I say? My mind blanks with fear, with hurt.

"The Press has been around a long time, and the people who work here have given years, sometimes decades, to the cause. Do you really think that after twelve short months you have a clearer picture of what's happening here than the rest of us?"

I stare at him, confused.

"This whole thing is upsetting my life. It's upsetting our work here. I can't think of anything else, and the fact that you have a lawyer working on this. And now the Press has a lawyer." He shakes his head. I can see his pain.

"Richard, I don't want a horrible fight," I say, wishing I could assure and comfort him.

"What do you call it when you bring in a lawyer?" he spits in fury.

"What else can I do? No one pays any attention to my need. Bohner never responded. He still hasn't. It's been weeks and he's never said anything except, 'No woman is ever going to get head-of-household.' "

"He's an old man. Change takes time."

"Don't you think a hundred years is enough time?"

He stares silently.

"Richard, not one woman in this whole place earns head-of-household, even though many of them are the only support of their families."

His eyes glare. He shakes his head. "Look, I just want this thing to end. I just want us to get back to work, editing."

"I'm working," I say.

"I know. I know." he nods. His lips squeeze together in a long, tight line. He shakes his head as if he has nothing more to say. I walk back to my office.

❧

There is talk that Gus is going to be "called" to Germany. A "call" is a denominational invitation to work at a certain school or hospital or publishing house. A "call" is infused with importance, with the feeling that God himself is asking. There is often a deep sense of obligation to accept such a job offering.

If Gus and Lorna leave, I don't know what I'll do. She knows where all the records are. She can cite specific examples of women who have trained in their male bosses decade after decade and never received a promotion, never received pay commensurate with their work. She knows the people and the stories and the statistics that I need to create a change here. If she goes to Germany . . . .

"Everyone's just talking," she says to me. "They're moving Gus' magazine to the German publishing house, and it seems logical that they'll ask him to move there, too."

"But do you speak German?"

She smiles, "A little. I can stumble along."

I wonder if there's some connection between Lorna's and my asking for policy-and-practice changes at the Press, and Gus's magazine being transferred to Germany.

Bietz is here and he's visiting Lorna! I'm scared to death. A man from the factory knocks on my door and says Bietz will see me next.

I phone Joan Bradford. I can't see Bietz! Not after his letter bawling me out. He'll yell at me, and say I'm evil, and I can't take any more of that.

"Bietz is here and he wants to see me, and I don't want to get yelled at." I'm frantic when Joan comes on the line.

"He can't see you without me," she says. "I'll call Bohner's office immediately. I'll be there in half an hour."

At least Joan will be here when Bietz comes; at least she can help explain the law. I know that things would change here if the men could hear about the law from someone other than Lorna or me. They don't take us seriously. We're just workers, not lawyers. But if they could hear from Joan, I'm sure they'd take the whole thing more seriously.

In a few minutes Joan calls back. "He refuses to see us," she says. "He'll only see you alone, and I can't allow that. You must have counsel so that there is a record of what's said."

I hang up, relieved that I don't have to see Bietz — and at the same time disappointed that he can't learn the truth about the law.

Lorna stops by later to say Bietz was very general in his comments.

"He urged me to stop stirring up trouble," she says. "The men around here think I'm behind it all. They think I'm putting you up to it." Her eyes crinkle into laughter. "They think you're too young and innocent."

I groan. Since May I've felt very, very old.

"He assured me that the Press would obey the law, and said that we should always tell the truth forthrightly about our employment and monetary practices. He said he would see to it that that was done and asked me not to tell other women what was going on, since that would just stir up trouble," she says.

"Who wants to stir up trouble?" I ask. "We've got more than we can handle now. I sure don't want any more trouble!"

We both laugh. It eases the tension. That's one thing I like about Lorna, she can always laugh. We laugh now and it feels good.

Then she says, "There's going to be a Press Board meeting next month, and Bietz told me I had a right to address the Board. I thanked him and told him I would like that, and he said he would let me know if they plan to take this subject up. I'm sure that Bietz came here to feel us out so that he can present some changes at the Board meeting."

Her words give me hope. Maybe this whole thing will be resolved in a month. I hope so.

During the past few days Lorna has met both with Elders Robert Pierson and R. R. Bietz. Elder Pierson, a small bald man with a gentle voice, presides over the General Conference of Seventh-day Adventists. Most of us just call it the GC. The GC is the governing (or management) body of the Adventist denomination. It is located in Washington, D.C.

"Pierson assured me that he's confident the brethren here will do whatever's necessary to comply with the law, if indeed they are breaking any laws," she says.

It sounds like politician's talk to me. It reminds me of the evening news, with everyone talking about Watergate and coverups, and administration spokesmen saying they have full confidence in the president.

"Bietz said almost the same things to me as Pierson did," Lorna says. "But he has more personality, more style."

I think about Elder Bietz, a big, handsome, silver-haired man with an easy smile.

"He asked me to go easy on the brethren. He asked for patience and understanding."

Then her voice grows serious. "He said that if we don't ease up, if we insist on pursuing this thing, the brethren will burn us at the stake."

Our eyes meet. The first out-and-out threat.

"Like Joan of Arc?" I grin. "Can he promise that we'll be in the history books and everything? We'd better get all that in writing." We laugh until we have to wipe our eyes.

"I asked him what he'd do in our place," she says. "He said he'd address the Board. So I asked to do just that, but then he hedged and said October's agenda was already full."

For a few minutes we share silence. Then she sighs. "He asked me to refrain from distributing copies of the Title VII law to other women. I think everyone should have a copy of it, but I told him I'd wait."

I nod. Perhaps if we are quiet and well behaved the brethren will see the justice of our requests. I hope they'll notice and take action to correct the wrong.

## September, October 1972

(Five months since my visit with Bohner)

The October Board meeting comes and goes. The Fall Council meeting (when church leaders from all over North America, including GC president Robert Pierson and GC vice president Neal C. Wilson, gather to discuss problems and solutions) comes and goes.

Numerous weekly Executive Committee meetings pass, and still there is no word on my request, no movement toward equality for women at the Press.

Silence. Silence. Silence.

It is as if we, our needs, our requests, do not exist.

Gus sits across the desk from me telling me he has received the official "call" to Germany.

"Please don't go," I beg.

"I must, Merikay," he says in his gentle Swiss accent. "It is where I'm needed."

"But I need you here. And I need Lorna."

"I haven't given my answer yet. But even if I go, it won't be until December; and I am hoping this situation will be resolved by then. If it is, you won't need us here. And if it isn't . . ." He pauses. I can see the concern flowing across his smooth features. "Well, Lorna will stay."

I look at him, wondering if I've heard correctly. "You don't think she'd leave in the middle of this, do you? That's not Lorna," he smiles. "She'll stay until it is straightened out. I hope that will be soon."

"So do I!"

I feel a burst of love for him, for her, for them.

"Don't get discouraged, Merikay," he says. "The brethren are hardheaded sometimes, but I can't believe they're hardhearted. Give them time to change. You are definitely right in this matter, and I feel that in time they will recognize that fact. But don't let their unreasonableness destroy your faith."

There is a rumor that someone has filed a complaint with the Wage and Hour Division of the Department of Labor.

Richard thinks I filed it, and he's not talking to me again. In fact, he's not even looking at me. We pass in the hall, but it's as if I don't exist.

I wonder if Lorna or Max filed the complaint. I don't dare ask. It's an unspoken rule that we don't ask. If one or the other of us volunteers information, okay; but we don't ask. That way, should someone quiz us about what the others are doing, we can honestly say we don't know.

On the home front, Kim's classwork is going well. He's getting high grades and likes the subjects he's studying.

I love my classes. Children's literature and American literature help me keep a sense of balance while editing manuscripts such as *Tent By the Sawdust Pile* and *Give Your Guilt Away*.

And last week I received the "go ahead" on my magazine idea. I will create and publish a magazine on Adventist women as an independent project under the direction of Dr. Marian Robinson. I'm excited about the magazine. I see it as a kind of "Reader's Digest" of articles, stories, thoughts, and statistics concerning the Adventist and/or Christian woman.

Since it's a school project, I can use student loan money to finance it. The magazine will give Kim and me something exciting and positive on which to focus. We certainly need that.

When I come home from class, Kim and Max are sitting in the living room talking about the Department of Labor complaint.

"It's official," Kim says. "Someone turned in the Press."

"I wonder who?" I smile accusingly at Max.

"Lorna thinks it's someone from the factory or bindery," he says, ignoring my suspicion.

"How do you know it's real?" I drop my books on the table and sit down next to Kim.

"Richard saw the letter. We're going to be investigated," Max says. "Someone's going to come and interview us all and check out the pay scales and find out if we're breaking the law."

I feel excited and relieved. Maybe my part in this is ending. Maybe I've just paved the way and now the Lord is bringing in someone else to do the legal clean-up work. Maybe I won't have to play insistent, women's rights pioneer any more. Maybe I can just fade into the background.

"Well I hope you're happy!" Richard stands just inside my door. "Now you've got the government on our necks."

At least when I'm in his office I have the option of leaving. When he corners me in mine, I feel more helpless than ever.

"Richard, I had nothing to do with this."

"You have everything to do with it!" Again I hear how he stuck his neck out to hire me despite the fact that I don't have a college degree. Again I hear that I should have taken him with me to visit Bohner last May. He could have eased Bohner into the idea of giving me some extra money.

"Richard, do you realize that not one woman receives head-of-household here?"

"All you ever think about, all you ever talk about is money!" I hear his angry disgust. His eyes narrow behind his glasses. The dark mustache which used to spread out easily above his smiles, twitches with rage.

I say, "Women are suffering because they aren't being paid fairly."

He leaves, then returns.

"You think you have all the answers. You haven't even worked here two years. Some of us have our lives wrapped up in the Lord's work, but you wouldn't understand that.

"Some of us have a quarter of a century or more in this labor, and our wives and our parents and our children work for the church. And here you are, not even two years in the work, and totally disrupting everything for everyone.

"You know more than all the rest of us. Well, I hope you're proud of yourself. I wouldn't be a bit surprised if you, single-handedly, kicked off the time of trouble."

He slams my door.

## November 1972

Six months and nothing has changed, yet everything has changed.

Kim and I live in San Jose.

Gus will move to Germany.

Max and Lorna and I exist on the edge of constant tension.

Richard spends hours chastising me after days and weeks of ignoring me.

Not a word from Bohner.

Not a word from Bietz.

## November 7, 1972

Lorna and I drive to Joan Bradford's office to file official complaints with the Equal Employment Opportunity Commission (EEOC).

Joan suggests that I begin immediate lawsuit proceedings, but I can't. I hope the government will apply enough pressure that Press management will voluntarily bring our employment practices into line without my having to do anything else. If the government can persuade them, I might be able to get on with my life.

Perhaps my official complaint will help.

On our way home, Lorna and I conjecture about the future. "It can't go on much longer like this," she says. "What does the Press have to gain? If discrimination is found, as it will be, it's far more expensive to fight than to comply."

I cling to her words. They make sense. And I long to believe that she knows these Press leaders better than I do. She has worked for the church for nearly twenty years; surely she knows how these people's minds work.

Guy Guerrero is a small man of Puerto Rican ancestry, with a soft voice and probing brown eyes. He is the Department of Labor investigator, and he is in my office interviewing me. I must list all the tasks I perform while on the job — every single task, from reading and evaluating manuscripts, to editing, to sitting on various committees must be listed for him.

He says that after he completes his investigation, everything will be straightened out.

Press employees are stiff with fear. There has never been a government investigator checking us out before. Tension fills the halls. Adventists have always believed that the government will single us out for persecution because of our "nonconformist" beliefs. Now here is a government investigator, invading our publishing house, asking all sorts of questions.

Since the pressure is almost unbearable, I throw myself whole-heartedly into my magazine project. I'm writing to *Insight, Liberty, Ms., Psychology Today, Christianity Today, Review and Herald, Sunday Digest,* and other magazines, asking permission to reprint articles I've clipped from their pages.

I've already written to Leona G. Running, professor of biblical languages in the SDA theological seminary at Andrews University in Berrien Springs, Michigan. She published a paper on the role of women in the Adventist church. Max recommended her and her paper, and I'm grateful for an excuse to contact her.

I wrote to Chuck Scriven and Pat Horning from *Insight* magazine and to Kit Watts, whose writings I've admired for years. A request letter goes to George Target. The more I think about all the people who may contribute to this project, the more I'm convinced it's going to be *great!*

I can't wait to see it all come together. I can't wait to have something positive to give to people. Anything to help counter the impression that all I am is a trouble-maker.

Wes Siegenthaler has come to reason with me.

He sits on the other side of my desk in his gray suit and urges me to "go easy" on the brethren.

The leaders really have my good at heart, he says; they are simply "thickheaded," and new ideas take a long time to sink in.

"I know," I say. "So far it's taken more than a hundred years."

He tells me about all the sacrifices he and other men have made over the years — how they have been passed over for promotions, how they have been mistreated.

I appreciate his stories. I sympathize with anyone who has been mistreated. But while he talks about isolated instances of personal abuse, I am concerned with institutionalized discrimination. When I mention this, when I point out that all women at the press earn thousands less than all men — whether they are the sole worker in their family or not — he grows serious.

"Well now, Merikay," he shakes his head. "I don't know if a woman is really worth the same as a man. Honestly, I don't know if they can do the same amount of work. You do have your monthly cycles...." His eyebrows rise as if he is making a vital point.

"Wes," I lean forward, as earnest as he. "Wes, I don't edit books with that end."

A fine, pink color starts at the top of his white collar and spreads up his neck and face, coming to rest in bright red cheeks and ears.

He smiles.

I smile.

We change the subject.

∾

Kim has secured a couple of student loans. They will ease our burden. Between his school loans and my credit union loans, we should be able to hold out for a few more months.

But sometimes we have to improvise. Like yesterday. We didn't have any gas money left, and I have to fill up the tank in order to get to work. So we hunted through the cupboards until we found a few canned goods and a box or two of food we probably won't use. Then we put them in a sack and tossed a coin to see who would get the illustrious privilege of walking to the grocery story and turning the stuff back in for a refund.

He got the job. Am I glad!

## December 1972

(Seven months since I visited Bohner's office asking for head-of-household allowance)

Guy Guerrero has completed his investigation.

"Did you find discrimination?" I ask.

"Yes, but that will be taken care of."

I love his confidence. Like Lorna, he knows that Press management will do what's right once it's pointed out to them. I hope that a man doing the pointing out will improve our chances for correction. Maybe by the first of the year this whole thing will be over.

"My report goes in next week, and then it will be a couple of weeks more before the Press hears," he says.

"Do you think everything will be settled by the first of the year?" I ask, hoping.

He shrugs. "Maybe not by the first, but shortly afterward."

I'm relieved that soon we'll be able to get back to normal.

Since it's December, everyone's in the Christmas spirit — exchanging cards or little gifts. Richard is talking to me again.

I'm receiving responses to all my "may-I-reprint-your-article" letters. Everyone has said "yes." I'm thrilled!

And all the people I asked to contribute stories have agreed, with one exception. So it looks as if I'm going to be able to produce the kind of magazine I dream about.

Kim and I have decided on the name *HERS* for it. We'll work on *HERS* all next semester and should be able to bring it out in the spring.

And maybe, just maybe, the Press will grant me equal pay in a few more weeks. What a Christmas present that would be!

∾

Gus left today.

Lorna stayed.

Everyone is shocked that she's still sitting at her desk working as Lawrence Maxwell's secretary. Yet there is no move to correct the wrong here.

Doesn't anyone care that women workers at Pacific Press are suffering?

Experiencing something suddenly opens your eyes to all the other people who experience it too. You buy a Datsun, and suddenly you notice all the Datsuns on the highway.

I'm suffering because of the Press' wage scale, and suddenly I notice that many other women are too. Only they've been suffering for years, and what they've endured is much worse than what I'm experiencing. They have lived in cramped studio apartments, have forgone the "luxury" of owning an automobile or buying new clothes, so they could put their children through church school on their Press salary.

I *know* how much I hurt. I can imagine how much worse it has been for them. And yet no one in leadership seems to care. No one seems even to notice that there is unfairness in our business operations, that oppression is built into the very fabric of our system.

Instead of tenderhearted understanding, instead of the brethren trying to work justice, angry emotions strike out at personalities — mainly me, and Lorna, and anyone else who dares say Pacific Press should clean up its act.

# January 1973

I'M IN THE PHOTOGRAPHY STUDIO TALKING ABOUT THE COVER illustration I want on one of the books I'm editing, when PPPA treasurer Bill Muir brings our first paychecks of 1973.

Opening my pay envelope I discover something interesting. My check is for the usual paltry amount; but on the stub, in the box entitled "total to date," more than a thousand dollars is typed in.

"Maybe the Press has finally decided to equalize our income." I think excitedly. "Maybe they made a New Year's resolution to be honest and fair."

Hurrying to my office, I call Kim. "Guess what, it looks like the Press is going to give us head-of-household after all," I say. "They've got more than a thousand dollars on my stub, as if they're going to pay that much to me."

"It's about time," he says. We talk, relieved, and plan to go out for ice cream tonight as a celebration.

After lunch I phone Bill Muir's office to find out what the "total-to-date" amount means. The secretary sounds nervous and puts me on hold.

When Bill Muir comes on the line I say, "Hi, this is Merikay."

"I know." His voice is flat, unemotional.

"I was just wondering what this amount in my 'total-to-date' box on the stub of my check means. It's over a thousand dollars more than you've paid me."

Silence.

"I mean, is there some mistake?"

"No, there's no mistake."

"Well, what does that figure mean?"

"I can't talk about it. It's part of the investigation." He hangs up.

I phone Guy Guerrero and tell him about the fact that my "total-to-date" box has more than a thousand dollars typed in.

"That's your settlement amount," he says.

"My what?"

"That's what the Press owes you in back pay, and they've agreed to give it to you. They are settling up, bringing everything into line with the law. You should receive your check within the next few days."

I can't believe his words. A thousand dollars does not begin to equal head-of-household. "There must be a mistake," I say. "How did you arrive at the thousand-dollar figure?"

"Mr. Bohner showed me what you earn and what Max earns, and the difference over a year is about a thousand dollars."

"There's got to be some mistake," I start to laugh. "I earn 40 percent less than Max."

He is silent.

"Well, look, we just got our W-2 forms. I'll quote you the exact figures. Just a minute." I run down the hall to Max's office.

"Guerrero is on the phone, and the figures he has for your earnings and mine are way off," I say to Max. "I need your W-2 to read him the figures." He hands it to me and I go back to my office.

"Here it is," I say into the phone. "Max earns $11,000 and I earn $6,676.41."

Silence.

"Are you there?" I ask.

"Yes. Please read me the figures again."

I read them.

"Will you please copy those forms for me? I'll be in your office tomorrow."

The joy I felt earlier in the day evaporates. Like all my hopes for the past nine months, it is gone; and in its place settles despair!

∾

Guy Guerrero sits solemn faced in my office. "I never thought they'd lie to me," he says. "I'm Catholic. I know what love of church is, and I never thought they'd lie."

He is on his way to Bohner's office to confront him with the xeroxes of Max's and my W2 forms. "I'll call you after I meet with them," he says. "Don't cash any checks."

All morning I edit. I work at making the point of view consistent. I try to make the order of events smooth and sensible. I concentrate on the manuscripts crowding my desk, but every few minutes Guerrero pops into mind and I wonder what's happening in Bohner's office.

After lunch Guerrero calls. His voice is strained. "Bohner threw me out of his office," he says. "He told me that the next time the Press sees me will be in court."

I am stunned.

"Do you want us to file suit for you?"

"No, no. I can't make a decision like that here, now, on the phone," I say, feeling drained.

"Well, whether we file for you or we file on our own, we will sue," he says. "I'm starting the process today."

I hang up, thinking about Bohner lying to him and throwing him off the premises. I realize that the thousand dollars I'd thought was the start of equal pay is no longer in my grasp. I realize that I don't want the government taking my employer to court. I don't want a government versus Pacific Press battle. For the rest of the day I sit thinking about all the possibilities, all the problems.

January 1973, a brand new year. I am twenty-six years old. I feel like a hundred.

God, what do You want me to do? When I started this whole thing I knew what was right. I knew You were with me. But nothing's happening. There's no indication that the Press will be fair. And now, throwing Guerrero off Press grounds, threatening to see him in court. Does the Press *want* a lawsuit? What am I supposed to do?

Kim and I pray about it. We're in debt. The stupid car keeps breaking down, and I keep borrowing more credit union money. Kim will graduate this spring, but what will we do in the meantime?

All evening we talk about the possibilities. I could just float along and let the government drag the Press to court. The thought frightens me. The government doesn't understand about our church and the love we have for each other. I dread what they might do.

I could file my own lawsuit. At least *I'd* be more understanding than the government. And if I filed, I'm sure the management would get serious about straightening things out. If we could work together to correct the inequities, the government's suit would automatically disappear.

Or I could quit, leave the Press and find other work. I am young and talented, and I could get another job easily. But what about all the other women, the ones who cannot quit, who are afraid to speak up for themselves? My actions have done nothing but make their lives harder. They all have to punch time clocks now. If I quit, just walk away from the mess, they will be left worse off than when I came.

I will not quit until we have equality at Pacific Press.

"Well, I think you should file suit," Kim says. "It's the only thing they'll take seriously. What's it been, eight or nine months of prayer and letters and begging, and what's happened?"

My days are filled with confusion. What should I do?

All the love, all the idealism, all the pride I've had in my church and its institutions bubbles to the surface, only to be snuffed by the reality I've experienced.

In the past eight months I have never once been listened to — not by Bohner, not by Richard, not by Bietz, not by the Pacific Press Board or the Executive Committee, not by the General Conference. Not one person has said: "I can see why you feel as you do. It's obvious that something's wrong. Let's work together to find a solution."

The only communication Joan Bradford's office has received is letters from Attorney McNeil denying discrimination.

And the government inspector is thrown out of Bohner's office.

It's clear to me that management (or the church leaders counseling management) are not going to change without being forced to. These men will not do what is right because it is right, will not obey the law because it is law, will not treat their employees fairly because it is the moral thing to do.

I must file suit.

I hate what I must do.

"You know, if I file suit, it could end my writing career," I say to Kim over supper. He nods.

Writing is my life. What will I do if I can't write? Ever since I was a youngster, writing has been an irresistible drive, linking actions and concepts in a continuing organization. Writing helps me sort out my thoughts and experiences. It gives form and structure to my ideas. It's my way of communicating, of sharing what I've learned.

I love to write. I need to write and see my writing published. But the possibility of an end to my writing for the church looms among my fears.

"Are you willing to sacrifice that?" Kim asks gently.

"I don't know. I don't know." I turn away irritated at the question.

I wish I could unhesitatingly say, "Yes. I'll sacrifice anything for principle, for justice, for equality." I wish I could be the way I am in my idealistic fantasies — ready to cast everything at the feet of Jesus in some noble gesture of self-sacrifice. But I honestly don't know if I'm willing to sacrifice my writing career.

"I'd sue them," Kim says, "to teach them a lesson." His words are uncommonly harsh.

"Well, look," he says. "They need to be taught that they cannot get away with mistreating women forever. And all it takes is one woman who says, 'Stop,' and means it. I think they deserve to be taught a lesson for all the injustice, all the hardships they've been forcing on women for years."

He's right, of course. Like Lorna and Max, Kim is usually right. But I keep thinking about how my heart aches whenever Richard ignores me, how my stomach knots when he yells at me.

I keep thinking about how difficult it is for me to go to Book Publishing Committee, to sit there with all those men who discuss me during Board meeting — all those men who have personally voted against giving me head-of-household pay, even though they know it causes me extreme financial difficulty.

What will it be like for me to sit on those committees after I file suit? What will the halls of Pacific Press be like for me after that?

We talk all evening. If I file suit, will it just drag on for another eight or nine months? Can we stand that?

When we go to bed I cannot sleep. I think of all the people I've loved: my academy teachers, my ministers, Elder Detamore who first published my story *NOW!* Will they understand? How can they? They're another generation, a generation which believes that you endure and wait for the Lord to act.

If I file suit I may lose them. Can I bear that?

To me the most important thing in life is the relationships I have — my husband, my family, my friends. In addition to my relationships, there is nothing that brings me the pleasure, the feeling of accomplishment and growth, that my writing brings.

If I file suit, I may lose the two most important things in my life. Can I bear that?

And what if it does no good? Nothing I've tried so far has done any good. Even the government inspector hasn't accomplished anything. What if I go ahead and give up all that is meaningful to my life and accomplish nothing? What if the Press just goes on its merry way discriminating from here till the end?

Tears gather as the questions tug at me. I'm the only woman in the entire company with a clear-cut male counterpart; so it's obvious if anyone is going to sue and have a chance at winning, it has to be me. I feel helpless, hurt and angry and helpless.

For nearly a week I go to work and come home and go to class and come home and battle over whether or not to sue.

I'm on the brink.

I'm on the doorstep, with my hand on the knob.

To sue or not to sue.

I'm the only one who can do it successfully. I alone am in the employment position necessary for a victory.

The fact that I have no children frees me from the worry of how my actions might affect little ones. My youth should give me some sort of resilience. I don't have years of retirement benefits which I must protect, built up within the system.

But I know if I say yes, things will never, never be the same again. And I'm frightened when I try to imagine what they will be like. I may be saying yes to the ruination of my life.

Yet, the other side of my brain and heart admits that things are pretty miserable now.

Kim and I drive to Joan Bradford's. It's sunny for January, but the sunshine doesn't cheer me. I'm agitated. We drive in silence, all the words having been said again and again.

In her office Kim paces. I sit. We want to know if I can be fired should I file suit.

She says, "No." She says it's against the law to fire someone for reporting illegal practices or for filing suit because of illegal employment practices.

"But other things are against the law too, and the Press keeps right on doing them," I remind her.

She assures us that I won't be fired.

"If I file now, can we prevent the government from taking them to court?" I ask. "I'm worred that the government would be far harsher on them than I want." There are thousands of people who might be hurt by a government suit. I'd like to do what I can to prevent that.

"If Merikay files suit, how soon do you think things could be settled?" Kim asks.

"They could be settled tomorrow if the Press would negotiate," she says. "It's been my experience that a lawsuit speeds the negotiation process considerably."

Kim looks at me, his eyes bright.

Less encouraged, I ask, "What's the longest it could take? If the Press fought it every step of the way, if they didn't negotiate, if they kept doing just what they've done so far, what's the longest it might take to get this whole matter settled? A year or two?"

"It could take as long as five years." She speaks slowly, emphasizing each word.

I look at Kim. "Five years." He doesn't seem to care. "Kim, I'd be thirty-one in five years. You'd be almost thirty-five. Can you take five years of this?"

"It's not going to be five years," he says confidently. "Those guys aren't going to drag it out that long. It's too expensive."

I walk out to the lobby to think. I can hear Kim and Joan talking. They're intense, dedicated people. I love them both. I need them both. If I go into this, I desperately need all the love and support I can get because I know I'm not going to get much.

Lord, what do You want me to do?

But the question is foolish. The answer has been obvious

almost from the start. I must do what I am able, what no one else can do. I must file suit.

God, please give me the strength to carry through on this.

I walk back into Joan's office. "Okay, it's got to be done. I'll file."

Joan draws up the papers. This will be a class action. That means I am suing on behalf of myself and all others "similarly situated."

"I don't want just simply to sue them," I say. "I want to change the employment policy that discriminates against all of us."

Joan nods, "That means a class action."

She also draws up a contract between the two of us. She will not charge me any attorney fees, and she will pay all court costs out of her own pocket. She is taking this case on a contingency basis. That means if we win, she gets one-third of the amount awarded, and I must reimburse her for any costs. If we lose, I must reimburse her for costs only.

The first order of business is writing to the EEOC and requesting a right-to-sue letter. Once I receive my right-to-sue letter, Joan will file our papers.

## January 22, 1973

Excerpted from Attorney Bradford's letter to the EEOC requesting right-to-sue letter:

> Mrs. Silver and I will appreciate your forwarding a right-to-sue letter at the earliest possible date. It is our belief that recent incidents between Mrs. Silver and her employer indicate the importance of filing a civil action at once. The employer in this case is a religious publishing company and is, I am convinced, engaged in tactics of unusual harassment of the charging party by sermons and conversations directed toward convincing her that she is "sinning" by her attempts to seek legal remedies rather than submitting to the employment practices of her employer.
>
> Because of the unusual nature of this kind of harassment and pressure upon an employee, I would like to file a complaint immediately, and will then ask the EEOC to intervene.

# During

When you start dealing with real change
you are talking about
interfering
with those
who are in possession of something.

Carl B. Stokes
*Promise of Power*

# January 31, 1973

(Eight months and one week since I asked Bohner for head-of-household allowance.)

TODAY MY CLASS ACTION LAWSUIT AGAINST PACIFIC PRESS is filed.

Civil Action #C-730168 CBR charges that Pacific Press is violating the Title VII section of the Civil Rights Act.

It charges violations in four specific areas:

1. The Press' wage scale is based on sex without regard to any standard of job performance.
2. The Press pays women workers below the job category in which their work is actually performed.
3. The Press denies women substantial fringe benefits based on head-of-household status.
4. The Press retaliates against women employees in an effort to make them abandon any legal remedies for their employment problems.

## February and March 1973

The Press receives the papers. A federal marshal serves them.

The place is like a tomb; deathly silence haunts all the halls.

I try editing, try working with the art department and typography, try to phone authors to discuss changes in their manuscripts. But I notice I'm holding my breath most of the time. Waiting. Hoping this will be the event which will spur the change.

Waiting.

In midafternoon I receive a call from the receptionist at the front desk of the administration building.

"There's something over here for you," she says.

I'm afraid. What could it be? I walk slowly to the ad building.

At the desk I notice a beautiful bouquet of bright roses. "They're yours," the receptionist smiles.

Opening the card, I read: "To the most courageous woman I have ever met. Love, Kim."

Teary-eyed I carry the flowers back to my office.

With a man like Kim, I can face anything.

Silence.

It's been two days, and still no response.

Midmorning the receptionist calls to say I have another present at the front desk. Again a bouquet of flowers greets me. Opening the card I read, "Right on! Fight the good fight! And thank you from all of us." It is signed by Pat Horning, Kit Watts, Rosemary Bradley — three women working for the church in Washington, D.C.

I walk back to my office, stopping by Lorna's on the way.

"News travels fast," I say, showing her the card.

So there is support for what we're doing. The flowers and what they symbolize help make the silence bearable.

"Bohner sent me a letter today," Lorna says, popping into my office after lunch. "He says he expects me to leave the Press and join Gus by April 1."

I look at her, afraid that she'll go. She just shakes her head with a quiet little Cheshire cat smile.

"If you don't go, what'll happen?"

She shrugs.

I can't believe her. She has more nerve than I. I'm always so frightened by authority. Maybe that's why the brethren here have not taken me or my case seriously. I always shake and cower. I don't stop doing what needs to be done, but I do it with knots in my stomach and tears in my eyes, and I'm not at all the image of confidence and power.

"I'm just going to ignore it," she laughs.

A knock interrupts my silent afternoon. It's Dr. Chaij, the man who asked about my college degree way back when Richard was trying to "sneak me in."

Dr. Chaij edits the Spanish publications we produce. He's an older man, well into his sixties, with a large nose. He says he's come to talk about the women's problem. Then he tells me that his wife worked for many years without any pay at all "because she loves the Lord," he says. "And I was receiving enough for both of us."

I nod. "But what if she didn't have a husband?" I say as gently as I can.

"But she does."

"Yes, but what if she was all alone, like so many women here who are raising families without husbands."

"Well, that's another item," he says. For a moment he is silent, then goes back to his first message.

"My wife is a good woman. She loves the Lord."

"So do I."

He nods. "I'm sure you do. I'm sure you do or you would never have come here to begin with. But you must have faith. You must let the Lord work things out in His own way. You must not try to take matters into your own hands. Patience is what's needed now."

"Brother Chaij, the Press is breaking the law."

"Maybe, but I don't think so."

I gaze at him. He is a dear, devoted old warrior of the church. I cannot contradict him. If only he could understand me.

"I don't think the good brethren whom the Lord has placed at the helm would do anything illegal on purpose. But even if they did, and I don't believe it for a minute, but if they did break the law, then we must let the Lord settle it. We must be patient and wait on the Lord."

"Brother Chaij, I think the Lord is working it out — through me." My words don't seem to register. "The men have never spoken out against the unfairness of our system," I say slowly, softly. "And the women are afraid to. Perhaps the reason the Lord brought me here was for this very thing."

He sadly shakes his head. "We love you," he mumbles. "I just wanted to encourage you to wait on the Lord."

We sit in silence, each of us longing for the other to recognize our truth.

"May we pray before I leave?" he asks.

"Of course."

We slip to our knees. He prays long and earnestly for God to change my stubborn heart, for Him to forgive my foolish, youthful impertinence — warning me with his pleas, trying to comfort me with his professions of Christian love.

When we rise I see tears on his cheeks.

"Thank you," I say shaking his hand, wishing I could comfort him.

He nods, his shoulders drooping, and gently closes my door behind him.

Letters come in by the droves concerning *HERS*. Everyone is enthusiastic.

Today I received a letter from Chuck Scriven, associate editor at *INSIGHT* Magazine, giving me permission to reprint "Christianity and Women's Lib." He and Pat Horning, one of the women who sent the flowers, work together in Washington, D.C., editing *INSIGHT*, the church's youth magazine.

At the bottom of his rather formal, secretary-typed letter, he added in his own hand:

"P.S. Keep up the good fight. Blessings on your work — all of it!"

Thank you, Lord, for the little encouragements you sprinkle along my path.

Joan's office calls. The Press has made an offer of settlement. My heart soars. They're going to settle!

"Wait till you hear it," Joan cautions. Then she reads me the offer. In effect the Press offers me $10,000 and they want me to drop the class action.

In other words I get $10,000 to split with Joan. No other women receive anything — not money, not the promise of equal pay in the future, no opportunity to move up through the employment ranks to higher positions.

Nothing but $10,000.

I obviously cannot accept. I am no longer alone in this. I don't know when the focus shifted from me and my financial need to all the women at the Press. Maybe it was in Bohner's office when he said if I received head-of-household, "all those women out in the bindery would want it." I don't know. But this is no longer Merikay Silver's struggle. It is a struggle for equality, for justice for all the workers here.

And $10,000 just doesn't do it.

---

Pacific Press and I came fairly close to settlement in November of 1973 and again in late 1974. Both settlement attempts foundered on the same point: The Press refused to accept monitoring of potential settlements by anyone except Pacific Press or General Conference appointees.

Board Chairman Bietz had chapel this morning. It was all about being content with your lot in life, working hard, keeping your nose clean, being patient, and waiting on the Lord. The Lord takes care of those who don't make waves, according to Bietz.

He used as illustration examples of ministers and leaders who had accepted paltry wages to work for the Lord; later they were very blessed. His message was crystal clear.

I'm upset because he asked Lorna and me to be patient, and we've tried. Then he asked Lorna (and, of course, me) to be quiet, not to spread information around the Press. And we have both complied.

And now, up there in the pulpit, in the position of ordained authority, he preaches for forty minutes against us.

Rumors against us fly, not only here at the Press but all over the denomination. No one seems to try to stop them or to set the record straight.

I've received phone calls and letters saying people have heard that I'm suing the Press for five million dollars; that the Press has offered a fair settlement which I refused; that I am determined to bring the Press to its knees; that I am a bitter troublemaker.

And Bietz asks me to be quiet and patient — and now he pulls this. Just what type of people am I dealing with?

## March 26

The Press has responded. Don McNeil filed an answering brief with the court denying sex discrimination and asking the judge not to certify the class (other women who are similarly discriminated against).

"Many if not most of the members of the alleged class do not wish to make use of the civil courts to determine disputes," he wrote.

Now a new fear grows. Will the judge dismiss the class action? Will the whole thing end up just a personal complaint, a personal suit of mine?

Chapel periods grow more intimidating. No one speaks to me when I enter. The comfy, good, family feeling is gone.

I usually come a few minutes late so I don't have to mingle with everyone and endure their silence.

Most of the period is absorbed with announcements by Bohner or Muir, followed by exhortations to be true and faithful to the original vision of the publishing work.

I have written to both Southern Publishing Association and the Review and Herald Publishing Association, attempting to assure them that my disagreement is strictly local — with the Press, not the church.

The book editors of each house write back saying they will honor the publishing contracts they have with me.

Raymond Cottrell, Review and Herald book editor, writes:

> I am sure that you have given careful thought to the course of action you have taken, and I hope that things will work out to the mutual satisfaction of everyone concerned . . . .
>
> For more than a year there has been serious talk here about the wage scale adjustments of which you write. I was told more than a year ago that such changes would eventually come. The mills of the gods usually take longer than we wish they would, but if we are patient they usually accomplish what they should. After all, patterns more than a century old do not usually change over night.
>
> Best wishes, Merikay. Remember Bill Shakespeare: "All's Well That Ends Well." So may it be with you.

## April 5, 1973

Elder R. R. Bietz, Chairman
Pacific Press Board

Dear Elder Bietz:

As I have said before, I am also distressed about the legal action which seems to be pending on the question of equal treatment for women employees. I am distressed for two primary reasons: 1) I believe God's people ought not to go to court with one another. 2) This problem seems to be blocking our efforts to get our message out through trade books.

The time has come for me to speak out clearly in this matter.

I have been a friend of Merikay Silver, who has initiated this legal action, since the time we attended Andrews University together. At the time she came to work here I was unaware of the extent of the difference in remuneration between what she and I were receiving. I assumed that she would be getting somewhat less than I, but when she told me what she was actually receiving annually, I was shocked. Including what is normally paid in weekly, monthly, and yearly (wage adjustment) checks, she was receiving sixty percent of what I was receiving. In addition, I was receiving such forms of remuneration as spouse medical benefits, automobile insurance, automobile club membership, theft insurance allowance, and life insurance, which she was not receiving.

In my opinion, a case can be made for some difference in our respective remunerations based on these objective considerations: 1) I have been working here three years longer than she. 2) I have an advanced degree, whereas she had not yet graduated from college. But based on those objective considerations alone, can a case be made for so large a difference?

To my knowledge, no difference at all is made in remuneration between men of varying academic degrees who perform similar work at the Pacific Press. Some men working here (in fields as much benefited by formal education as the field of editing) do not hold college-level degrees. And yet some of these men are in the highest salary brackets.

Obviously this cannot be the reason for so large a difference in remuneration between Sister Silver and me.

Nor can it be the difference in my three years' seniority, since nowhere else here does so large a difference apply in seniority cases among men.

Nor can so large a difference be made on the basis of our day-to-day work. Some difference can be made over the fact that my higher degree in theology and philosophy enables me to do more precise work on manuscripts in those fields. But on the other hand Sister Silver's wide experience in being published qualifies her more than me in some other areas. Is the value of her specialty worth forty percent less than the value of mine?

Sister Silver is an editorial assistant. I am an assistant editor. Yet our day-to-day work is so similar that the difference in titles "assistant editor" and "editorial assistant," for practical purposes, is meaningless. The Pacific Press now requires an assistant editor to hold a ministerial license. I hold one, but she does not. Nor can she ever receive one, since women are not given these credentials. This rule was made after Sister Silver accepted employment here, since her predecessor, Sister Barbara Herrera, was in fact an assistant editor just as I am. It appears to have been made precisely to keep Sister Silver from becoming an assistant editor. Yet the ministerial license cannot qualify anyone to be an assistant editor. You cannot take a licensed minister out of the field somewhere, hire him, and say that his license qualifies him to be an editor!! Yet that is what we are trying to say with this rule!! The fact is that this requirement serves not as a job qualification at all but as a barrier to exclude women from advancing in editorial work beyond editorial assistant.

It seems clear, Elder Bietz, that so large a difference cannot be construed to be based on job qualification at all, but on sex discrimination, which has always been wrong on principle, but which is now illegal as well.

In fact, our whole Pacific Press policy discriminates against women employees in the areas of hiring, advancement, salary, fringe benefits and other forms of remuneration. Such a policy cannot be defended on the basis of the Bible or the writings of Ellen G. White. To the contrary, Sister White bore plain testimony from on high that "the wages of the woman should be *proportionate to her services*" (CH 365) and that "her work should be estimated *according to its value*" (7T 206) and not determined on the basis of sex. (See also Ev. 491-93.) Our present troubles in this area, including the fact that we are being hounded by the law, can be traced to our long disregard of that divinely-inspired counsel. A legal defense based on the supposition that our religion demands discrimination against women will not stand, because our religion does not do so.

A defense based on the supposition that our policy of remuneration is based on "need" will not stand either. We pay a considerable rate (once termed "head-of-household") *to all married male employees*, whether or not they have dependent children, whether or not their wives also earn incomes (even if larger than their husbands'), whether or not they also receive (in some cases huge) extra forms of income (such as book royalties). Yet *to no female employees* do we pay this rate, whether or not they are widowed or divorced with dependent children, whether or not they must support invalid dependent relatives in their homes, whether or not they are putting their husbands through school (as is the case with Sister Silver). In all honesty, is there any form of valid "need" argument here at all?

I took this matter up with the general manager long before I had any idea Sister Silver might take legal action. I pointed out the same arguments I have outlined here. I discussed this matter with him privately in his office more than once. And I wrote him letters. I warned him patiently and clearly that the day might come when the Press would be seriously embarrassed over this problem. I must now say kindly but candidly that to this day I have received no viable response from him.

When Sister Silver began to voice her grievance, I, at the request of the general manager, went to her more than once trying to reach some solution. But the proposals made by the management did not attempt to solve the underlying problems. Communication broke down. And Sister Silver retained a private attorney as counsel. I did not know that she was going to do this.

As I said in the beginning of this letter, I do not believe God's people should take each other to court. I feel that Sister Silver, failing to reach an acceptable understanding with the general manager, should have pressed the matter with the chairman of the board (in accordance with Jesus' counsel in Matthew 18:15-17). She will have to answer for her own course of action. But we will also have to answer for ours.

There are two sides to this matter of going to court. Both parties have to decide to go to court. The Press also has to decide whether or not to go to court. Sister Silver has offered to negotiate the matter, with both sides retaining private counsel. But I understand that the Press wishes to pursue the matter to its ultimate conclusion through the court system. Now is this not as much a violation of the apostle Paul's counsel (1 Corinthians 6) as Sister Silver's original decision to seek legal remedy?

Let's carefully examine 1 Corinthians 6. This chapter is part of a section which concerns itself basically with abuses among the Corinthian church members and the proper ways to end these abuses. The proper solution, Paul points out in chapter 6, is not to take one another to court. He shows great concern (6:2-6) that they seemed unable to settle their own disputes. "I write this to shame you," he said.

I maintain that Paul in these chapters shows more concern over the fact that the abuses exist and that they seemed *unable* to settle them than he does over the fact that they were going to court to settle them. If the abuses did not exist, then there would have been no reason to go to court. He says: "To have lawsuits at all with one another is defeat for you. Why not rather suffer wrong? Why not rather be defrauded? *But you yourselves wrong and defraud, and that even among your own brethren.*" (6:7).

We have shown great concern over the fact that Sister Silver chose to go to court. And we quote statements from this chapter to prove our point. But do we show the same great concern over the abuses that caused her to seek legal redress for her grievance? If we are going to apply the wisdom of this chapter, then let us apply it correctly and according to the spirit in which it is given. And that is to make remedy among ourselves.

We have applied this chapter arbitrarily. We read it through special filtering glasses which make it read like this: It is wrong for an individual church member to take a denominational institution to court for redress of grievances, but all right for the institution to take an individual church member to court (as in, for example, the collection of debts). But this is not what the chapter says. The chapter does not make this distinction. The chapter says: Do not let abuses exist. And where abuses do exist, get rid of them through the methods of Christ, rather than through the legal system.

We quote verse 7 to Sister Silver: "Why not rather suffer injury? Why not rather let yourself be robbed?" But do we quote this when attempting to recover a bad debt from a brother? If we are going to apply this chapter in our dealings with one another, then shouldn't we apply it in the way that it was intended?

At any rate, I incline to think that this counsel is not absolute. (And I do not say this in any way to justify Sister Silver's action.) I certainly do not place it on the same level with the Ten Commandments. Paul gives this counsel because he knows that Christians through the power of Christ are well equipped to settle differences without resort to legal redress. "Do you not know that we are to judge angels?" he asks. "How much more, matters pertaining to this life!" He is telling us not to take matters to court because we can settle them ourselves.

There may be cases, however, as in the collection of some bad debts, when there is no other alternative. Perhaps Sister Silver felt this way in her situation. Whatever the case, God will judge her. We need not do so. We do know that Ellen G. White did not make the matter one of absolute black-and-white. She wrote, "Brethren should not go to law *if it can be possibly avoided*; for they thus give the enemy great advantage to entangle and perplex them." (1T 201).

The question that faces us *now* is not how wrong Sister Silver was to take this matter up with the legal authorities. It is rather one of what is the right thing to do *now*. On the basis of Paul's counsel, I do not think it is right for the Press to pursue this matter through the court system. This, especially in view of the fact that Sister Silver still leaves open the possibility of negotiation. If it does go through the courts, the church will be exposed to ridicule and the cause of God will suffer.

I have a difficult time believing that the cause of the church will suffer by paying women their just due. Quite to the contrary, I believe that the church suffers more when the services of women are accepted without remunerating them according to the value of their work and in proportion to their services without making a difference on the basis of sex. Ellen G. White has written the following:

> If a women is appointed by the Lord to do a certain work, her work is to be estimated *according to its value. Every laborer* is to receive his *or her just due.*

> It may be thought to be a good plan to allow persons to give talent and earnest labor to the work of God, while they draw nothing from the treasury. But this is *making a difference,* and selfishly withholding from such workers their due. God will not put His sanction on any such plan. Those who invented this method may have thought that they were doing God service by not drawing from the treasury to pay these God-fearing, soul-loving laborers. But there will be an account to settle by and by, and then those who now think this exaction, this *partiality in dealing,* a wise scheme, will be ashamed of their selfishness. God sees these things in a light altogether different from the light in which finite men view them.

> Those who work earnestly and unselfishly, be they men *or women,* bring sheaves to the Master; and the souls converted by their labor will bring their tithes to the treasury. When self-denial is required because of a dearth of means, *do not let a few hard-working women do all the sacrificing. Let all share in making the sacrifice.* God declares, "I hate robbery for burnt offering" (Ev. 492).

Now, although Sister White here refers specifically to women who were not being paid at all, it is plainly evident that her principle was that of equal treatment of men and women in payment according to the value of their work done. It is clear that *on principle* she opposed "making a difference" and "partiality in dealing." And it is that principle which our policy now violates. Let us change our policy to accord with the principle of equality which came to us long ago from God Himself through His prophet Ellen G.

White. Let us do it ourselves before the law of the land forces us to do so, thus putting the church to "open shame."

Sincerely your friend and brother in Christ,

Max Gordon Phillips
Assistant Book Editor

xc: L. H. Bohner
    W. L. Muir
    R. H. Utt

There have been several negotiating meetings with Joan and Don McNeil and Len Bohner and Bill Muir, but with no results. Joan says they won't negotiate. They won't give her any information, and they won't respond to the information she has. They simply demand that I drop the suit, accept $10,000, period — and then sit there silently, refusing to interact.

Today I hear that management is arranging a meeting with the women employees here. Lorna and I can't believe it. "They can't do this," she says.

"They can do anything they can get away with," I say, picking up the phone to call Joan Bradford.

# April 12, 1973

(Excerpts from Joan Bradford letter to Don McNeil.)

. . . Yesterday, I was shocked and dismayed to learn that management of the Press had, without any notification to me . . . called a meeting of certain employees which it set for April 17, 1973, at which time management would, without attendance of attorneys, discuss employment policies with female employees. I am shocked because such scheduled meeting with women employees is in direct contradiction to management's expression, through you, that management would meet with me, provide me with personnel records, and attempt to set up employment guidelines before our meeting jointly with interested and affected women employees at the Press. I regard management's calling of the April 17 meeting to be another demonstration of the Press' pattern of expressing superficially its desire to conform with the law while, at the same time, preserving its own authoritarian position over its female employees — instructing them without allowing them to receive information of appropriate employment practices from anyone other than their own employer.

By timing its closed meeting with female employees for the day following its meeting with me as Merikay's attorney, management places itself in the position of standing as sole interpreter of the meeting it requested with me so as to provide itself with the opportunity to convince these women of the wrongfulness of their participation in Merikay's suit as members of the class.

Can you or management seriously state that these women will not be intimidated by hearing the voice of management on the subject? How many of these women, once having heard the voices of management, can afford the bravery of free expression or participation when their paychecks and their consciences are controlled by management?

I view these tactics by the Press to be another form of intimidation and coercion of its female employees . . . .

. . . I have taken considerable time to attempt to meet and cooperate with the Press in all good faith for the purpose of bringing about amicable reform of employment practices. Now I find that secret meetings have been set up behind my back without notification or invitation to me. I can only conclude that the purpose of such meetings is further coercion and intimidation of female employees of Pacific Press who also happen to be members of the class of *Silver v Pacific Press*.

Another "rah! rah! management" chapel period. This one's by Bohner — extolling the virtues of the denominational work-pay structure.

I don't know why I even go to chapel any more. It's never spiritual; it's always political.

The management is flexing its muscle.

The management is encouraging unquestioning obedience.

The management is chastising discontent.

And all I can do is sit, listening, like everyone else. Is it any wonder the women here are afraid to openly support me?

Is it any wonder that they fear asking for what is due them? Can they even afford to think about the problem?

Lorna and I go to lunch together. It's fun to get away from the strain of the Press, if only for an hour.

"Lawrence wrote me a letter today," she says.

"Boy, everyone is writing letters to you," I tease, and we both smile.

"You know I ignored Bohner's deadline of April 1 for me to go join Gus in Germany. Well, so now Lawrence has set a June 1 deadline for me. He wants me to leave by then, to move to Germany."

We both laugh. Such insistence. I know what Lorna will do. She'll ignore it. And she does.

## April 18, 1973

Letter to Merikay Silver
from
Norma K. Bork, Ph.D.
Associate Professor,
Speech Pathology and Audiology
PACIFIC UNION COLLEGE
Angwin, CA

I just wanted to let you know that my prayers and best wishes are with you while you are going through your difficult time with Pacific Press. The pressures and emotions that are bound to be stirred from your action I am sure will be difficult for you, but I am equally certain that what you have done is necessary. By now you may have heard that the General Conference has reversed itself and is asking that the college remain on the two-level wage scale. This is a blow for us at PUC. One of these days one of us will have to make the same move that you have made.

Thank you for your courage.

## April and May 1973

Kim and I have been working every spare minute on *HERS*. The articles are coming together beautifully. I have plenty of photographs, and Kim is doing an excellent job designing the magazine. It's fun. It's exciting. And as I watch *HERS* take shape I'm happy. It's going to be a good-looking publication.

I concentrate on *HERS* because it's the only positive thing I have in my professional life right now. I want it to be the best magazine I can create. I want it to show that the Press can be as tough on me as they want, but they can't crush my creativity.

## May 17, 1973

Letter to Merikay Silver
from
Jonathan Butler

Dear Merikay,

Only a brief word from a "fellow traveller" to say I'm pulling for you in your legal confrontation with the Pacific Press. I would guess there is something like Elijah's seven thousand hoping for your success.

As Graham Maxwell said to me over a meal a couple of weeks ago, "There are a lot of little ladies all over the denomination hoping Merikay succeeds so they won't have to stick their necks out."

I've enjoyed so much your literary contributions and pray that this legal entanglement with the church visible will not smother the flowering of your spirit.

Yours,

Jonathan Butler

Bill Muir spoke at chapel this morning. Bill Muir has always impressed me as a soft-spoken, Christian gentleman. He has the unwrinkled features of a man at peace with himself. I've always thought he had a certain strand of integrity. But now I wonder. Maybe his shyness was strictly shyness. Maybe it has nothing at all to do with integrity.

His chapel period was another in the continuing barrage of management propaganda.

I grow angrier, more frustrated as the months pass. No one listens to me. No one invites me to share my viewpoint and facts with the workers. I have no way to communicate with the other women here — and I've promised not to "stir up trouble." Thus, I've stayed quiet and courteous in my office, practicing patience.

And every week or so management flaunts its position, power, viewpoints, control.

I dread chapel. What a *powerful* tool the pulpit is — even if it's the management-controlled podium at Pacific Press. There's a feeling of "sanctified truth" to every word uttered from it.

What a discouragement!!!

*HERS* COMES OFF THE PRESS!

Actually, Kim picked up the blueline today, and we've spent all afternoon checking and rechecking it page by page, noting errors and corrections. He'll take it back to the printer for corrections Monday, and then it will be a matter of only days until the magazine will be finished. I can't wait!

I can't wait to ship off copies to all the people who helped make the dream a reality.

I know I'll get an A for this project. But that's incidental. The important thing is that I'll have a magazine full of information about the value of women's contributions throughout the development of our church, and all this information will be neatly packaged in my magazine. I can just hand it out to whoever wants it.

All that information in one easy-to-give-away package.

Three very heavy boxes of magazines sit in our living room. I had no idea how many or how heavy 1,000 magazines would be.

*HERS* is beautiful. Ninety-six slick pages of information, inspiration, and education. It covers the arts, business, education, medicine, history, religion, and the family. I even dedicated one whole page to quotes from Mrs. White about equal pay. My introductory blurb to the page reads: "Decades before equal pay for equal work became an issue, the co-founder of the Seventh-day Adventist church wrote widely on the subject. Here is a chapter from her book *Evangelism.*"

Kim and I go through the magazine again and again, examining every page, complimenting ourselves on how it looks, what it says, the fact that we really published it.

It feels so good to have all this information available in one neat, well-designed package.

Now comes stuffing envelopes and mailing *HERS* all over the country. Boy, has this project been fun!!

The spring Forum newspaper comes out with a news story of the lawsuit. It's the first objective information released anywhere. The Forum newspaper is published at Andrews University — the same Michigan university where Max and I worked on the student newspaper so many years ago. Forum newspaper is published by the Association of Adventist Forums, a national SDA organization, supposedly independent of the denomination but serving "thought-leaders" within the Adventist community.

I'd heard rumors that Forum was going to publish information about the case. But when I received my copy of the newspaper, I noticed another article stating that Larry Geraty, national president of the Association, had resigned. It turns out there was a much bigger story behind the Press lawsuit article than most people realized.

Dr. Larry Geraty, president of the Association of Adventist Forums, is employed as a teacher at the Seminary at Andrews University. Geraty "oversees" Forum newspaper — helping direct its student editors and staff — to keep the publication objectively serving its readership. Geraty shares the following information with me during a telephone conversation.

"When Eric Anderson (co-editor) showed me the draft of the Press story, I felt we should get the Press' side," Geraty explains. "I felt the story presented Merikay's viewpoint without any response from the Press.

"Eric felt that if we contacted the Press, they'd try to keep us from publishing the story at all.

"I said that would be foolish because it would be to their advantage to have their side of the story told. I also felt that Forum must stand for a thorough, objective, all-sides-of-the-issue-researched story — which meant contacting the Press for their viewpoint."

(Eric Anderson began making phone calls to find out the Press' viewpoint.)

"The next thing I knew, within 48 hours or less, I was called into President Hammill's office," Larry Geraty says. Hammill is president of Andrews University.

"President Hammill said that he'd been told by Robert Pierson (GC president) that Forum was making inquiries about the denominational position on the Silver v. PPPA case, and that Pierson said that was none of

Forum's business.

"This story was something that the GC didn't want publicity on; and if I knew what was good for me, I would use my influence to make sure that nothing about the case appeared in the Forum.

"I was shocked!

"I said, 'Are you threatening me with my job?'

"President Hammill said, 'I don't like to put it in those terms, but we are a denominational university. And when Pierson says we shouldn't be involved in something, we take that seriously.'

"I said, 'What you're asking me to do is choose between putting out a fair report or resigning my job.'

"He said, 'I don't want it to be a threat, but I think it's important that you not allow this article to appear.'

"I said, 'I've always felt I was a moderate influence within the Association, but in order to continue to be that moderating influence I have to have credibility. If I go around saying you can't print this or you can't print that, I lose my credibility and my influence. I'd rather resign as president of the Association than to say that Forum cannot print this article.'

"He said, 'That's your decision.'"

Draw. Lawrence Geraty chose to resign rather than bar the article from publication.

Geraty's resignation was announced April 24 in a letter to each board member.

"I told the Forum's board that it was clear that a denominationally employed person could not serve as president, because the denomination could put pressure on that individual to do what it wanted. I said that the Association can serve its constituency only if it is free to pursue what's best for its members."

The Association of Adventist Forums has followed Geraty's advice. Dr. Larry Geraty was the last denominational employee to serve as president.

## June 11, 1973

Dear Merikay,

While we never got very well acquainted, I have this com-
pulsion to write to you in the common love we share for
Christ and His church. Since your story hit Forum, I suppose
you have had an increase of assaults from the not-so-well-
meaning brethren and sisters.

My purpose is not to attempt an analysis of your situation,
which, of course, I do not understand, but to attempt to
counter the onslaught which might cost you your soul.
Sometimes our people are not very good at being kind, and I
fear you are being judged and condemned more than you are
being loved and supported through your *Anfechtungen*.

But hang in there, Merikay. We need you. Our need is par-
tially measured by the response you have undoubtedly already received from the stumbling saints. There are many of
us who are praying for your survival — spiritually and
denominationally.

Rest in Jesus,

[Name withheld on request]
General Conference Employee

Lawrence Maxwell spoke at chapel this morning. It was the worst chapel so far. He talked for almost an hour about modern Judases who sell the Lord's work to the government for a few pieces of silver. The accusations and insinuations are impossible to answer because Lorna and I have no forum. We have no way to defend ourselves against these chapel periods.

But I'm sick of it. This is exactly the kind of indoctrination and intimidation that keeps women afraid to speak up for themselves — either to complain or to simply ask questions. And I'm finished being quiet.

I phone Joan Bradford and say I want to hold a meeting for all the women working at the Press. I want them to hear about the lawsuit from my side. She agrees. After all, she is the attorney representing all of us.

Kim and Lorna and I go to her office to discuss how we will announce the meeting and what we will say during it. Joan will write a letter explaining the lawsuit from a legal standpoint. I'll write a letter explaining what caused me to file such an action. And we'll invite every woman to a meeting on Monday evening, June 25.

I work on my letter.

So many, many months have passed while I sat quietly in my office — doing my work, wanting to tell people my side of the story, but not being able to — that now the words gush like a waterfall.

I want to explain that I am not fighting for myself alone. The goal of head-of-household allowance for me and Kim disappeared long ago. The goal is total equality, fairness to each woman worker at Pacific Press.

I want each woman to know that she is noticed, that someone here realizes she has been taken advantage of, that her labor has been used without being fairly paid for. I want each woman to feel good about her contribution, to realize she doesn't have to apologize for seeking fair wages for her labor. I reiterate all the steps I took trying to get management to correct the situation before I finally filed my lawsuit.

I write:

> Since January, management of the Press and the Press' attorney have met several times with my attorney. I have received two offers of settlement. But both were offered with the stipulation that I drop the class action.

> I don't believe I should accept the back-pay money offered to me for myself alone while you are denied it, unless you decide for yourself that you don't want the back pay. And I think you deserve to know what the law and the lawsuit are about before you decide. That is where the Press and my attorney have disagreed. The Press wants me to accept settlement without your knowing what this is all about. I don't want to do that. That's why we're calling a meeting.

> I refuse to drop the class action because I want to make it possible for women to freely choose employment at Pacific Press over outside employment. As it is now, many talented women do not consider Press employment because they simply cannot live on the salary paid to females here. And I want those who deserve it to receive equal pay and benefits with men.

I quote Mrs. White. I encourage the women to think for themselves, to come to the meeting so that they can base their opinions, their decisions on facts. I ask them to pray with me that God will bring about the needed changes, so that we can all work as equals under the blessings of the law.

For too long I've been bottled up in my office, sneaking in and out, hoping I don't run into Richard, hoping no one yells at me. And now at last I'm going to be able to explain myself. I feel freer than I have in a long time. The other side of the story will at last be heard.

We've rented the Adobe Building, less than a mile from the Press for the evening of June 25. Our meeting will start at 5:30 p.m.

I take my letter to Joan Bradford and she shows me the letter she has prepared. It's very long (aren't all the letters pertaining to this problem?), but it is beautifully written. In it she explains and assures the women that we are not trying to force them into anything they don't want. Part of her letter reads:

> Merikay cannot and would not desire to include you in a lawsuit against your will. If it is your desire not to share in the results of this legal action, you are free to remove yourself from the class and, in so doing, either to relinquish your claim or to institute a legal action of your own.

> Please remember that neither your employer nor Merikay nor any other person can coerce you into or out of participation in legal action in which you hold an interest. If anyone attempts to coerce you, either directly or indirectly you may wish to report the matter to the Equal Employment Opportunities Commission, 1095 Market Street, San Francisco . . . or directly to me . . . .

She explains the main obstacle to settling my complaint:

> At the present time, one obstacle to settlement of this suit is the Press' limitation of settlement offers to one person only, MERIKAY SILVER, without recognition of other women employees who may also wish to recover back pay or to achieve future changes in employment practices.

> It is Merikay's position that she has taken on a certain duty toward you in this lawsuit; therefore, she is not favorably disposed to settling on her own behalf without other women also benefiting.

> Neither Merikay nor I can or will decide for you the extent of your participation in the pending litigation or settlement. That matter is to be decided by each of you as a matter of free choice. We are addressing this information to you and scheduling the meeting of June 25 so that you may base your choice on free access to information available to you.

Along with our letters we decide to include a copy of that first letter Joan wrote to Bohner. That way the women can see that from the beginning our desire was to help the Press legalize its employment practices.

Lorna compiles the names and addresses of every woman at the Press, as well as women who no longer work here but are still part of the class.

Lorna has an "underground" network which feeds her information from all over the Press. I don't know who the people are or how many there are, but Lorna can almost always produce any information for us that we need.

I'm grateful that she is still here. Without her I don't know where we'd be.

I wonder if anyone will come to the meeting. What if we hold it and everyone is too frightened to attend?

Most of the women are so scared they don't even look at me anymore when we pass in the halls. What if they are too frightened to even find out what their rights are?

## June 20, 1973

Dear Merikay,

. . . It sounds as though they are quite paranoid out
there, and if they had the arm of the Inquisition they
would gladly use it! They can't actually fire you until
things are settled, can they? *Make a diary* of how they
treat you! It might make interesting reading in a future
issue of *Forum* — or **HERS**! Right on! SISTERHOOD
IS POWERFUL!

Love,

Leona G. Running
Andrews University

All weekend we talk about Monday's meeting.

"What if nobody comes?" I ask again and again.

"They'll come," Kim assures me.

"But they're all so scared."

He shrugs. "I'll bet there are a lot more women on your side than you know. They'll come."

The pressure grows. I'm tired. I cry a lot. Most of the time I feel angry. Most of the time I'm scared. Kim deals with me as best he can; but I can see that my strain affects him, and I don't want it to. I don't want his life to be as miserable as mine.

We talk about *HERS*. That's something positive. Maybe we'll make the magazine a regular publication. Maybe we'll print other issues. The response has been encouraging — nearly 100 letters ordering copies since it was published. Libraries at Christian schools and colleges want copies. People from all over the United States are requesting copies.

We talk about becoming magazine publishers. It's fun to dream.

## The Morning of June 25, 1973

It's Monday morning and I'm excited.

The Press has been buzzing ever since the women got their letters last week. Today's the day. I walk to chapel, hoping that the women will come to my meeting, hoping we don't have to sit through another typical management-dominated chapel period. I climb the stairs to the balcony. I sit in the balcony because it's dark and most of the others who sit here are student workers. They're not concerned with the lawsuit, which makes the balcony more comfortable for me.

Four men walk out onto the stage. They are Len Bohner, R. R. Bietz, Bill Muir, and Press attorney Don McNeil. I can't believe it. I sit up straight in my chair. A hush falls over the chapel as Elder Bohner walks to the microphone.

"Some questions have arisen that we believe need some answers," he says in an authoritarian voice. "We want it understood that nobody has to remain. You're all invited to remain if you wish, but it's not required."

Elder Bietz takes over. He talks about the unfortunate state of affairs — that someone was so unhappy that she went and hired a lawyer, and now the Press is all entangled in legal arguments and the filing of endless documents. And since this whole unpleasant incident affects every worker, the Board and the management decided it was time to bring it to "the family" and share information with all of us.

"I appeal to all of us that we be patient in correcting what needs to be corrected," he says. "Let's be patient, and I can assure you that Pacific Press is working very diligently."

I am chilled. I am shocked. After this show of power and control, who will have the nerve to come to my meeting tonight? Angry tears rise, but I blink them away.

All these months management has had exclusive control of communication here. All these months they've preached and warned us, telling us to be loyal, trusting, and patient. And now when the women have an opportunity to learn the facts — to ask questions and make their own decisions — now the Press stages this.

Bietz introduces the attorney, and McNeil takes the

microphone. Briefly he describes some selected facts of the case and then opens the floor to questions.

Someone asks if the lawsuit will affect the men. He says no.

Someone on the floor below stands and says, "I just want to let the management know that there are a whole bunch of us working here who support you."

Bohner's and Bietz's faces light up with smiles.

"We don't run around making speeches or writing letters about it, but we love this work," the voice concludes.

The auditorium fills with applause.

Other people stand and shout support for management.

Somebody asks how a person can withdraw from the class.

"Okay, here's the hustle," McNeil says. "We have a relatively formal document that people will be free to sign. I want to make it clear that I don't intend this to be, nor I think does management intend it to be, a situation where there's any kind of pressure on employees to get out . . . . But, yes, I think it's important for the viability of the Press that this not be a class action.

"We have attempted to avoid it, to avoid the implications of the class action. That makes the settlement clumsy. And anybody who opts out is appreciated."

I can't believe this! They're all sitting down there like a row of godfathers, asking the women to defeat the very legal action which will give them employment equality here. I can't believe it. I'm reeling from shock.

Ross Wollard is in the aisles with a hand-held microphone, walking up and down, passing the mike to anyone who wants it.

"I just want to say that I've been in this work for thirty-nine years," someone says. "And I've never felt mistreated or abused. This is the Lord's vineyard, and I'm grateful to be part of it."

A woman's voice rings out clearly, "As far as I understand, there is a great majority of us who are not in favor of it at all. Is it not possible for us to sign a disposition of some kind disassociating ourselves from this action?"

McNeil nods. "We do have a semiformal document that you can sign if you want to, which we will submit to the court indicating that the individual signing does not want to be part of the class."

Lorna takes the mike and asks McNeil to explain which General Conference wage guidelines and which federal laws the Press has been breaking. McNeil says that the Press does not feel it is breaking the law. Lorna insists on an explanation of the Press' position.

Finally McNeil admits, "The Press, as I understand it, is going to take every step to see to it that — where its conscience permits — it will comply with the law."

But no one seems to care about the issues. People stand to pledge allegiance to Pacific Press management.

"Well, I've been in denominational work now for a number of years," a woman says, her voice shrill with emotion. "I think a good share more than some people here. And it's true that if anyone is unhappy within the work, they're not required to stay within the ranks of the work."

Applause rings from every corner of the chapel.

I want to die! I stand and pace at the back of the balcony. Lots of people are standing. The place is frenzied. People are talking loudly, raising their hands and voices.

"Don't we think that perhaps the General Conference is aware of the law of the land?" a woman says. "This thing is not only against the denomination, not only against Pacific Press. It involves the General Conference, and basically it is against God."

Applause explodes, filling my ears.

My knees shake so hard I can barely stand. What is going on here? What are they doing?

"I think if anyone isn't happy here they should leave," a man yells.

The applause deafens me. I stumble down the stairs and over to the editorial wing. Max's office is empty. So is Lorna's. Everyone is gone. I'm all alone in the editorial wing. I can hear the noise from the chapel.

My knees are shaking. My heart is beating so hard it hurts. I'm out of breath. I can't believe that they all want me to leave! I feel sick. I phone Joan's office and tell her what is going on.

"Go back and take notes," she instructs.

I don't want to go back. I don't want to ever show my face around here again.

A little scene plays in my mind. In the scene I walk with calm dignity to the front of the chapel auditorium. I take the microphone from Ross Wollard and say:

"I've been struggling with management for you. No one else has ever been willing to do that. No one else has ever pointed out how the Press is breaking the law and withholding wages from you — wages you have earned with your labor. But I have pointed it out because I want to work for an employer who is just and fair, for an employer that is moral, for an employer that does not abuse its workers.

"According to the federal law, according to the counsel of Mrs. White, you deserve what I have been asking and struggling for. You deserve it.

"But you don't want me around. You don't want someone to urge the Press to obey the law, to pay you fairly. Okay. I'll leave." And then I'd stand there and just look at them, let my eyes touch each face in a very long moment of silence.

And then I'd just say, "Good bye," hand the mike back to Wollard, and walk out.

But it's just a fantasy. Its comfort is momentary at best.

I swallow my tears, try to stop my heart from racing, and go back to the chapel. My knees won't stop shaking. I feel cold and helpless, drained of all life.

Finally Elder Bietz says we've had a good meeting and now it's time to get back to work.

"Something has been said about certain blanks if certain individuals want to sign them," he says. "We're not asking you to sign them. We're not telling you to sign them. But if you want to sign them and take yourself out of that class action, they will be available at the door, and you can pick up your blank and sign it. Go to the door and they'll be there."

A few more people want to make statements or ask questions.

Then Bietz says, "I hope we have enough individual conscience so that we will tend to business here. I mean our business that we're being paid for. We're not being paid to start a crusade. We're being paid to do the job. And let's be true to our individual conscience. I'm sure that if we aren't careful we can spend hours and hours of time developing documents and talking here and there and everywhere on this case when we ought to be tending to business. And I'd like to appeal to you to tend to the business that you're being paid for."

We stand while Bietz prays for God's blessings on the Press and the management. And then it's over. Everyone hurries to the doorway to grab a copy of the form.

I go to my office and sit shaking half the morning. I call Kim, sobbing. He comforts me via Ma Bell.

After lunch Max visits. He says, "I can just feel the waves of Pacific Press hatred rolling all over the place."

I nod, silently. I have never been so humiliated, so attacked, so devastated before. And there was no chance to reply. What do you say when everyone is yelling at you and saying you are attacking God and saying they wish you'd leave?

I cannot speak. I have nothing to say. I only wonder if any women will come to the meeting tonight. And if they do, how in the world can I face them after this morning?

## Evening, June 25, 1973

At five o'clock I drive to the Adobe Building. Joan is there. Her husband helps her set up chairs in a semicircle facing a table. On the table sits a huge bouquet of flowers.

"They're from Kim," Joan smiles. "He wanted you to have them tonight."

I can't believe how supportive he is.

I walk up and stick my nose in the middle of them, inhaling their rich sweet fragrance, letting it fill and soothe me. The pain from this morning is so strong; I feel empty and ravaged. The sweet fragrance comforts me. Just what I need.

Lorna comes carrying bulging notebooks.

When the chairs are arranged in a semicircle Joan's husband leaves. "He said he might stick around to make sure no men from Press management try to disrupt things," Joan says lightly. Then she laughs. "But I told him I didn't think he had to worry."

Women start arriving. In tight little groups of two or three, they timidly enter and take seats. I count twenty, then thirty. They keep coming, their demeanor subdued, their hands clutching the letters we mailed them, or Bibles, or books by Mrs. White.

There must be nearly fifty women by the time Joan starts the meeting. I sit with the women rather than up in front with Joan. I cannot bear to sit in front. I am too raw to expose myself to all those eyes.

She welcomes them, tells them that she's going to describe what is going on, and assures them that this is a forum where they can ask questions and make statements. Joan can be very gentle when she wants to. Tonight she wants to. Her face softens. Her eyes grow tender, and her voice takes on a comforting, almost loving tone.

She explains the months of attempted reasoning before I filed suit. She explains that the Press has two wage systems — one for men and one for women — and that this practice is illegal. She explains that I want to equalize pay and make advancement possible for the women at the Press, so that qualified women can be promoted to higher positions within the company. She talks for twenty minutes and then accepts questions.

The queries are timid at first. Someone wants to know

if she has to stay in the class if she doesn't want to. Someone else asks if she remains a part of the class and is awarded a sum of back pay, will Press management know that she chose to stay in? Some women read passages from the Bible or Mrs. White.

I am amazed at the spirit here, the sense of really searching for facts, the hunger for information. No one is shouting or condemning. Everything is quiet and earnest.

Someone wants to know how long the whole process will take. Someone else says that she was told I'd sue her if she talked to me. Other women nod. Suddenly I realize why I've been so alone. These people have been told not to talk to me because I'll sue them.

Joan talks about equal opportunity at the Press.

"You mean we could become anything we want, if we're qualified?" one woman asks.

Joan nods.

I watch the woman's face open to the possibility.

"You mean we could be a supervisor or anything at all?" someone else asks.

"Yes, if you're qualified."

Light flickers in faces all over the room. As Joan explains that every job would be available to whoever qualified (whether male or female), the shadow of hopelessness vanishes from one face after another. The glow of possibility, of hope, fills eyes which long ago acquiesced to exclusion from "men only" jobs.

When the meeting ends I gather up my flowers and head for home. This day I will never forget.

"Management is trying to find out who went to your meeting last night," Lorna says.

"Do you think they can?"

"Well, they'll sure try."

We talk about the meeting. Only about a third of the women employed here attended.

One of the women from the factory stopped by this morning to say that the word going around the factory and bindery is that "the management's meeting was like a circus, and Merikay's meeting was like a prayer service."

I smile, filled with gratitude. At least some people can see the difference in our styles.

**June 28, 1973**

Dear Ms. Silver:

It was with great interest that I read the article in the *Forum* regarding your courageous stance on sex discrimination in denominational employment.

You no doubt have been the object of a great deal of pressure from denominational people to refrain from "publicly embarrassing" the church. I want to encourage you because there are many denominational employees before you, and perhaps many will come after you, who have had to suffer helplessly as a result of discriminatory employment practices.

. . . Be strong for the task you have undertaken not only on behalf of your fellow employees but, in the long run, in the best interests of the denomination as a whole.

. . . May God give you continued strength and courage to continue this noble effort on behalf of thousands of employees and for the denomination as a whole.

Sincerely,

Wesley L. Nash
Los Angeles

# July

Joan and Don McNeil are starting the "discovery" process. They're both seeking information so that they can file briefs with the court in preparation for trial.

I feel dazed all the time. Nothing is working out the way I thought it would. We are not moving toward a solution. There is no attempt to cooperate, to work together, to seek an answer. All I have received from Press management has been a continual, arms-folded "try-and-make-us" attitude.

I go to work each day, do my editing, go to my various committee meetings, try not to cross paths with anyone in the halls, and drive home each night exhausted. I live for the weekends, when I can breathe out from under the excruciating burden of the Press.

And poor Kim; my misery has infected his life. He has opened his own graphic arts studio. It's exciting for him, but I'm so exhausted I can't really give him the support he needs.

My paycheck is significantly larger than usual. So are many other women's around the Press. Management says they are equalizing pay, according to Department of Labor recommendations. Joan thinks it's a trick. Lorna is also suspicious and is comparing new statistics with old.

Wouldn't it be wonderful if the Press truly has worked out an equitable, nondiscriminatory pay scale? That would be the best news ever!

Within a week Lorna has it figured out. Instead of having two kinds of pay — basic wage and rent allowance — the Press has now combined them both into one system called base pay. Base pay is based on the job that's being done. In the past, if you were a female and your basic wage was 50 percent of the pay scale your wage is still 50 percent of the pay scale; but in addition you now also earn 50 percent of the rent allowance.

Instead of the old 30 cents per hour rent allowance for women, now, at 50 percent, your rent allowance is 50 cents an hour — quite a substantial increase.

However, it is still discriminatory. All single men in the plan had their "rent allowance" portion of the new base wage raised to $1.00 per hour. No woman received that kind of raise. Women are paid strictly according to the percentage they earn in basic wages as compared to the wage scale. So there's no way any woman will ever receive $1.00 per hour for "rent allowance" because no woman earns 100 percent of the basic wage scale.

When Lorna explains it, showing the figures, comparing what men and women earn, I am furious. And discouraged. They will lie; they will cheat; they will scheme; they will do everything and anything they can to keep from paying women fairly. I never realized how deep and determined their bias was.

It's seems so simple to me — you pay a fair wage for fair labor. Whether the worker is female or male makes very little difference. If the worker performs well and reliably, you pay a fair wage.

There is no attempt to treat women with respect here. All my beliefs of equality in Jesus Christ — "There is neither Jew nor Gentile, there is neither slave nor free, there is neither male nor female for we are all one in Jesus Christ" — all that, as far as Press management is concerned, is just so many empty words.

My heart has been aching for so long that I hardly feel it any more. The new pay scale is just one more fact in my growing case.

## August 1973

Press management ignores all Joan Bradford's requests for information. Joan has called me several times expressing her frustration.

"Don McNeil can't control his client, and it infuriates him as much as it does me," she says. "The Press acts as if they aren't part of the world as the rest of us know it. They simply do what they want or refrain from doing what they don't want."

It's clear Joan Bradford has never dealt with anyone like the Press before. If she doesn't get the answers to her interrogatories, we can't move ahead and neither can the Press. And I guess that's what they want.

Several scheduled meetings have been postponed because the Press won't cooperate. Joan has finally informed McNeil that she will go to the Press herself and search their records on Friday, August 17. I'm embarrassed at how the leaders in my company are acting. I wanted Joan to see that Adventists are different from the world. And she is certainly seeing it, first hand, and in very graphic terms.

Joan and her law clerk spend the day reviewing **PPPA** records, books, and files, trying to gather the information she needs for the battle ahead. Lorna helps, telling Joan exactly where to look for the facts.

"If you'll notice," Lorna says, spreading out the pay scale records, "there is not one woman in the entire Press, paid on the salary scale. Every woman worker, including Merikay, is an hourly employee."

Lorna's finger traces down the list of names, "Here," she stops at my name. "See, Merikay is being paid at the clerk-typist level." Then flipping through the records, Lorna points out that all the males in the editorial department are salaried on the administrative level.

Lorna and Joan's law clerk photocopy all the pertinent forms and records for Joan. After eight grueling hours, Joan still has twenty-one separate areas for which she has requested but received no information. She begins the process of writing another of her many letters to McNeil requesting information.

I'm amazed at how involved the legal process is. There are so many steps, so many places where someone can stall or stonewall.

The campaign to get Lorna out is gaining strength. Gus wrote today saying he was under tremendous pressure from the Euro-Africa Division (the denominational division with authority over Hamburg Publishing House).

Lorna's worried and so am I. How can I bear working here, walking these somber halls, facing these angry people, without her good humor? How can she stay if Gus's job is in danger?

She assures me that she isn't leaving until this Press matter is corrected. She's staying and that's all there is to it.

Dear Merikay,

How are you today? Better I hope. Merikay, I have thought about that chapel meeting; all the Press did was beat you to the punch — they got wind of your proposed meeting and had theirs first to discourage anyone who planned on attending yours.

I know you are right in what you are doing. So keep up the good work and keep smiling at everyone. Don't give any suggestion of defeat.

Pray that the Lord will guide you; then leave it in His hand and He won't let you down.

Honey, I wish there were something I could do to lighten your load. My heart bleeds for you. I wish I could just wipe out this whole year and tell you and Kim to come home here and forget all about those people at the Press. But I know you have a work to do. I am praying for you, and I know in the end you will be victorious.

I love you.

Love,
Mom

The summer passes in a flurry of letters, affidavits, depositions, and bitter, angry words from Richard and others.

One moment of warmth stands out in my mind, a little event, something that would never have made an impression were it not for the fact that I exist in an emotional desert — a hostile lions' den for eight hours every day.

I was in the women's room combing my hair when another woman entered. She was older, maybe in her sixties; but she looked like a loyal sister who would gladly give her life for her church. As I headed out she grasped my arm in a firm, loving squeeze.

"Thank you," she whispered.

And then it was over. That touch, those words, kept me going most of the rest of the summer. Women may be frightened. They might stand and scream, "Leave!" at me. But out there in the factory, in the bindery, in the hallways and offices, there were some who silently hoped that justice would be done. And I'd just heard from one of them.

## September 1973

I escape into classes. At least I have peace while at school. At least there I can forget the Press.

Kim is unhappy, very unhappy. He was hoping that the Labor Department would take over the case and I could get back to "normal." Then in July when I got "the big raise," he was sure the Press had stepped into line with the law and we could drop the suit. Now pressure is building again.

"Why don't you just drop it," he says more than once. We both know that's not possible. But that's what he'd like.

"You're no fun anymore," he complains. And he's right.

I don't feel fun. I don't feel giddy or hopeful or loving anymore. I feel only disappointed, angry, and unhappy. I don't sleep well. My eyes hurt. And I don't have much energy left for anything "extra" besides work and school.

We quarrel often. It saddens me, but I can't seem to stop. The pain from the Press has come between us.

Len Bohner is in the process of being fired. The rumor is that he's being replaced because he couldn't deal with "those girls." A man named Jack Blacker will become general manager. Blacker is currently here part time.

Max thinks that Neal C. Wilson, General Conference vice president for North America, is behind Bohner's firing. Wilson's responsibilities include keeping tabs on what's happening at church institutions throughout North America. He's been to the Press a few times — during various religious business gatherings and to some of the Board meetings. I've never met him.

While Robert Pierson is General Conference President, it is generally accepted that Neal Wilson is the real "power behind the throne." Most people expect Neal Wilson to be elected president at the next General Conference session.

"Wilson is a political fox," Max says. "He's probably really angry that this equal pay thing isn't cleared up here. I'll bet he's bringing Blacker in to settle the dispute."

Gus is home for a visit. He whisks into my office, just like old times, full of gentle enthusiasm. How good it is to see him!

Gus has a sanctified innocence about him. He always seems to be in the process of discovering something exciting and meaningful, like a child watching a butterfly emerge from a cocoon. He says he will visit Blacker and Muir. He says he is disappointed that we don't seem any closer to a settlement than when he left.

I can see that my lawsuit saddens him. But he encourages me to be true to my own conscience.

Late in the day Lorna drops by. She is worried. She says that while Gus was talking with Muir, Muir expressed concern because he had heard that Gus might lose his job over this whole situation.

## October 1973

Gus has been here almost a month. His visit is nearly over. It's been fun having him here again.

This morning Lorna is very pale. "Gus got a long distance call this morning from Elder Powers," she says. Elder Powers is the president of the Euro-Africa Division, the division which has authority over the Hamburg Publishing House where Gus works.

"He ordered Gus to bring me back under any circumstances."

"What did Gus say?"

"Well, you know Gus; he said he couldn't exert pressure like that. He said he does not control the conscience of anyone other than himself."

Lorna and Gus Tobler are a rare breed. Devout, sincere, but neither of them has the spiritual dominance so often exhibited in fundamentalist Christians. They don't force their beliefs, their interpretation of Truth, on others.

"But Powers is adamant. He wants me at Gus's side when Gus returns."

"Are you going to go?"

She shakes her head. "Not until this equal employment thing is settled."

# October 12, 1973

Dear Sister Tobler:

Yesterday Elder Bohner called from Washington, D.C., and asked that an item be presented to the Executive Committee for action. It seems that the President of the Euro-Africa Division is quite insistent that you return to Hamburg, Germany, with your husband Gustav at the end of his vacation, which he is spending with you here in Sunnyvale.

I am sure that this comes as no surprise to you, as Elder Powers has been in touch with Gus by phone.

Elders Bohner, Blacker, and Bietz discussed this request; and they were agreed that the Executive Committee should take an action notifying you that your services be terminated on or before October 31, 1973, in order that you may return to Germany with your husband.

We are perfectly willing to pay your salary until October 31, even though you may wish to actually cease work almost immediately in order that you may pack up for the move to Hamburg.

If you have not yet taken your annual vacation, you would be entitled to pay for that, which I presume is 152 hours. In addition to that, we would prorate next year's vacation from the anniversary of your beginning date of employment. I believe you started work for us about June 27, 1960. If you have not already taken your vacation, then your pay would be extended until near the end of November, and that would mean that you would have an additional 63 hours of vacation time to be added to that which you have earned towards this year's vacation.

Also, if you have any medical expenses to report, those should be turned in to us so that we can give you reimbursement before you leave. You also would be entitled to a prorated portion of the annual bonus, which I will compute as soon as we determine what your total annual pay for 1973 will have been, including the vacation time to which you are due.

We wish you and your husband the blessing of the Lord as you continue in the service of the Master in this new field of labor.

Sincerely yours,

William L. Muir
Secretary-Treasurer

cc: L.F. Bohner
    R.R. Bietz
    W.J. Blacker

## October 19, 1973

To: Bietz, Bohner, Blacker, Muir, members of
    Executive Committee

Dear Brethren and Sisters:

I have received the enclosed letter Brother Muir wrote me
regarding the action Brethren Bohner, Blacker, and Bietz
requested the Executive Committee to take. Although the
language of Brother Muir's letter is unclear on the point of
whether I have actually been terminated, it seems to show
the intent of termination. Since the date in question,
October 31, is close, I respectfully request an early response to this letter.

I was surprised to see such an extraordinary measure taken
against me — especially in view of the fact that we are
nearing a settlement of the problem of sex discrimination
that we have worked so hard to keep out of court and
public view.

Now this action complicates everything. It would certainly be viewed by the law as a reprisal, and I myself can
explain it in no other way. Ostensibly the letter "encourages" me to go at once to Hamburg with my husband. But
the Press is not in the habit of coercing the private lives of
its employees as long as they remain upright.

Brother Muir has assured me that there are no charges of
personal or professional misconduct against me. He said
also that he knows of no similar action ever taken by the
Executive Committee.

I can think of no less appropriate action for an executive
committee to take than one presuming to interfere in the
personal relationship Gus and I have with each other and
to attempt to force personal decisions on us that we feel
before God we must make for ourselves.

Ordinarily I feel no particular obligation to keep people
informed on the state of our marriage, but under the
circumstances I will tell you that Gustav and I think we
have a great thing going. We wouldn't trade our marriage
for anybody else's. We feel that unity of heart and mind is
more important than any other kind. Sometimes that sort
of unity calls for temporary physical separation. This

experience is well known to Adventist workers, many of whom spend long months away from their families. They do this because of the love they bear not only for God and His work, but also for their united goal. For this reason I agreed that Gustav should go to Hamburg before I myself could go in good conscience. It has not been easy for either of us, and we have been looking forward to the day in the near future when I would be able to go, too.

In view of all this, and considering the further difficulties it places on the Press from the standpoint of law, I earnestly and respectfully request that you ask the Executive Committee to rescind any action it may have taken against me.

I appeal to you as friends and brothers and sisters to look beyond any personal misunderstandings individuals may harbor because of one aspect or another of this problem, to withhold judgment, and to accept my request as coming from one who, with you, has committed her life to God, His children and His message of love.

Sincerely,

Lorna Tobler

Lorna files charges of retaliation with the Equal Employment Opportunity Commission, charging that she had been discharged in retaliation for her support of my case.

Joan Bradford fires off a letter to Don McNeil about Lorna's termination. Part of that letter reads:

October 24, 1973

> ... I realize that you cannot entirely control your clients in this matter. However, the Press' termination of Lorna Tobler after her opposition to discriminatory employment practices and her cooperation as a witness in the *Silver* case can be regarded only as retaliation. Settlement conferences are futile during such a period. Until we have written notice of the continuing employment of Ms. Tobler at the Press, no further conferences will be held
> ....

Two days later the Press Executive Committee officially "clarified" their use of the word "terminated." They said that the word meant Lorna was free to return to Germany with her husband. The Board said they thought perhaps she felt she *must* stay here, and the letter was merely their way of saying, "You are free to go, and thank you for your work."

Nothing more was said about the letter, the word "terminated," or Lorna's going to Germany.

After his Mountain View vacation, Gus flew back to Hamburg alone.

Tension is my daily companion. My insides feel like a tightrope most of the time.

People I do not know write me letters of condemnation. Others shove hate mail under my office door.

Men come to my office to "reason" with me, pointing out all the trouble I am causing. They pray with me. But always, even in their prayers, they are trying to force me to submit to whatever the Press dishes out. I am amazed at their blatancy — telling me that I must go on suffering, that all women here must suffer simply because that is more convenient for the Press.

And the tension which keeps me taut like a bow string at work invades my home life. My husband is restless and unhappy. He doesn't like my nervousness. He doesn't like my disillusionment.

"You're hard and cynical," he says, making me want to cry. If he could have his way, I'd forget everything that has gone on for the past year or so; and I'd go back to being the trusting, happy Merikay who prayed so long and hard for this job.

But I can't erase what I know. And I know more than I ever wanted to. I know what the leaders think about women, about me and every other female. That knowledge pierces so deeply I can't even put it into words. I am not an equal human being; and should I ask to be viewed as such, I suddenly become despicable.

They will take my talent, my labor, whatever they can get from me; and I must always be grateful to them for taking it. I must never ask for a fair return, an equal exchange of labor and wages.

I feel the hatred. I see the looks of repulsion. I watch as people who see me coming hurry into their offices so they won't have to speak to me. And I realize that I am the object of all this simply because I am female, a woman asking to be treated in the same way and with the same respect as a man.

Just treat me as a person; give my requests the same hearing you'd give any person's; just listen to what I'm saying, please. But no one listens. No one cares. Is it any wonder that I am in constant turmoil inside? Is it any wonder that I can never go back to the trusting innocent who wrote the story *NOW*!

And poor Kim suffers too. Poor, patient, hurting Kim. I am no longer the pollyanna he married.

## December 1973

Len Bohner is out. W. J. Blacker is in — full-time general manager of the Press. A squat, plumlike man, he has steely gray hair and steely gray eyes. His face is nearly square with post-midlife jowls. He rarely smiles.

Bohner was a big, loud man, blustering through the halls like a friendly whirlwind. Blacker is silent, almost shadowlike.

I've heard that he is here for one purpose, to end this equal-pay mess. I have also heard a rumor that Neal Wilson said, "We'll hire the best lawyers we can; and we'll show those girls who's running things."

I can't believe a GC vice president would make such a remark. All the evidence is against the Press. How could he dare encourage them to fight? I know all the rumors going around about me. All lies. Perhaps this is just a lying rumor about him. I hope so.

Blacker visits Lorna today.

Her face shows the tension of all the months of harassment, of the painful separation from Gus, of working day-in-and-day-out in a hostile atmosphere.

"I'm really worried for Gus," she says to me. "Blacker told me that the Euro-Africa Division is absolutely insistent that I join him in Germany. He said that if I don't, some serious action will be taken."

"Like what?"

She just shakes her head.

"Gus has too many years in; his entire life is the denomination," her voice trails off.

"You think they'll really try to fire Gus — because of you?"

She simply stares at me, her eyes large and worried. Then she says, "Blacker's message was a clear threat."

Lorna receives a letter from one of the officials of the Euro-Africa Division, ordering her to "get over here." The letter, written in German, warns that if she doesn't move to Hamburg immediately, something terribly serious will happen.

She calls Gus. He says that Elder Powers, president of the Euro-Africa Division, and Elder Vogel, manager of the Hamburg publishing house where Gus works, have been pressuring him to write Lorna and demand she move to Hamburg.

"I told them that they should write you, and express their desires," he tells Lorna. "I thought they should write their own letter. I didn't want to."

"Well, they did," she says. "And it's strong! They say it's my duty to obey and move to Germany, whether or not it seems good to me."

Later in the afternoon she calls to say she's decided to contact R.R. Bietz to see if he will help.

The rumor is that the General Conference has instructed all the publishing houses to stop publishing my writings.

"Can they do that?" Kim asks.

How do I know? I don't know anything any more. I feel afloat in a strange world where there are no rules, no principles, no standards. Nothing is familiar.

"I'll phone the book editors at Southern Pub and the Review tomorrow and ask if they've heard anything," I say. I'm just so glad that both of those publishing houses have accepted manuscripts lately. And the Press has a little booklet of mine coming out soon.

If the GC begins telling publishing houses to stop accepting my material, then the GC is going to be in trouble because that's retaliation. I can't imagine why they would want to retaliate. Don't they want the Press to abide by the GC wage guidelines? Don't they want the Press to obey the law? I don't see where my employment fuss is any of the GC's business. But then, I don't understand much any more. Except that everything is wrong, and I'm a nervous wreck.

Ray Cottrell at the Review and Herald Publishing Association says he hasn't heard anything about a letter. He is such a kindly gentleman. I'm sure he doesn't approve of my lawsuit, but he is so gentle in his statements to me.

Gentleness is rare. I never noticed before how I starve for it. I feel raw most of the time — pained and hurting. And everyone keeps telling me it's my own fault; if I'd just be more patient everything would be fine.

It's so comforting to have someone speak gently to me.

When I phone Richard Coffen, the book editor at Southern Publishing, he says there is indeed a letter going around. But he can't give me any more information than that.

I call Kit Watts and Pat Horning to see if they can get me a copy of the letter.

I call Joan to see if she can request a copy of the letter.

I *must* see the letter.

My hopes that this disagreement would not affect my writing career begin to dim.

Today I receive a copy of the letter.

It is written on General Conference stationery, and is signed by Bruce M. Wickwire. I have never heard of Bruce M. Wickwire. The letter:

December 10, 1973

Dear Friends,

RE: ARTICLES AND MANUSCRIPTS BY MERIKAY SILVER — PACIFIC PRESS PUBLISHING ASSOCI-ATION EMPLOYEE.

Due to the fact that Merikay is presently at variance with the church, and because, by her tendency to ignore Christian counsel, and inasmuch as she has involved the PPPA in civil court litigation, it is hereby requested that before any further production or promotion of her works is done, counsel be sought from General Conference administration and the General Conference Publishing Department, this request to apply until further notice. Thank you for your cooperation.

I sit at my desk reading and rereading the letter. Who is Bruce Wickwire? I shake my head in disbelief. Someone I don't know. Someone who doesn't know me, who has never asked me what I am doing or why, who has no idea of who I am and what I care about and whether I love the Lord or if my writings embody a vital message . . . a stranger . . . a stranger has ended my writing career within the church. I am numb. By now it is a very familiar sensation.

# January 10, 1974

LAST NIGHT LORNA MET WITH ELDER R. R. BIETZ. THE Board chairman is in town because tomorrow is Board meeting. They discussed what's happening to Gus.

"I showed him the letter I'd received from Germany," she said. "He read it and said it was too strong. But when I asked if that meant that Gus's job was safe, he didn't respond.

"I said I was afraid that Gus would lose his job after all the years he'd been a faithful servant of the church. Bietz said, 'Well, those are some of the hazards.' He said I should just test my influence and see if I could prevent Gus's job loss."

"I said, 'That sounds to me like some little game or something.' And he replied, 'It's not a little game. It's a big game.' "

Lorna and I stare at each other in shock.

"You know, Merikay, this is the worst thing, the very worst of all that has happened," her eyes are sad, rimmed in red.

"The most important person in my life is being attacked and I can't prevent it," she says, her voice sadly subdued. "I can't do anything unless I want to sacrifice my principles. And even then, nothing is certain. There's no guarantee Gus wouldn't be fired."

The pressure shows in Lorna's face.

"I asked again if I could address the Board today," she

continues. "But he said that wasn't possible."

Frustrations mount. There's no way we can communicate with the leaders or with the other women. And the threats and the harassment continue.

Kim is unhappy.

And Joan is sick. She's going into the hospital for tests. She has been working so hard on this case for so long, and I haven't had any money to pay her; the stress is getting to everybody.

And then that stupid Wickwire letter. That's the end of my writing; I just know it. Who is going to say "no" to the General Conference?

Sabbath we drove to Sacramento to visit some friends; and they said that Neal Wilson was at Walla Walla College a few weeks ago, and he spread all kinds of vicious rumors about me. I don't understand all this rumormongering among the leaders of our denomination. They are a group of men who are supposed to be dedicated to the Lord. Yet not one of them has ever contacted me to ask about my actions. Robert Pierson never even acknowledged the letter I sent him more than a year ago.

No one's interested in the reason behind this entire situation. No one cares. And yet they're all out there writing letters and making speeches and spreading rumors.

I called Mike Jones, editor of *Insight* magazine, to see if he'd received the Wickwire letter.

"No I haven't, and no one has asked me to stop publishing your work," he said. "I love your writing and will use it as long as I can."

That encouraged me. Maybe the Wickwire letter won't have the effect I fear. Maybe . . . I can always hope. I always do.

## January 14, 1974

I spend today working on *Sigi's Fire Helmet,* one of the manuscripts I'm currently readying for publication. It's not as bad as some. But it is difficult to work on dry, dusty material when there are so many explosions happening in my life.

As a break from editing, I write Neal Wilson a letter. Since he has made no move to contact me, I've decided to take the initiative and contact him. I ask to meet with him, to explain my side of the PPPA situation, and to see if perhaps there isn't some way to work out all this unpleasantness.

After work I drive to Joan's and file retaliation charges with the EEOC over the Wickwire letter. It is so exhausting to keep complaining about the treatment I'm getting. The treatment, itself, is fatiguing enough. You'd think "the boys" would rest sometime. If they aren't doing one thing to one of us, they're doing something else to the other. It's all so wearying.

Kim and I have started attending Milpitas Church. The Mountain View congregation is filled with Press employees. I don't feel comfortable there any more. At Milpitas my old friend Elder Leonard Mills is pastor. Elder Mills was a friend back in Michigan when I was a teenager. Now he wants us to join his congregation. He and his wife come over Sabbath afternoon and spend most of their visit asking Kim and me to transfer our membership to their church.

"I'd love to be a member at your church," I say, "but I don't think that will be good for you."

He smiles. He's a tender man with a peace-filled heart.

"The brethren are just crusty and hardheaded," he says. "But they won't hurt you. Not really."

I don't tell him that they already have, and that the hurt grows daily. I hesitate to say yes to his request. Fear nibbles at the edges of my mind. Things are not harmless any more. There is a creeping, horror-filled feeling of evil; and I don't want a sweet Christian man like Leonard Mills to get caught in it.

Yet it feels so good to be wanted somewhere. Kim's eyes glow for the first time in months. He has also suffered from exclusion and ridicule. He married a woman who was highly respected. And now he is married to a woman who is despised. Not an easy situation to deal with — being the husband of a troublemaking, crusading, anti-sex-discrimination pioneer.

It's late when the phone rings. The voice on the other end is familiar. It's Roland Hegstad, editor of *Liberty* magazine (past editor of *Insight*) and crusader for religious freedom.

Roland and I have always had a great telephone relationship. He loves my writing and I love his. When he was acting editor of *Insight*, he bought almost everything I sent his way. Now he phones from D.C. with concerns. "I'm calling to urge you to get together with Blacker and settle this thing," he says.

I can envision him standing in the pulpit, preaching with power and emotion. I always love Roland Hegstad's sermons because they are about justice and religious freedom. He always tells stories about people who almost lose their jobs because they refuse to work on the Sabbath, and how the GC goes to their defense and saves their income.

Now I'm glad to hear his voice. If anyone can understand my position, it will be Roland. After all, his department has used the same law I'm using (Title VII of the Civil Rights Act) to protect the rights of Adventist workers all over our nation. For an hour I talk with him, explaining all that has happened, all the stalling by the Press, all the threats; how management does not want to pay women fair wages; how the Press is in opposition to Bible morality, the counsel of Mrs. White, and even Title VII.

But he doesn't seem to listen. He just keeps saying that I should talk with Elder Blacker and work things out.

"But don't you see that he won't talk to me," I finally say. "I've been trying for a year; they will not negotiate."

The more he talks, the more I realize he isn't listening. Like the others, he just wants me to stop causing trouble.

In my mind I see him in the pulpit, extolling the virtues of the laws which protect Adventist workers from religious discrimination. Yet because my employer is an Adventist institution, he cannot see the justice of my cause. My heart aches.

He is very disappointed in my stubbornness. His voice is not friendly but frustrated. He will pray for me and the Press situation, he says. I thank him.

❧

I've decided to take up skydiving. I've always wanted to jump out of an airplane and soar. Maybe skydiving will help take my mind off the Press mess.

Kim thinks it's a great idea.

I hope it will help me relax. The stress is getting to me in physical ways. Lately I've lost my sight on several occasions. The experience starts with sparkly light at the outer limits of my peripheral vision; and then slowly my vision gets narrower and narrower, until I can't see anything but these sparkly lights. My eye doctor says it is a migraine headache without the ache. She says it is caused from stress and tension.

"The muscles in your neck and the base of your skull contract until they cut off the flow of blood, and it affects your vision," she explains.

I must learn to relax. I must somehow get away from the tension. Perhaps flying through the air under a parachute will help.

Joan had surgery and is feeling better. The rumor at the Press is that she has cancer, that God has struck her with cancer just as He struck Naaman with leprosy. I can't believe people's cruelty, their "thank goodness" attitude over her illness.

An editorial on the authority of the church was published this month in the *Review*, the denomination's official magazine. The *Review* comes from and bears the sanction of the General Conference. It is probably the most influential publication the denomination has. The *Review* is mailed weekly, bringing the power and patronage of the General Conference to church members throughout North America.

Mother phoned to say the editorial worried her. "I think they're gearing up for a real battle," she said, her voice fearful.

"Well, Mom, they're battling truth and justice and law and things that are a lot bigger than they are."

"But, Honey, I don't want you to be hurt."

"Don't worry about it. I'm doing okay." I laugh.

I'm amazed that I'm still functioning: still walking, still editing manuscripts, still sitting on the committees offering my opinions. You'd think with the continuing pain and tension that I'd be collapsing in a corner somewhere like a wax statue in a fire. But I'm not.

I just keep going and going. Sometimes I think I'm a robot that someone set on "go"; and I just keep "go"ing, mechanically. I won't run down until this whole situation is resolved.

A phone call from Neal Wilson! Contact, real contact with someone from the General Conference. He wants to meet with me on February 22. I can't wait. I'm going to tell him everything. Maybe after he meets me he'll see that I'm not an "evil troubler of Israel," that all I want is simple justice. Maybe he'll use his influence to end this fuss.

How I hope he'll make a difference!

Kim and I go out for ice cream to celebrate the possibility of an understanding ear.

## February 1974

Parachuting is one of the best things I've ever done in my whole life. The equipment is bulky and heavy, but the experience is like paradise: swaying with the plane as it roars down the gravel runway, watching the earth fall away, watching the hills sink to soft round mounds and the sky flood my view, climbing out onto the wheel and feeling the prop wind suck my breath away.

Jumping. Falling free and fast, the air roaring past, the earth a dizzying patchwork below — nothing beats that for excitement!

Floating gently and silently under the parachute umbrella, steering toward the target — nothing beats that for peace!

Kim spent a day making a super-8 movie of my jumps. He went up with me to get shots from inside the plane, and he filmed me landing and everything. It's going to be a neat movie. I can't wait until it's finished.

This is one activity that takes me completely away from the Press. When I'm out there falling through space, I don't have one thought in my head except "pull that cord." There's no hassle with Richard or Blacker or anyone.

Just me and the sky. And I love it!

Well, I've jumped from an airplane ten times.

I've been scared spitless. I've rolled over and over instead of maintaining my stability in the air. I've landed on target and far afield. I've had the excitement of not being able to find my rip cord and having to pull the cord on my reserve chute. I've had the hypnotic desire to refrain from pulling the cord at all.

And today I broke my ankle.

I miscalculated and landed about a fifth of a mile off target, in a cow pasture. When I was coming down I was so mad at myself and concentrating with such fury on *not* landing in some cow pie, that I hit on one foot, heard the snap, and felt the pain.

So now I wear a cast from toe to knee and hobble around feeling rather foolish.

When I call home to say I've broken my ankle, mother is all concern and sympathy. But when I tell her *how* I broke it, she says, "That's the craziest thing I've ever heard of. Jumping out of planes! People are going to think you really are insane!"

So much for comfort.

Jack Blacker dropped by my office today.

"Just came by to see your cast," he said.

I walked around the desk and showed it to him. He wanted to know how scary parachuting was.

I said it was the scariest thing I'd ever done . . . and the most exciting.

He stayed about ten minutes, and not a word passed between us about the equal-employment issue. Maybe this broken ankle is a good thing — helping break the ice that has formed between me and the rest of the people here — giving us some level other than the lawsuit on which to relate.

I prepare a document for Neal Wilson. It's important to have my thoughts and viewpoint organized for him, and the best way I can do that is to write it all down.

In my document I talk about my hiring-in impression — how I thought I'd earn about $600 a month, when in reality I received less than $400. I talk about Kim losing his job, thus making me economic head-of-household, how I was refused proper compensation, and how shocked I was to learn that *no* woman who needed and qualified had ever received the allowance. I talk about the Department of Labor's investigation and how management lied to the investigator. I tell about trying to be patient, about the many letters from and meetings with Lorna and Gus and Max, and how nothing, absolutely nothing came of it all.

I write: "After eight months it was clear to me that women would never be treated fairly at the Press unless some kind of force was applied. We may be God's people but we are still very human. And the selfish human heart does not identify with the needs and suffering of many financially mistreated female employees . . . .

"The Press did not respond to the suit as I'd thought they would. There was still no attempt to get together and talk this thing out. Instead there was the same silence."

I go on and on for nearly twenty pages.

I write, "If a woman does not ask for what is rightfully hers, no one will give it to her. The Press management said, 'Well, I don't hear any women complaining.'

"But when a woman does complain, Press management either ignores her, tries to beat her down with emotional rumors and group pressure, or tries to starve her out by not paying her what she needs to live.

"Either way the woman gets hurt . . . .

"So many women have said to me and others, 'I can't bear to think or talk about it or I'm afraid I'll lose my religion.'

"This is the broad, underlying base on which we are operating. I think it is disgraceful. I think it is a situation that should cause tears to stream from the eyes of the more faithful men in our church.

"I am only one of many who have suffered from this system."

I go on and on, pouring it all out on paper for Neal

Wilson. I describe the farce of negotiation sessions. I tell
about my upset with the Wickwire letter, and that now
Gus' job is being threatened — not because he has done
anything wrong, but because his wife is supporting justice and morality in this case.

I describe what I have heard about Neal Wilson himself:

"I heard from friends at Walla Walla that Neal Wilson
was there and publicly represented me as having filed a
second, a personal lawsuit for damages; and that the General Conference was very disappointed in this action of
mine and couldn't condone it.

"All over the country General Conference people are
saying this or that about me; and usually what they are
saying is not only untrue but also calculated to hurt or
destroy me personally.

"From my viewpoint, the entire issue has been lost in a
sea of politics and a struggle to maintain authority. I can't
take part in that kind of game. I refuse to consciously play
the political odds."

The last four pages of my document are lengthy quotes
from the Bible, stressing honesty, justice, fairness in
dealing with employees as well as widows and orphans:
Proverbs 28:5, 9; Proverbs 81:8-9; Jeremiah chapters 21-23;
Micah chapters 2-3; Mark 3:5; Matthew 12:28-31; and on
and on.

## February 22, 1974

(One year and nine months since I asked Bohner for equal pay. More than one year since I filed suit.)

Neal Wilson comes early, about 9:30 a.m. I hobble in my cast to greet him.

"Hello," he says, smiling down at me. He seems very, very tall. Removing his black overcoat, he tosses it on the couch. "Well, Merikay, today is your day," he says. "I've set the whole day aside for you."

I can tell from the way he says it that that is an impressive gesture.

I have seen Neal Wilson for years. As a child growing up in Michigan, I watched him speak during campmeeting. He was one of those movers-and-shakers in the church. A politician with skill and knowledge and a kind of charisma that either drew or repelled people. There are very few who hold neutral opinions about Neal Wilson.

Now, close up, I see that he is older than I expected. He is tall and almost skeletally thin. His ears stick out like half-saucers, giving his face more fullness than it really has. His eyes, deep set and dark, look as if they're hiding in crevasses behind his glasses. He has a large nose and a thin-lipped mouth.

"How'd you do that?" he asks, pointing to my cast.

"Parachuting."

"You skydive?"

"I'm a beginner."

He laughs.

"Hey, you want to see a movie of me skydiving?"

"Do you have one?"

"Kim just finished editing it. You want to see it?"

"Well, of course."

I set up the projector and screen; and we watch as I suit up, climb into the plane, climb out and let go of the strut, and fly away. Then we watch as I float down to earth. It's fun to show my parachuting film to someone.

After my film I pour us both a glass of juice.

"My son and I climb mountains," he says. "That's about as dangerous as I care to get."

He talks about mountain climbing — how you must not do anything hastily or thoughtlessly; how it takes all the physical and mental stamina you have. His eyes shine. His enthusiasm softens his features, giving him an almost warm appearance.

We talk about our families and our "dangerous" sports. Then the doorbell rings, and a messenger delivers an Easter lily plant — a gift from my parents to say they're sorry about my broken ankle.

The morning passes quickly with laughter and warmth. I think Neal Wilson is a nice man. I'm grateful that he is taking the time to get to know me. I am glad that he doesn't spend the whole morning preaching at me. My hopes grow as I realize he is really concentrating on Merikay the person, rather than Merikay that-trouble-maker-who-is-trying-to-destroy-the-Press.

"Well, maybe we should get down to the business of my visit," he finally says, settled comfortably on my couch.

I pull out the document I've written. "I've prepared this for you," I hand it to him. He scans the first page. "Maybe you can read that while I fix lunch, and then we can talk about it."

"All right, Merikay," he says.

While I clean lettuce and slice tomatoes and green peppers into a big yellow bowl, I pray that the Lord will touch his heart, will bring us together in understanding, will use Elder Wilson to help end the Press mess.

When I place our plates on the table, he joins me. While we eat, we talk about the Press problem. He asks me what I think of Blacker, and I say I haven't had a chance to know him very well because he rarely talks to me. Then Wilson says that he has the utmost confidence in the men in leadership at the Press. He believes they are well-meaning Christians, although they may not see things quite the way I do.

When we finish with lunch, I clear the dishes; we remain at the table talking. He asks me about the negotiating sessions.

"There are none," I say.

"It's my understanding that your attorney has been meeting on a regular basis to negotiate."

"Well, we were meeting regularly up until they tried to fire Lorna; but even during those meetings there was no negotiation."

He looks confused and I start to grin. I enjoy this man. He seems earnest. He seems sincerely interested, and all my ham comes out.

"Watch, I'll act out a negotiating session for you," I say. "First, here's Blacker." I puff out my cheeks, lower my mouth, and knot my eyebrows. I cross my arms and sit down with serious finality.

"Now Blacker never looks at us, never speaks to us, never does anything but come in like this and sit down. Then here's Bietz."

I stand up straight and dignified. My face is emotionless. I carry a piece of paper in my hand. Sitting down, I throw the paper on the table, and cross my arms.

"That," I point to the paper, "is the Press' final offer." Wilson starts to laugh.

"They always throw their final offer on the table and sit there with arms crossed and never say a word.

"And here's McNeil," I say; and I get up and pace back and forth, back and forth on my cast, running my hand over my head in frustration.

Wilson chuckles, his eyes shining.

"That's the Press management side of the negotiating table," I say. "The other side, the side where my attorney and sometimes I sit goes like this."

I pick up the paper, study it a minute, and say as sincerely as I can; "Mr. McNeil, I'm looking at item A2 on your offer, and I wonder exactly what your client means by such and such."

Then I look at Wilson and wait expectantly for an answer. Of course Neal Wilson doesn't say anything; he just looks back. So I stammer around for a moment, and then turn the paper over and say; "Well, how about item G? Mr. McNeil, do you think your client would be willing to do such and such. I know Merikay is willing to reword her requests to read that way."

Again I look at Wilson, and he's laughing at me.

"Don't laugh," I say, "that's how we negotiate. There are *no* negotiating sessions. The Press throws its last offer on the table, and we keep asking a stone wall to discuss it."

"You're quite an actress, Merikay," he grins.

"Well, you know, I'm just trying to get beyond icy formality."

We talk a few more minutes about the negotiating problems. Then he picks up my document. "You know, Merikay," he says, rolling it into a long, thin tube, and pointing it at me, "you aren't shooting all blanks in this."

My heart skips. Maybe he agrees with my position or my motivation or with the texts I've quoted. I grasp at any little flicker of agreement. If he can see my side, if he can understand, even a little bit, maybe he can explain it to the others; and maybe together we can work this whole thing out.

"The main thing that bothers me about all this is that I don't think the government has any right coming into our publishing house and telling us what to do."

"Well, if we were living by our own guidelines, if we were obeying the law, there'd be no danger of that," I say.

He shakes his head. "It's a very dangerous precedent." He pauses for a long moment and then says, "The feeling around the denomination is that you are at odds with the church."

I smile and shake my head in disagreement.

"I just want the Press to obey GC wage guidelines," I say. "I want the fairness and justice advocated by the Bible and Mrs. White. I'm not the one at odds with the church. The Press is."

He looks at me with a long, steady gaze that starts out serious and full of authority. I match his gaze with what I hope is clear, innocent, brave sincerity. After several seconds his eyes soften and he breaks out in a smile.

"Well, what can we do to end this thing?" he asks.

"Talk. Negotiate. Do what is right and lawful," I say. "I don't know what is so all-fired difficult about doing what's right."

He unrolls my document and starts going through it. "What about this?" He points to some item. "What could we do about this?"

As I talk, he jots notes. I can't believe it! He's actually listening to me and taking notes. My spirit soars. The Lord has sent an angel! Someone who will listen. Never once in the last year and a half has anyone listened to me. They've talked at me and endured my replies until they could speak again, but Neal Wilson is the first leader who has listened. If he can just get the management to listen, to talk and communicate, we can settle this problem.

About thirty minutes before he has to leave, Lorna arrives to plead on behalf of Gus. She says it is grossly unfair to pressure her husband, who is innocent of any wrongdoing.

I leave the room and thank God for sending Neal Wilson to my house. I feel happier than I have for months. I feel hope, something that's been missing from my life lately.

Lorna will drive him to the airport. As he pulls on his coat, I realize that we have not prayed all day. Grace before lunch, but not any real prayer.

"Let's have prayer before you leave," I say.

"Yes, of course," he says. He comes over and stands next to me. He is so tall and dark in his black overcoat. He puts his arm around me, so I put mine around him and around Lorna and pull us together in a close, tight prayer circle.

He prays first. He prays for a solution. He asks that the Lord will work with me and the Press brethren, to help us find a solution.

I pray next, asking that the Lord will soften hearts, will guide me and guide Neal Wilson. And I ask that the Lord keep Wilson safe on his flight back to L.A.

Lorna says a few words, and then it's over.

He looks at me for a long moment before he leaves. "It's been quite an experience," he says. We both smile, and he and Lorna head for the airport.

I sing and pray for the rest of the day. If I didn't have this clumsy cast on, I'd dance. The Lord has sent a wonderful man to work this whole thing out. I just know everything is going to end up well. He said I wasn't "shooting all blanks," and he took notes.

When Kim comes home, I go over my day moment by moment. We laugh and hug each other. Maybe the end is within sight. We pray, thanking the Lord for Neal Wilson, hoping that this man from the General Conference will be the key we need to open the doors to negotiation.

Lorna and I talk about Neal Wilson. She agrees that he seemed interested and sincere.

"Oh, I'm so excited! I just know that he can change this whole thing around," I say, still high from my meeting with him.

"He certainly can if he wants to," she says.

I'm always sure something wonderful, or something horrible, is going to happen; but she's more cautious. And, of course, she's usually closer to right than I am.

## March 1974

March rushes by in a whirl of phone calls and letters. About a week after his visit, Neal Wilson phones to say he's been talking with the brethren; he feels they are more open to compromise than ever before. My hopes rise on his words. It is so good to talk with him because he really listens and seems to care.

Then a week or so later he phones again.

"I urge you to have an open attitude at your next settlement conference," he says. "Merikay, I'll be very disappointed if you can't find a compromise."

"Boy, not half as disappointed as I'll be," I laugh.

"Try, Merikay," he says. "The brethren have good hearts. Try to find a compromise."

How I long to find the key to settlement! Maybe Neal Wilson's encouragement is the catalyst we all need — maybe through his efforts communications will begin and we can correct the inequities at PPPA. I hope so.

Mike Jones, *Insight* editor, calls to ask if I'd mind using a pseudonym until after the lawsuit is settled. *Insight* buys many of my stories and essays.

"People on the publishing committee here are saying your name makes it very hard to sell *Insight* to the churches," he says. His sympathetic voice is warm, but the words still hurt.

I tell him I'll use a pseudonym.

Near the end of March Lorna has an unexpected visitor — an Elder Seton. Seton is one of the vice presidents from the Euro-Africa Division. His visit is friendly, something very unusual these days.

When she expresses her concern for Gus and refers to the threatening letter she received ordering her to come to Hamburg, Seton suggests that she try negotiating with Hamburg.

"If you feel you cannot leave by the date they set for you, offer a date of your own. Often that kind of negotiation is acceptable. Why don't you try and see if it works?" he says.

So Lorna composes a letter to Elder Powers, promising to come to Hamburg as soon as the trial is over. She explains her involvement with the proceedings and promises to leave for Hamburg on the first plane, once the situation here is settled.

After she checks it out with Joan Bradford and Gus, she mails it. We both hope it will do some good.

## April 1974

At our April settlement conference — the one Neal Wilson has been phoning about — Jack Blacker sits stiff and unsmiling. He refuses to talk and seems as immovable as ever.

I wonder what Wilson was referring to when he said he hoped we could reach a compromise. If the other side won't talk, I can't do anything. I don't think we're terribly far apart; but when no one talks, you can't close even a tiny gap.

Later in the day Max stops by to say, "Richard's laying the groundwork to fire you. Be sure to keep a diary so you can document things he says and does and thus protect yourself."

Sigh! Self-defense is so exhausting.

And even my homelife has soured. Kim and I quarrel — a lot. He wants more time for us. I spend too much time on the Press case. All I ever talk about is the Press case. Or my classes. But even my classes are "extra."

Kim's business is not going as well as he had hoped. I think it's fine — he has an employee and many clients, but he's not happy with it.

And he's not happy with me. Who would be? I'm miserable. I'm either discussing strategy with Joan or Lorna or I'm studying or I'm ranting about the unfairness of it all or I'm sleeping. I'm exhausted all the time. It takes all my energy just to go to work each day and endure. I have nothing left when I come home. And Kim needs me. He needs more than I have to give.

It seems that almost any time we talk, we argue. I feel so miserable, so helpless. And there is no way out.

For months now the Press has been trying to get Judge Charles Renfrew to decertify (throw out) the class part of my lawsuit. They don't want a class action, but that is exactly what I want. What will I have gained if I win a lawsuit in which I am the only plaintiff? I might get my money, but every other woman deserving equal pay would still have to go through this hellish experience to get hers. A successful class action can assure all the women workers here of equal treatment. That's my goal.

For months now we have been filing papers and going into court to argue for the class, while the Press has been arguing against it. Today is another hearing. Judge Renfrew's courtroom is on the seventeenth floor of the federal courthouse in San Francisco.

Renfrew is a rather pale man, with freckles and thinning strawberry blond hair. He has never seemed friendly to my side of this case. Today he sits high up behind his bench, listening to one item after the other on the docket. When he finally gets to us, number thirteen, all the attorneys go forward and put their briefcases and piles of papers on the two counselor tables. Then, one at a time, each pleads before Renfrew, who seems tired, casting down sarcastic remarks now and then.

But when it's all over, he does not throw out the class. He says he'll allow the women to decide by secret ballot whether or not they wish to receive their benefits. I breathe easier. The class action still exists.

However, Jack Blacker effectively destroys my relief when he reads a letter from Attorney Don McNeil at the April 8 chapel period. The letter, addressed to the women at the Press, says that if the Silver lawsuit goes to court, every woman's name and how she voted (on whether to accept class-action benefits or not) would be revealed.

I am furious. These people will stop at nothing to keep women cowed and "in their place."

All morning Lorna's phone has been ringing as women workers call to say they cannot risk asking for their rights under such "your-name-will-be-revealed" conditions.

∾

The two attorneys — Joan Bradford and Don McNeil — met with Judge Renfrew last week to work out the particulars on the "vote letter" which will be mailed to the women. The letter is supposed to explain the litigation and give each woman a chance to mail back a form stating that she wants to be "out" of or "in" the class action. Or, if a woman doesn't return the form, it will be automatically assumed that she wants "in."

I hope and pray that the management tactics haven't frightened every woman at the Press into asking "out."

This Sabbath Kim and I joined the Milpitas Church. We were voted into membership, and after the service the congregation had a potluck for us. It feels so good to be welcomed for a change. Most of the Milpitas Church members are not Press employees and have no interest in the struggle going on there.

For me, personally, it is wonderful to be in Elder Mills' congregation. He represents all that was good during my youth in Michigan. He's a gentle man with a good heart and a tender sense of humor.

His wife is just as friendly and seems to have boundless energy. She is raising funds to build a day-care center. She believes strongly in the next generation and in living out your faith by doing something positive and constructive in your community.

The Mills are so full of hope and joy. Just being around them raises my spirits.

The daily news often reads like a parallel to my life. Nixon and his people are swearing that they are not breaking any laws; but the more information that emerges, the deeper their deception appears. That's how it is at the Press. Management continues to say they are doing right by the women, that the judge has denied the class action, and on and on. But as time passes, it becomes clearer where the hearts of the leaders are. Their hearts are hard and totally unconcerned with the suffering that women endure.

However, now and then during all these dark months some spark of joy lightens my day. Neal Wilson is one of those sparks. Even though nothing has come from our meeting, I'm still hopeful he'll help us move toward settlement.

Attorney Warren Johns is another of those sparks. Johns, an attorney in Sacramento, has started a specialty publishing house. He's hired Kim to design the jacket and cover for one of the books Johns is publishing. The book will be super deluxe, and Kim is going all-out to give it the right look.

I've talked to Johns now and then when he's phoned Kim. Through the weeks that Kim and he have been working together, we've become better acquainted. He seems like a good-natured man with a strong Christian vision. He is enthusiastic and creative. He wants to go skydiving with me some weekend. He's friendly, and friendliness is rare these days; so I rejoice whenever I hear from him.

We have briefly discussed the legal position of the Press; and although he didn't state any strong views, he did not condemn me or my position.

Lorna's letter to Powers concerning her move to Hamburg must have done the job. Gus called to say that even though the pressure is continuing, there are no longer any threats of losing his job.

However, the brethren recently brought out their "really big gun."

Gus grew up in Switzerland. His father worked for the Swiss publishing house, and in the back of Gus's mind he has always dreamed of going back to the Swiss publishing house as someone with influence. He would love to become editor there.

He phoned to tell Lorna that the Euro-Africa Division has offered him the general manager position at the Swiss publishing house. His dream position offered to him on a silver platter, with only one string attached — Lorna. He can have the position only if Lorna is at his side.

## May 13, 1974

Today is Constituency Meeting at the Press. This day comes once every four years. It is when the constituency elects (or re-elects) PPPA officers. Jack Blacker will be re-elected general manager. R. R. Bietz is resigning; so a new Board chairman will be elected. It will no doubt be Neal Wilson. Any really important business, major changes, or acquisitions will be discussed and voted on. And all those PPPA employees who have been hired since last constituency meeting will be voted into membership today. That means that I'll be able to be a member of PPPA constituency, and perhaps I can have some say on the policies and practices here.

Today is a fun, party-type day. Everyone is keyed up; and tonight, after all the business, we'll have a big banquet and celebrate. The chapel is overflowing. Even the balcony is full today. Neal Wilson is here, along with others from the General Conference. Bietz presides, discussing past accomplishments and future plans. After all the opening exercises, the prayers and hymns and announcements, the meeting gets down to business.

One of the big propositions is that PPPA management wants to make the Press directly responsible to the General Conference. They want the Press to become part of the General Conference in a legal, structural sense. Such unity would strengthen their position in our struggle for equal pay. If they were incorporated into the structure of the religious headquarters for our denomination, then the argument that any court interference would be interfering with religious freedom would be a much stronger argument.

Men stand to argue for or against the proposal. The discussion rages for nearly an hour. Finally one of the GC men, Walter B. Beach, stands to say he is definitely against any such close association between the GC and the Press.

"We don't want anything you do wrong out here to come back on us. For the simple reason that after they take your money they might take ours too," he says. The entire auditorium erupts in laughter. "That's what I'm concerned with."

Neal Wilson suggests that a committee be appointed to

study the proposition, and everyone votes to move it to committee.

There are other issues, other proposals. Then near the end of the day comes the chance to vote all the new employees into membership. Lorna and Max and Richard have explained how this is done. Bietz will read through the list of names, ask the constituents to admit these employees to membership by a voice vote, and everyone is automatically accepted. That's how it has been done from the beginning. I am glad there won't be another hassle about me.

But when it comes time to vote, Bietz says there has been a change of procedure. "We're going to have a secret ballot vote," he says. "You will receive a sheet of paper listing the names of all those applying for membership. You can check yes or no beside each name. Some of the brethren will tally up the vote, and we'll inform those who are accepted. I know this is different from what you've been used to in the past, but I think it will work just as well."

Men walk the aisles, handing out the voting sheets. I go back to my office. It's obvious what is happening. I might as well do some more editing.

I'm busy working on *Sigi's Fire Helmet* and *I Heard Singing*. Both manuscripts are nearing completion, and I want to have them done by the time we all go to Editorial Council in June.

It's a strain to keep going over and over these manuscripts. But I must make sure that the viewpoint is consistent and that the dates flow chronologically; and most of all, I try to interject some kind of spiritual lesson into the story.

Many of our manuscripts lack that; and it seems to me if we're a Christian publishing house, the first requirement should be a spiritual lesson. I go from one manuscript to the other as my interest wears thin.

A knock at my door gives me a welcome break. It's Wes Siegenthaler and Shirley Burton. Shirley Burton works for the Pacific Union Conference. She edits the *Pacific Union Recorder* and about once a year visits the Press.

Now the two of them come in and sit down for a visit. At first I'm grateful for the break, but their conversation soon changes that. They urge me to stop harassing the Press.

Shirley says that she's been in the work for decades and that things are changing. "They change slower than we'd like, but they are changing," she assures me. "The Lord moves in mysterious ways. And sometimes He moves much slower than we'd like. But it's my belief that things are best left to Him."

Then Wes starts in on how good women in America have it. "There's no other country in the world where women have so many privileges," he says, detailing some of the horrors of women's lives in other countries.

The two of them talk for nearly an hour. I try to answer but I am weary, really weary of it all; and most of the time I just sit and listen.

Finally I say, "Look, do you think I'd put up with everything the Press has dished out if I wasn't convinced that what I'm doing is right?"

Neither answers.

"I think I'm here for this very reason. I'm doing what I feel the Lord wants me to do. And I'm the one who must live with my conscience."

They change the subject to Editorial Council. Next month editors and public relations people and the publishing leaders from the General Conference will meet for three days at Pacific Union College in the Napa region of California. It will be an exciting time, with speeches and workshops and fellowship. It will be a time of spiritual and professional refreshing. We talk about Editorial Council for several minutes. Then they leave. I go back to my manuscripts.

The rumor going around the Press these past few days is that everyone was accepted into the PPPA constituency except for me. This afternoon the rumor was substantiated. I received a letter from W.J. Blacker saying that the majority of constituents voted against accepting me as a member.

Sigh!

One more rejection.

One more little pain.

I will no longer be silent. I've been silent far too long already. The management has busily spread their rumors and falsehoods. They've usurped most chapel periods and used interoffice mail to spread their viewpoint, while I've sat "patient and silent." People are always coming to my office to pray or preach at me. Well, I'm through being meek and humble and quiet. I'm going to start communicating.

I phone Joan and say I want to start sending women information sheets on the lawsuit. I want the women to know that the judge has *not* thrown out the class. I want the women to know that the Press has refused to negotiate concerning anyone except me.

Joan says I can do anything I want, as long as she checks it.

At home I discuss my idea with Kim.

"You should have done that sort of thing long ago," he says. "Being quiet never works."

I spend several hours composing my first information sheet.

## *Excerpts from my first information sheet*

The reason two lawsuits are presently pending against Pacific Press (Silver v Pacific Press, and Brennan/Dept. of Labor v. Pacific Press) is that the Press has been and is still breaking the law. The Press hires, pays, and promotes one group of workers differently from another. It makes a difference in remuneration, benefits, and promotions not just on the basis of job performance, but on the basis of sex. This is against the law.

The Press is involved in these two lawsuits because in the ten years since the 1964 Civil Rights Act and the 1963 Equal Pay Act became law, Press management has not voluntarily complied. Even now, instead of trying to work out a system whereby the Press can bring its employment practices into line with the law, it maintains it has a right to do as it sees best because it is a religious organization.

### WHY IS THIS IMPORTANT?

The Civil Rights Act, Title VII, protects you from ruthless employers who would fire you because of your religion, refuse to hire you because of your race or national origin, or pay you substantially less than other workers because of your sex.

It is protective legislation. As a church we have gone to court in support of Adventists who have lost jobs because of Sabbath observance. Title VII of the Civil Rights Act protects Adventists from this kind of treatment. It also protects women from discrimination on the basis of sex.

### WHAT DOES MERIKAY WANT?

Merikay is asking that the Press pay its workers according to the work they perform, rather than the sex they happen to be.

Merikay is asking that women be encouraged to move up in the organization, just as men have been moving up for years, and thus have a voice in decision making.

### WHAT'S KEEPING THE SUIT FROM BEING SETTLED?

Once a suit is filed, the two sides try to find common ground on which to negotiate. Merikay and the Press are quite close to agreement when it comes to the financial part of the suit.

The amount of money which will be paid to women as a token for their years of underpaid labor, has nearly been agreed upon.

The biggest area of disagreement concerns future changes in policy and practice. Management has not yet agreed to search for, hire, and train women for administrative and supervisory positions.

Management does not want to change to a system of remuneration and benefits paid according to tasks performed.

Management does not want auditing of its compliance with the court order. Management does not want to publicize the settlement, once agreed upon. Management does not want to institute an affirmative action program to begin utilizing the talented women now employed by the Press.

At the same time, management has not come up with any idea of what it *does* want. Merikay and her attorneys have suggested more than one plan and have asked management to suggest alternate methods of complying with the law. A variety of ideas can give a wider choice.

But there have been no ideas from management and management's lawyer. Thus, as of this time, negotiations seem bogged down, with management disliking the solutions Merikay suggests, but refusing to suggest any solutions of their own.

My document covers many more topics and ends with more than a page of quotations from the Bible. At the end I list three steps people can take if they believe the Press should obey the law.

1. They should make their views known to management.

2. When they receive a letter from the court, they should write their own views to the judge.

3. They should write the General Conference brethren and urge that they assist the Press in bringing its practices into compliance with the law and the counsel of God's Word.

I feel good about the information sheet. It's four pages of solid, single-spaced typing. It's the first real defense

I've offered for my position.

Soon the letter from the court will go to each woman, and each will have to check yes or no on the class action. I hope that the information I'll pass out will make their choice more informed.

I'm stirring instead of simply sitting in my office. And it feels good for a change.

Yesterday I sent seventy of my information sheets through intercompany mail. I put them in the morning mail delivery pile and they were automatically distributed by the mail carrier.

In the afternoon Lorna stopped by. She had visited Blacker right after lunch and said he was so agitated he couldn't sit still. "I'm going to reply," he said again and again. "I don't know how, but this has got to be answered."

He called the mail carrier into his office and grilled her about who mailed all those lawsuit sheets. She said she wasn't sure.

Today Jack Blacker replied. His two-and-a-half page letter sits in a photocopied stack at the reception desk in the Administration Building. Anyone who wants can pick up a copy.

I picked up a copy for me and a copy for Joan Bradford. I feel his letter is very misleading. He says things like, "To a very large degree these are matters which are beyond our ability to solve without General Conference approval."

He says the Press has made numerous attempts to settle. "The demands on behalf of Mrs. Silver have been extraordinary," he says. But he never mentions a desire to do right by the other women at the Press.

I immediately respond, answering each item he has addressed — from back pay to job categories to attorney's fees. Joan checks it, and then I photocopy it and take it over to the reception area and set it next to his stack.

Late in the afternoon Lorna calls to say someone has photocopied my first letter and set a pile of them next to Blacker's. So now there are three stacks of information sheets on the receptionist's desk.

❧

Richard is furious!

"You're spreading a manure pile full of misinformation!" he shouts.

He storms into Arbie's office while I'm asking her to retype part of a manuscript I'm editing — yelling at me, blocking the door so I can't leave.

"Your facts are so warped it would be laughable if it wasn't so serious!" He scowls.

What can I say to such fury?

"Where did you ever get the idea that you alone have an avenue to the truth? You know the Press' policies better than management? You know the law better than attorneys?"

For the next half hour he tells me what a bad influence I am, what a disappointment, how the devil is blinding me, and that if he were me he'd be on his knees pleading forgiveness before it's really to late.

Arbie pipes up once or twice in her shy little voice to say she agrees with him.

I try defending myself but it's useless. I find my statements serve more as an exercise to remind me that I'm alive and breathing than to convince them of anything. When I finally go back to my office, I sit shaking, on the verge of tears. Nothing changes. No matter how many times I'm yelled at, no matter how common the ocurrence, it never gets easier. It never hurts less.

Arbie knocks timidly at my door and then peeks in. Her face is flushed. She carries a stack of photocopied papers.

Handing me a sheet she says shyly, "This is my information sheet." She smiles half apologetically, half pleased with herself.

I look at her sheet. It is filled with Mrs. White quotes against lawsuits. I feel a slight pleasure in the fact that she had the nerve to do this and give it to me.

"Are you going to put these over at the receptionist desk?" I ask, grinning.

She grins back, nodding.

"You know, we're going to have an information library over there," I say.

"Well," her shyness returns and she starts for the door, "I just wanted you to have it."

Within a couple of days there are eight piles of information sheets and open letters at the receptionist area. Everyone is getting in on the act.

Lorna and I giggle about all the paper communicating going on. Maybe if we'd tried negotiating via letter and interoffice memo, we would have had better luck.

It pleases me that people are thinking and getting personally involved, because the issues behind this whole situation affect everyone here.

Lorna brought me a copy of the four-page letter Dr. Chaij has written and stacked over at the receptionist area, along with all the other stacks of information and letters.

I wasn't going to read it. After my horribly frustrating meeting with him, when he did not believe anything I said and he just kept telling me to be patient, I didn't want to read what he said. But my curiosity got the best of me. Here are some excerpts from his open letter:

". . . Probably most of us who have worked some years in the cause of God could remember some moment of crisis in our life when we had to suffer some kind of misunderstanding, or probably some real or apparent injustice that we had to undergo in our work. After all, all of us are human; and we have human frailties. But God in His mercy permitted these injustices to afflict us in order to prepare our character for heaven and develop patience, forbearance, and humility. In these experiences He offers us the possibility of learning the most wonderful lesson of our lives.

"After the years pass by, we can look back retrospectively and thank God for the victory He gave us by His grace, considering it as the greatest blessing of our life when we humbled ourselves before Him and asked Him to conquer self in us and create in us the same mind which was also in Jesus Christ (Phil. 2:4, 5).

"After all, if we have to forgo some conveniences of life, and if we fail to receive as much money or benefits as we think we are entitled to, that money is left in the cause of God and is used to further His work.

"In fact, although some of us are very sad for what is happening, this does not take us completely unaware, neither is it very strange to us, because we are entering in the time of the shaking. Actually, more of these incidents are going to occur.

"But these occasions show what is inside of each one. They separate the wheat from the chaff. And eventually the people who do not have a real experience with God, those who put self above the interests of the cause, and the present temporal benefits above the eternal destiny of their souls, will be separated during the great reformation that will bring about the outpouring of the Holy Spirit and the finishing of God's work . . . ."

Fernando Chaij is Fernando Chaij is Fernando Chaij. For four pages I read the same words, the same "be patient, trust the leaders, be patient" that I heard in my office.

I know the man means well. I know he thinks he is right and "has the Truth."

And I know, just as certainly, that his trust is misplaced, and that he has no idea of the evil which pervades our system.

# June 6, 1974

Excerpts from

An Open Letter To My Friends At The Press:

by: Elise Schirmerhorn

. . . What does it matter if we as women make less money than we deserve? So what if there are inequities? Do we not have enough faith in our Jesus to believe that He sees these sacrifices and records them? Does it not mean that we have stored up more riches for ourselves in heaven? And even if that is not true and we will never be rewarded, so what? What are we anyway? Are we not to be the outpouring of the Holy Spirit upon a dry and barren earth? Are we not vessels of God, completely nonimportant except that His glory shine within us? If this is so, where is there more room to be concerned with ourselves? The Lord takes care of His own. If there are inequities at the Press (and I do not say there are not), haven't we enough faith in our Jesus to believe that He has the power to take care of them without our puny efforts — and indeed without the efforts of the world? Like the mother of James and John, it seems to me that we are jockying [sic] for positions of selfish importance. What does it matter where we sit at the table, as long as we sit there? . . .

I beg of you who have entered your names in this action, or who are considering doing so, to reconsider. Our time on this earth is so short. What does it matter if you are being treated somewhat unfairly? Do you have enough food to eat? Is there a roof over your head? Of course you do, and of course there is. What more do we need. Do you want to reach the courts of heaven to face the horrible responsibility and judgement that because of your concern with yourself you have slowed the work of God and perhaps caused some soul to lose out? . . .

In my interoffice mail today, I receive a sheet of paper with the following words typed in the middle of it:

Can't you think of aything but money????? You remind me of the fable of the goose and the Golden Egg.

A little later someone pushes an envelope under my door. Inside the envelope is a photocopy of something called "Let's talk about company loyalty." The following words were underlined in red:

Don't let criticism develop to the point of disloyalty to your company.

But just before leaving for the day, I receive a letter from a woman named Julie Hardin, who works for the Michigan Conference of Seventh-day Adventists. Her words of encouragement help balance out the negative barrage.

... I'd just like to thank you personally for using your influence in such a courageous stand. And on behalf of hundreds of women in denominational employ, thanks for what you've done to our pocketbooks.

Lorna writes an information sheet today.

Like Arbie's, it's a whole collection of quotes from Mrs. White. But unlike Arbie's, it supports what I am doing. Lorna found quotes telling people to think for themselves, not to be cowed by authority, to stand for the right though the heavens fall.

In the late afternoon Max came in to say that Richard is going to hire another editor. We certainly need one. The work load is nearly unbearable. But the real blow was that Richard wants a man. There are women working here who could be promoted to an editor position, but Richard will go outside to find a man.

"Hey, Max, I don't need that kind of information," I say. "Don't tell me that."

"Well, I just thought you'd want to know," he says somewhat playfully.

I don't feel playful about it; I feel discouraged, depressed, miserable.

I don't want to go to work today.

I don't ever want to go to work any more.

Every day is the same. The alarm awakens me. I lie there orienting myself to where I am and what day of the week it is, and then all of a sudden the whole horrible world I live in comes roaring into my consciousness and I feel miserable.

Another day at the Press!

I don't want to get up. I don't want to go to work.

But I always do. The robot in me climbs out of bed, brushes her teeth, gets dressed, and drives to the Press. Day after day after day.

And I sit at my desk, working on manuscripts, hoping I can last until 5:00 and then I drive home exhausted.

What a life!

## June 27 - July 1

NORTH AMERICAN EDITORIAL COUNCIL
Pacific Union College
Angwin, California

This morning Richard Coffen, book editor from Southern Publishing, brought me my six author's copies of my book, *Luv Is Not Enough*. I am so excited! Another of my books is off the press! It may be one of my last. I treasure it.

I drive Max and Southern Publishing Association editor Gerald Wheeler, our old college pal from Andrews U. days, up to Pacific Union College. When I was a flunky freshman reporter, Gerald was copy editor and Max was big-shot columnist on the AU student newspaper.

We used to gather in the newspaper office and argue or discuss or talk. Now here we all are, "in the work," going to PUC for Editorial Council. It's fun being together again.

Neal Wilson and I had supper together the first evening. He wanted to know why we hadn't settled. I wanted to know why he hadn't helped.

"You know, Merikay, the brethren think I've fallen victim to your charm. They think that all I hear is your side," he said, buttering his bread.

"Oh, come on," I say. "You're too bright to fall victim to anybody's charm. But I hope you've shared part of my viewpoint with them. I hope you've pointed out where the Press needs to become legal."

We jostle each other, preach to each other, and finally settle down to talking about something else. I ask him how he sleeps with such burdens — the struggle at the Press and other problems at other institutions where he is board chairman.

"I have no problems sleeping," he says. "My head hits the pillow and I'm asleep. All these difficulties are just like water off a duck's back."

I look at him — his dark recessed eyes, his thinning black hair, his black suit, and long skinny fingers lifting his glass to his lips. He could look scary. If he turned his fury on someone he could be frightening.

"How about being friends?" I say.

"We're friends."

"No," I shake my head. "I mean real friends. Where we keep in touch, share what's going on in our lives, talk and write and kind of go through the years together."

"Boy, I don't know, Merikay. I'm so busy," he says. "The General Conference duties are so extensive; they take up so much of my time. And then I'm chairman of the board at Loma Linda, and we have such complicated issues to deal with there. And . . . I just don't know."

"You're too busy to pursue a real friendship, right?" I say. "You just have nodding acquaintance kinds of friends?"

"I'm afraid so."

I wonder how many men are so wrapped up in jobs and careers that they never develop any life outside of work. Are they the ones who drop dead two weeks after retirement? I wonder.

~

Elder Robert Pierson, General Conference president, had devotions this second morning. His whole talk was about harmony and unity. Now as I sit at lunch eating with Mike Jones (editor of *Insight*), Lawrence Maxwell, and others, we discuss Pierson's devotional. Our conversation is animated and enthusiastic.

Suddenly Lawrence glares at me and says, "You are one of the people trying to divide the church." His gray eyes, flat and emotionless, bore into me as though he is preaching to a crowd and I'm not even here; but every word in his torrent is aimed directly at me.

"You're a jealous, vindictive, bitter woman who only wants attention for yourself. You'll go to any lengths to keep in the spotlight," he says. "You don't care about the damage you cause others or the terrible damage you're causing the church."

I try to say that disobeying the law causes a lot more damage than I could. But I can't get a word in. I look around the table and see shock on every face.

Lawrence continues spewing the most personal attack at me, and suddenly Mike Jones stands up. "There's no use continuing the discussion," he says. "Come on, Merikay," he grabs my arm and literally pulls me away from the table.

Shocked, I stumble from the cafeteria, Lawrence's words reverberating inside my head.

Mike leads me to a bench and we sit down.

Sympathy covers his face. And suddenly everything is under water as my own eyes fill, then overflow, with tears.

The last morning of this conference is fascinating. Our devotion is on "unity" not meaning "uniformity." Most people confuse the two words, and it's good to hear a minister describing how the two are not the same. Next comes a presentation on change and how people introduce change into society, and how painful but necessary that always is.

Neal and I discuss the topic over lunch.

"You are definitely a change maker," he grins.

"I suppose so," I grin back.

"Merikay, you've effected great change in this denomination, from one end of the country to the other. Now why don't you rest a little?" Our eyes meet. I'm sure he can tell I can't rest. A little smile plays at my lips. I determine not to interrupt him. I'll let him say the preachy words he must say.

"Why don't you rest now and give the brethren an opportunity to do more, voluntarily?"

He laughs about my having more energy than the brethren and suggests that I should give them a chance to catch up. I say I'm glad about the changes, but they haven't come to Pacific Press yet; and that's where my energies are centered.

We don't mention the Press again but talk about families and vacations and those things which mean a great deal to us. I like him. I only wish he would have worked to settle the Press mess. I wish he would have rescued me from the clutches of illegal employment practices. But wishes are nothing more.

The conference is over. I've enjoyed the fellowship, the meetings, the lectures. And now I have to go back to the Press. What a sad thought after these few refreshing days.

Max and Gerald and I walk to my car. Gerald is leaving with someone else. This may be the last time the three of us are together. Gerald has always been a soft-spoken cynic. He once said, "Cynicism is cutting yourself on the shattered pieces of your own pink cloud."

Now as we walk through the parking lot to our respective vehicles, in a somewhat giddy mood, we talk about the future.

"Where do you think we'll all be thirty years from now?" I ask.

Gerald looks at me. "There's no question where you'll be. Out. On the garbage heap."

We all laugh.

"Yeah, Merikay," Max says. "You can have all the lunches and suppers with Neal you want, but you are definitely ruined."

I laugh. It's true. It's true. But it's also funny, at least right now it is.

"And Max isn't much better off," Gerald says.

"Yeah, I'll probably still be an assistant book editor, slaving away on inferior manuscripts, going crazy," Max says. "But Gerald — sneaky, silent, mild-mannered, cynical Gerald — he has just the qualities needed in a good General Conference leader," Max laughs.

Gerald thinks about Max's appraisal and nods agreement. "Yes, I might really go somewhere in this denomination," he says softly, smiling.

## July 10, 1974

Today Judge Renfrew, Joan, and Don McNeil tallied the womens' responses to the court's letter.

One hundred and ten women asked to be released from the class action. They don't want to accept any benefits which might accrue from the lawsuit.

Eight present employees and nine former employees voted "yes."

Sixty people did not respond. (It was agreed ahead of time that a nonresponse was an automatic yes vote.) So seventy-seven people chose to remain part of the class.

Judge Renfrew decided to continue the case as a class action.

That seems only fair.

If only one or two women wanted to be included, it seems that they should be allowed in. Since the abuse affects all women, it seems only fair that all women be included in the struggle to reduce such abuse and be included in the benefits if our struggle succeeds.

## August 5, 1974 .

Nixon admits today that he lied and aided in the cover up. The country's in an uproar.

I can't believe he allowed his daughter Julie to go to bat for him when he knew all along he was lying. He let her make a fool of herself; he allowed her to reveal her deep, daughterly love and trust; and he never stopped her. His use and abuse of his own daughter is despicable.

Everyone is calling for his resignation. The newscasts are filled with it. So are the papers.

Joan Bradford wants him removed from office by impeachment because if he resigns he gets $60,000 a year pension, which comes from taxes.

The tension between Kim and me is tremendous. I don't know what to do.

His twin brother, Marc, has phoned from Seattle several times and offered to get him a job and a place to stay if Kim wants to go back home. Kim is seriously considering this proposal. He says the pressure here is unbearable, and it is.

We can't seem to escape it. Our friends are all Adventists — so even when we're socializing we're with people who have strong opinions about the lawsuit. At church we feel immersed in "the organization." Any sermons or statements extolling church authority or leaders seem directed at us.

We seem always to be explaining, justifying with facts and figures, defending my actions. It is exhausting. It is miserable. We are totally enclosed in this world of church-Press, and it is overwhelming us both.

Kim says he's no longer happy in California; he misses Seattle.

I realize that I'm not a pleasant person to be around. I have no emotional energy left for him. I am drained day in and day out. I am angry and unhappy and exhausted; and those traits don't make for a happy wife or a happy home. But I don't want him to leave.

We talk about it. Should he go or should he stay?

## August 8, 1974

Nixon resigns.

We were in San Francisco all day, and everyone was out on the streets celebrating what they thought would be his last day in office. There were vendors selling Richard Nixon masks and Richard Nixon posters and cassettes of his speeches and tee-shirts and all sorts of memorabilia.

A really festive atmosphere filled the city.

At home we turned on his live broadcast.

There he was, telling us that the Watergate controversy was becoming so destructive that the wheels of government had come to a virtual standstill and that the country was suffering. Rather than see the country torn apart, he would resign.

And then he was gone.

One minute he's President. The next minute he isn't, and the TV screen is gray.

Kim talks daily about going back to Seattle.

I'm sure the memories of a peaceful, accepting town are enticing. If I could leave I certainly would. I'd go anywhere where people liked me and smiled when they saw me. But I can't leave.

He talks about the possibility more and more.

I feel like an emotional yo-yo. Up and down. Up and down. The Press is the most miserable experience I've ever had, and now my husband wants to leave me. I vacillate between thinking it's a good idea and panicking. I think perhaps he should get out while he still has his sanity and a certain amount of emotional stability left. And the next minute I'm crying, begging him to stay.

Then in my more rational moments I think that a separation might be good for both of us. It will give us a little space in which to breathe (or vent our anger and frustration) without affecting the other. It might be a good idea. And the next moment I'm on the verge of tears.

On top of everything else, I don't want to lose the man I love, the man who has stood by me all these many nightmare months.

## August 31, 1974

Kim leaves today.

He'd been packing and unpacking for nearly a week. I'd ask him to stay, and then say, "No, it's best that you take care of your needs; and if you need to get away from the pressure, go." And then I'd beg him to stay. And he'd pack and then unpack and then pack.

We both felt like we were on a roller coaster until he finally decided.

So I drove him to the airport this morning and kissed him goodbye. He looked as handsome and as apologetic as I've ever seen him. I only pray that he'll feel better in Seattle.

I have mixed feelings. I am torn apart that he is gone. I am lonely and disoriented. My husband, the man I've loved and lived with, fought and slept with, is gone.

But I also feel relieved. My problems, my anger, my pain will no longer affect him. He won't have to put up with a hurting and exhausted person tossing restlessly in bed next to him. He won't have to be wounded by my pain, and for that I am grateful.

Kim has always been a sensitive soul. He's always needed acceptance and love (as we all do); and for the past two years he has received rejection, ridicule, anger. He has watched me change from a starry-eyed pollyanna to someone who doesn't believe anything the leaders say.

My dear, wonderful Kim. I love you so much. May your life be full of happiness and love.

Dear Merikay,

This week I heard the question asked, "What have you done recently to rescue someone from the clutches of the devil, and what are you doing now?" Your name keeps popping into my mind, and I am unable to shake it; for I have followed you through your writings and otherwise for some time. You do not know me and wouldn't recognize my name if I revealed it to you. I am a woman and a little older than you. I have had occasion to brush up against your philosophies in various ways, and I must say, I can only feel you are caught in the clutches of the devil.

When you wrote that sensational story (*NOW!*) at Grand Ledge Academy a few years back, somehow it got circulated around where I was living; and a Christian psychiatrist friend read it and remarked that that girl has problems. I wondered how this person came to that conclusion, but I asked no questions. Now, as I learn of your activities at Pacific Press, I understand. To have a nature that can turn on an organization as you have, rationalizing that it is a righteous cause, certainly reveals a powerful lack of good judgment besides a seething bitterness that seems to be unbalancing. I write this in "love" (hoping it is not too late) simply to try and shake you to a realization that this is not the way Christ functioned when on earth or the way He desires us to function. "Our rights!" What are we really? True freedom comes from God. And when we have a converted relationship with Him, we have no worry about our rights, for we are working for others and not ourselves. You say you are concerned about others and are doing what you are for their sakes and not your own. That is a pretty phony way of serving mankind while crunching the work of the Lord.

The church has come a long way — I know for I have come along with it. One day a few years back I got notice of what my salary would be the next fiscal year. I looked at it in amazement and went dashing to the accountant to explain that the computer had gone crazy. He explained that it hadn't and that they were endeavoring to equalize women's pay. I appreciated this, and as far as I know there has been an honest endeavor on the part of the denomination to move in the right direction at the right time in all things. Now you come along and try to force their hand like someone riding in a dirigible attempting to make it soar to the heights by puncturing holes in it. It just doesn't make sense, Merikay — no way does it.

Somehow, Merikay, the bitterness in your soul needs to be drained off in a more healthful way. The path you are following at the present time is only going to cause you to hate yourself later. We may forgive you in time for what you do, but you will have a hard time forgiving yourself if you carry all your suits through to the bitter end.

Christ, our example, was certainly discriminated against; but He went to the cross as a beautiful Saviour. The only time we have record of His using force was when the temple of God was being desecrated; and He did that for His Father and not for Himself. If you feel discriminated against as a woman, I sincerely advise you to seek the help of a good Christian counselor. As women we have a beautiful role in life — please don't blow it for the millions of us who want to be women and not competitors with men. The route you are taking is going to keep you asking all through life, "Happiness, where art thou?"

A Concerned Fellow Female

The Press must not find out that Kim is gone.

If certain people know, they'll be like sharks sensing blood.

I spend the weekend wondering how to keep it a secret. I know the fact that he's left will (in some minds) discount or discredit anything I might say.

They'll say, "If her husband doesn't even want to be around her, if she can't even keep him, how can she be right about the Press issue?"

I decide not to mention him. People at the Press rarely see him anyway; so it could be weeks or months before they notice that he's gone.

Kim phoned this evening to say he is enjoying Seattle. "It's so good to be out from under the pressure," he says.

I'm glad for him. He deserves happiness. If he can find it in Seattle, then that's where he should be. I just wish someday I could be out from under the pressure. It's very lonely when you try to change things.

The Equal Employment Opportunity Commission files a preliminary injunction suit against the Press. This suit (the third now pending against PPPA) is to try to make the Press stop illegally harassing us — like trying to fire Lorna and trying to end my writing career via the Wickwire letter.

The preliminary injunction suit is supposed to make the Press stop the constant stream of retaliation.

It seems like every few weeks I drive to EEOC offices in San Francisco to file another affidavit complaining of some new retaliation. Between Lorna and me, the EEOC has volumes of retaliation complaints against the Press. Yet nothing seems to change. The same yelling, the same ranting, the same misinformation comes flowing out of Blacker's office. Chapel periods continue to be propaganda and indoctrination periods.

It is all so exhausting. I have no idea where it will end. I just hope I can hang on until it's over.

## October 1974

Today we had a good-bye party for Arbie. She is trans-
ferring to the Personnel Department.

Richard went on and on and on about what an excep-
tional worker she is. How reliable she is, what a good
typist she is — waves and waves of praise. All sincere.

But I couldn't help thinking that all she'll ever get for
her work is words. Just words of praise. She'll never be
able to move up in the company. She'll never get the title
or pay she deserves. And should she ever in a moment of
weakness or need or (God forbid) equality ask for the pay
or title she deserves, everyone will suddenly forget what a
good worker she is. They will only know that she is a
troublemaker.

## October and November 1974

Trips between San Jose and San Francisco. Trips to Joan Bradford's office. Filing affidavits. The process goes on and on.

John Rea, the attorney handling the case for the EEOC, interviews Lorna and me for hours. He asks us questions about our jobs, about the Press harassment.

John Rea is a mild man. He has warm blue eyes and an infectious smile. He often blushes when he smiles, which makes his eyes seem even bluer.

He is balding on top, with curly brown hair that grows down the back of his head and just barely creeps over his collar. He wears wire-rimmed glasses and seems to have a good grasp of the Press' position. He is always slipping in soft-spoken humorous jibes at the Press.

He relaxes the atmosphere with his jokes. I like him. He seems to have integrity as well as a sense of humor. Nice combination.

A few weeks ago Judge Renfrew asked Joan to submit to him our rock-bottom settlement offer. He said he'd take a look at it and see if something couldn't be worked out with the Press.

She doesn't think doing such a thing is a good idea. So she wrote him a letter saying that I instructed her *not* to submit a further settlement offer because (1) the Press had failed to submit one and (2) the Press had said it would not negotiate settlement.

## November 7, 1974

Judge Renfrew phones Joan today and blows up at her.

"I don't like Merikay's attitude," he said. "I want her to appear before me next Tuesday afternoon."

I am furious! *I* am the victim here. And he's supposed to be an impartial judge — not a biased, emotional participant.

I am *so* unhappy.

I don't think I can get much more unhappy than this. I have never felt so miserable, so isolated and upset.

## November 12, 1974

I wear the sweetest, most feminine dress I have.

At the courthouse I gather with Joan, Lorna, two law clerks, John Rea (the EEOC lawyer), Blacker, Muir, McNeil, and a General Conference attorney Boardman Noland.

We sit in the large, empty courtroom, with gray walls and marble floors, and long blond pews. The pews are uncomfortable, much worse than church pews.

We've all been here several times. The room feels familiar.

The two counselors' tables, with their thickly padded leather chairs, fill the space between the spectator seats and the bench.

Judge Renfrew's chair sits empty. The clerk comes out and leads us all back to the judge's chambers.

We sit there in his office, stiff and uncomfortable, waiting for Judge Renfrew. Lorna talks with Boardman Noland, asking about mutual friends in Washington; but I can tell that Noland would rather not visit, and eventually the chatter dies away to silence.

Then Renfrew enters.

He sits down behind his desk, very pale, his face freckled and tired.

He addresses his remarks to the attorneys, asking them what line of reasoning they will pursue during trial, asking if there isn't some way we can settle this outside the courtroom.

The discussion rises and falls, and he seems wearied by it all. He spends a great deal of time looking at me, sizing me up. I wonder if he realizes I'm doing the same with him.

His eyes seem open and friendly when they meet mine. I feel hopeful.

Renfrew asks what's the next step, and Joan says that she will be doing depositions very soon. This is the process of people testifying under oath in answer to questions the lawyer has prepared. A court reporter takes down their answers; and those documents, "depositions," are then used in the case as evidence.

"Discovery is proceeding with some difficulty," she says, "But I'm sure your honor is aware of that."

There is the feeling of a chuckle being restrained on the part of the Press personnel.

"I think you all should know that I see this case as a class action," Renfrew says.

My eyes meet Lorna's in a smile. No one from the Press smiles. I feel relieved and grateful. For now at least, I still battle for the others as well as myself.

Renfrew asks more questions, says he wishes we could settle this among ourselves, and dismisses us.

Not only has Bohner disappeared from the scene but so has Attorney Don McNeil.

The Press has hired the San Francisco firm of Brobeck, Phleger, and Harrison. Joan says they are a big, powerful firm and that they're probably charging the Press an arm and a leg.

And to think, all that money is going just so the Press might continue denying equal treatment to their female workers. And most of the women workers here are very loyal — giving ten, twenty, even thirty or more years of their lives to the publishing work.

Joan says the Press' arguments are changing from "no, we don't discriminate," to "hey, we're religious; and as such we don't have to answer to the government for our activities. The First Amendment protects us."

The new argument is strangely familiar. It's the same reasoning I heard from Neal Wilson the day he visited me at my apartment. Joan says the Press is determined to move from an employment-sex-discrimination case to a constitutional-religious liberty case.

The new lawyers for the Press are Malcom Dungan and James Quirk. I chuckle over the names of the people who have struggled for the Press' viewpoint: Bohner, Blacker, Dungan, Quirk. Whenever I think about the cumulative effect of their names, I laugh.

Dungan looks like a movie heavy — with a long, well-jowled, unsmiling face, immense eye bags, and a heavy, pear-shaped body. His voice is deep and melodramatic.

Quirk has nothing to distinguish him from anyone else in a crowd, one of those anonymous people who goes through life facelessly.

## November 21, 1974

Lorna and I have asked the court to let us intervene in the EEOC case. Intervening means that we have an interest in the EEOC case and wish to join our complaints or requests to theirs.

Today we drive to court to see if Judge Renfrew will allow us to intervene. The EEOC wants to secure a guarantee that the Press will stop harassing us. Renfrew listens to arguments, says he'll look at the papers both sides have filed, and sees no reason to rule against our request.

After the hearing, Joan and Lorna and I eat at a little cafeteria and talk about where we go from here.

"Merikay, I want you to file suit against Bruce Wickwire because of his letter," Joan says suddenly.

"Oh, Joan, I don't know."

She tells me how important it is from a legal standpoint; but I don't want to file another suit, and especially not against an individual.

"You know, I don't believe Bruce Wickwire decided on his own to write that letter," I say. "I hate to admit this, but I wouldn't be surprised if Neal Wilson made him do it. Neal is his superior, and Wickwire wouldn't have been able to do anything like that without Wilson's approval."

I look at my soup and think about how many more years I'll be adding to the horror if I file a new suit. And how can I justify attacking a little nobody who was only obeying orders. Nonthinking obeyers have always repulsed me. Those people who go through life as eager little machines for others' commands frighten and disgust me. But to file a lawsuit against him ... slowly I shake my head, no.

Anger and frustration fill Joan's face. "Merikay, if you tie my hands I'll just have to stop working so hard on your case," she says, her voice breaking with emotion.

I don't know how to respond. She works long hours, much longer than she should, considering her health. I don't have any money to pay her. She is definitely a selfless advocate. I love her.

But I simply cannot sue Bruce Wickwire.

The Press has a new argument. The latest briefs which Dungan and Quirk filed with the court say that the Press is the church, and all the workers are in reality ministers of the church.

The case has become a disagreement between the church and one of its ministers — me.

"I think I like that," I say. "I think I like being a minister. Now does that mean I get to preach from the pulpit? I get to stand up in Press chapel and admonish the people to obey the law and practice justice and fairness, right?"

Lorna and I laugh over the argument. Who will buy it?

Max, theologian that he is, is appalled at the argument.

In part, Dungan's brief reads:

Just as the initial freedom of selecting a minister is a matter of church administration and government, so are the functions which accompany such a selection . . . . Matters of church government and administration are beyond the purview of civil authorities.

Dungan argues that church policy forbids members to use the court system to sue a church institution for any reason, let alone to determine intra-church, intra-family disputes. By continuing my suit, I have put myself "at variance with the church" and have become "a prime candidate for early disfellowshipping."

I read those words with fear. What is this about "variance" and "disfellowshipping?"

The brief holds within it a dagger.

Lorna photocopies complete copies of Dungan's brief and ships them to people throughout the denomination. Requests for the brief are coming in from the Seminary. Many theologians want to see this "Press is church, Merikay is minister" reasoning the Press defense is arguing.

Attorneys from across the country phone, asking for copies of the brief. Lorna feels that the more broadly the information is disseminated, the stronger the grass-roots pressure against the Press' position.

Max comes into my office to tell me that Warren Johns, my friend from Sacramento who has the specialty publishing house, has received a "call" to join the General Conference legal staff.

My heart sinks.

I wonder if he'll go. I hope not. I hope he will maintain his freedom, his independence, his integrity. He is one of those little bright spots in my dismal existence, and I dread the thought of his joining the other side.

# December 4, 1974

Excerpts from:
Opening Brief for Defendants
In Support of Their Motion
For Summary Judgment

Attorneys:  Malcolm T. Dungan
James H. Quirk
(Brobeck, Phleger & Harrison: San Francisco)

Boardman Noland (Takoma Park, Maryland)

Donald McNeil
Ruffo, Ferrari & McNeil (San Jose, CA)

3: 23-30

Our submission accordingly is that the case should be dismissed *now*. Once it is made to appear to the Court, as we shall shortly do, that the whole subject of this litigation is ecclesiastical, the only proper disposition is to get this controversy out of the courthouse at once, and back into the Church where it belongs, and where it can be dealt with by the ecclesiastical authorities in accordance with received doctrine and the teachings of the Scriptures.

5:12-17

Seventh-day Adventist doctrine does not permit discrimination against any person on the basis of race, national origin, or sex. However, only members of the Church who are in good standing are eligible for employment by the Seventh-day Adventist Church, its departments and institutions, which are integral and vital organs of the Church.

29:3-27

The Church must have the right to screen and hire or to discharge ministers, editors, and other workers without challenge from the State. There is no possible way for the State or for a court to properly assess the circumstances, the needs, the implications, and the solutions that become a part of the operation of a church. The State must not find itself in a position of imposing control and thus endangering the freedom of the Church to achieve its divine mandate.

The relationship between an organized church and its ministers is its lifeblood. Just as the initial freedom of selecting a minister is a matter of church administration and government, so are the functions which accompany such a selection.

It is unavoidably true that these functions, among others, include the determination of a minister's salary, his place of assignment, and the duty he is to perform in the furtherance of the religious mission of the Church. Matters of church government and administration are beyond the purview of civil authorities. Determinations by proper church tribunals respecting ecclesiastical matters — even if they affect civil rights — are accepted as binding in litigation before the secular courts because the parties involved have made them so by contract and by willingness to work within a church structure.

What the Church cannot tolerate is for members to bring church disputes into civil courts.

61:17-21

In the Seventh-day Adventist Church, it is a matter of utmost gravity for a member to take a dispute with another member, or with the Church, before the civil authorities. All Adventists know this, and when such a thing occurs, as it rarely does, it is the occasion for sorrow, shame, and wonder.

73:3-20

The General Conference embodies the Church, and the institutions, including the publishing houses, are integral parts of the Church, established to carry on God's work. The ministry of editorial work is no different from the ministry of the pulpit (Wilson DE 37) and equally important to the fulfillment of the Church's mission.

As Elder Bietz put it, the Pacific Press was built "for the advancement of the Gospel of Jesus Christ." (DE 11.)

It follows that the Church, including the General Conference, the departments, and the institutions, are entitled to the protections of the First Amendment.

At bottom, this is simply a case of schism. Mrs. Silver and Mrs. Tobler have decided that they know better than do the Elders of the Church how the Church should behave itself in relation to anti-discrimination laws. The Church *per contra* has exercised its authority to declare that Mrs. Silver is at variance and has a tendency to ignore Christian counsel. Such disputes are not for judicial arbitrament.

89:9-11

Laws designed to enforce fairness to workers in a commercial setting are not designed to operate in an ecclesiastical one.

89:27-28

The wage policy of a church cannot be determined by government.

90:2-5

Those who work for the Seventh-day Adventist Church respond to a religious vocation in exactly the same sense as does a cloistered nun. Man's law is by its very nature not applicable. *Cessante legis, cessat ipsa lex.*

104:4-6

The Church does not consider the Government its antagonist; but it will not compromise its position in order to comply with regulations that weaken its mission.

104:15-17

The Church claims exemption from all civil laws in all of its religious institutions; although it seeks accommodation, it draws a line of its own when dealing with Caesar.

**December 9, 1974**

Merikay Silver
55 S. Sixth Street
#216
San Jose, CA

Dear Merikay:

In confirmation of our telephone conversation of yesterday, we are agreed that I will not file the complaint against Bruce M. Wickwire for libel (and other tortious acts). We have reached this decision in view of the amount of time and energy that would be taken from the main Silver action and EEOC action if the case against Wickwire were to be pursued. The decision has also been reached in light of the costs and fees that would be involved in another action.

You understand that the statute of limitations runs out on the Wickwire action on December 10, 1974, and that you will therefore have no further opportunity to bring suit against Mr. Wickwire for the alleged torts.

Best regards,

JOAN KURT BRADFORD

JKB/dj

## December 9-11, 1974

I am reading the affidavits of everyone deposed by Joan and John Rea: Neal Wilson's, Wes Siegenthaler's, Richard Utt's, Jack Blacker's.

They are *very* depressing. I am amazed at these men's facility for twisting and distorting incidents until they sound completely different from what they were. I am crushed when I read that they want me fired and the church "cleansed of the shame" I'm causing.

I feel *so* sad when I read their personal feelings toward me. Everyone hates me, but no one seems to hate (or even mind) the gross injustice that caused the suit. I feel sick at heart, totally crumbled on the inside. To be *so* hated when I'm really a nice person. And I'm only doing what I've been taught — to stand for the right though the heavens fall . . . to be true to principle.

Richard has been renewing his visits. But now he acts almost like the old days, sitting down and talking about manuscripts and laughing and being friendly. It's impossible to respond. How can he be so friendly after all he's said and done against me?

I feel sick and disoriented. I don't understand anything about human relationships. I'll bet a psychiatrist would have a field day with all of us involved in this thing.

## December 24, 1974

I am sending out resumes. I want to quit. I hate working here. I'm so tired of hostile surroundings. Few talk to me, unless preaching. Richard is friendly one day and attacks me the next. He yells at me two days a week, then asks forgiveness, then yells at me again. I just want out. I am tired . . . of the pressure, of the hatred.

Just before leaving for Christmas vacation, Richard stops by to wish me a happy holiday.

"Will Kim be with you for the holidays?" He asks.

I hope the shock doesn't register on my face. No one's asked about Kim; and I thought things were going smoothly, with no one noticing his absence. But now the word is out.

I nod yes.

The word is out. That means the pressure will increase. Just what I need, a little more pressure.

## February 17, 1975

I'M SICK. MY WHOLE BODY IS EXHAUSTED AND WEAK. I'M STAY-ing home, hoping to sleep. That's all I want to do these days. Just sleep and sleep and sleep. Anything to escape the pressure. But even in my dreams I face Bohner or Blacker or Utt, and they're yelling at me and railing at me and threatening me. Even in my sleep I cannot free myself from their hatred.

I phone the switchboard to say I'm sick, and the woman who answers the phone says that Max was called into Blacker's office. Last week Blacker began calling people into his office to admonish them to stay away from me and never, never to discuss the case on Press time.

In midmorning Lorna calls to say that Blacker initiated action during last night's Board Meeting at Mountain View Church to have her disfellowshipped. If Lorna is disfellowshipped (in effect, kicked out of her church by her congregation), then she can no longer work at Pacific Press, because only church members in good standing are eligible for employment here.

And if she is fired because of church standards, then she no longer can be protected by the court system. The Press could claim she was being "disciplined" or terminated because she was not an Adventist. As such, any remedy for retaliation would be out of Judge Renfrew's hands.

They can't fire her now. They'll try disfellowshipping her first. I'm frightened.

At lunchtime Max calls. "I'm calling from a pay phone at the post office," he says. "I thought I'd tell you what's been going on. I was called into Blacker's office this morning and really worked over. He told me I was giving aid and comfort to 'the girls.' He told me there was a strong feeling around the Press that I'm disloyal. He stressed loyalty over and over." Max is quiet for a long moment. I can hear him sighing.

"Look, I can't afford to lose this job. Jeanette hasn't yet landed a full-time teaching position, and we've got the mortgage and car payments. . . . I'm just asking that you don't come to my office any more and I won't come to yours. And I don't think we should give each other lifts home, or anything like that any more."

I listen to frantic words and I understand. "Sure, sure," I say mechanically.

"This is more to save me than you," he says. "Blacker's already crossed you off."

We hang up. I cry.

Max is my oldest friend at the Press. He and I have known each other since Andrews University days, ten years ago. And Blacker makes him so afraid that he doesn't dare even talk to me any more.

I am no longer an Adventist. The realization hits me in a rush of sobs. The church — that loving world I have given myself unreservedly to, that great feeling of belonging to "God's Family" — is no longer mine. I have been too isolated to ever be one of the group again. I just can't carry on.

The love or affection or idealism or whatever the connecting link was between me and the organization has been destroyed. I didn't destroy it. And I wish it wasn't gone. But it is.

I have been yelled at, threatened, criticized, condemned. My writing has been cut off. My actions, words, and motives have been maligned. Slanderous, untrue rumors have been spread about me.

My friends have been frightened away.

I am ostracized.

I am no longer a member of the group. I am "outside." I feel outside. I am treated that way every day.

I am no longer an Adventist. Every time I think about that, a new wave of sobs wracks me. The realization tears me apart.

But my life in the organization has been hell these last few years. I'm no masochist and I want out. I want to

get as far away from this torture as I can. I need a long,
deep rest from organized religion. I need emotional calm
and peace, and I'm not getting that in the church.

## February 18, 1975

Trial is due in March.

This is the EEOC trial for preliminary injunction. In English that means: "Judge, will you please tell the Press they can't get rid of these women until the Silver trial. Please ensure that the status quo remains until the Silver trial. Please make the Press stop retaliating, stop harassing, until the Silver case comes to trial."

Because the EEOC trial is coming soon, I'm at Joan's office almost every night working on my affidavit. Lorna is there too, working on hers.

So much has happened, so many individual incidents, such a complicated web of involvement, that sometimes it's hard to remember everything. And so we have to go over and over and over the dates and events until we have it all clear in our minds; and then we try to make it clear in our affidavits.

We've been working until 1:00 or 2:00 a.m. Joan Bradford, John Rea, Lorna, and I — all struggling with the records, our recollections, the dates and facts — all working until we can barely keep our eyes open.

Tonight I write and rewrite my affidavit. Lorna and I sit at a table together writing.

"Your affidavit flows much faster than mine," she says.

"That's because you use commas and I use periods."

After a while she goes in another room to work with Joan.

I try making my affidavit as clear and understandable as I can. John Rea helps by asking questions. He asks; I write. He reads it and asks more questions. I edit what I wrote and add to it.

He drinks cup after cup of coffee. I write.

I write about my Neal Wilson meeting. It was almost a year ago when he came to my apartment and my hopes soared. What a fool I was to think he'd help. He is the person behind the new Press argument. He spent a whole day listening to me, but his only interest is in devising an argument the judge will buy.

Nearly exhausted, I glance up from my work and notice John Rea standing on his head against the far wall.

"That's exactly how I feel," I say, laughing. "All mixed up, upside down, standing on my head."

"This is a good thing to do if you have to drive home tonight," he says.

He has to drive to Berkeley. I have to drive to San Jose.

By 2:00 a.m. I am so tired, so emotionally drained, that I actually start crying over typing errors. Everyone is punch-drunk, misplacing things, mismarking exhibits, giggling over things that aren't funny, and weeping over things that aren't sad. I hope I never have to go through this again.

As I drive home it is nearly 4:00 a.m. The freeway is empty and endless, stretching out before me like a great black ribbon, mysterious and lonely . . . like my life.

## February 20, 1975

I have barely seated myself behind my desk when Lorna enters, her face alive with emotion.

"John Rea just called," she says. "Dungan phoned him this morning and said the GC has told the Press to fire us."

"What?" I start to grin. Then I feel scared, so stop.

She nods; then we both start grinning.

"How many times does this make for you?" I ask. "Three? Four? We could write a country-western song about the woman who got fired again and again."

I laugh a little, although I'm worried. While we're talking, my phone rings. Picking it up, I hear the familiar cotton sound of long distance.

"Merikay?" A male voice says.

"Yes."

"You probably don't remember me. My name's Bob Ruskjer. You and I were freshmen together at Andrews," he says. "My brother works at the GC and he just called to say he heard you are going to be fired. Neal Wilson's behind it. He's trying to get you fired and disfellowshipped. And I wanted to call and alert you so you could prepare."

"Just a minute, Bob." I cover the receiver with my hand and repeat for Lorna what I've just heard. Then I go back to Bob Ruskjer.

"I'm just calling to encourage you, to tell you to hang in there, that there are a lot of us rooting for you. A lot of people, not only women, support your actions," he says.

"And I have collected about eighteen inches worth of evidence which your lawyer will probably want. These are all lawsuits that the church has been involved in. Most of them were filed by the church or by church officials. I have a letter here from Jack Blacker when he was Pacific Union president. In it he encourages a Dr. Brenneise, a church member in good and regular standing, to sue the Union.

"I have dozens of documents, and you can have them all for your case."

My heart beats so hard my chest aches. Someone to the rescue! Like the cavalry charging over the hill, Bob Ruskjer is galloping into the EEOC v Pacific Press case.

He gives me his work and home telephone numbers. I

give him Joan's number. He says he'll fly up today or tomorrow to deliver the documents.

I give him John Rea's number.

His voice is enthusiastic. "The men will never get away with the argument that we don't sue each other in the church," he says. "Their faces will be beet red, and they'll not be able to carry off that farce." He laughs and I laugh and we hang up.

Lorna is as excited as I am. "Do you remember him?" she wants to know.

I don't. But I don't care. If he has the information he says he has, we're going to do just fine in court. I phone Joan. Lorna goes back to her office to call John.

At noon Joan has lunch with us. Lorna and Joan and I go to a nearby restaurant and discuss the threatened firing.

"Take the rest of the week off," she says. "Get away from the Press as quickly as you can so they can't give you your termination notice. They'll try to fire you right before the weekend. That would complicate my attempt to get a restraining order from the court."

I go back to the Press and tell the secretary that I'm taking the rest of the week as vacation.

I am in the process of moving from the apartment Kim and I shared to an older, even less expensive place a couple of blocks away; so I spend the rest of the afternoon packing. I pack books and clothes and dishes and records.

Joan calls to say that I must not stay at my apartment because the Press is going to try to serve my termination notice to me at home. I can't believe this is happening. I pack my car with boxes and bedding and drive to my new apartment. I'll stay here, unpacking and painting and trying to get the place in order.

# February 20, 1975

Mrs. Merikay Silver
Editorial Office

Dear Mrs. Silver:

On Friday, February 14, 1975, the General Conference Committee recorded an action in which they recommended to the Pacific Press Publishing Association that you be discontinued from church employment as is provided for [in] the General Conference Working Policy, page 35, and in the *Church Manual*, page 48.

The recommendation was brought to the attention of the Executive Committee of the Pacific Press on February 19, 1975. An action was recorded that we support the recommendation of the General Conference and implement it. Thus by Executive Committee action we are terminating your services as of the close of this present week — Friday, February 21, 1975.

We enclose a final check covering your wages for the week ending February 21, 1975, plus vacation time earned, plus wages for seven weeks in recognition of approximately four years of service to the church.

You may submit any medical expense incurred up to and including February 21, 1975.

Please leave any keys with Elder Utt when you leave on Friday.

Thank you.

Very sincerely yours,

W.J. Blacker
General Manager

## Friday, February 21, 1975

The sun is shining as I pull up to the curb in front of Joan Bradford's office. I'm still breathless from all that's happened in the last twenty-four hours.

This afternoon Joan and John Rea will ask Judge Renfrew for a temporary restraining order (TRO) against the Press' firing of us.

Lorna and Joan are waiting for me. The three of us drive to the EEOC office in San Francisco, where John Rea and his boss are finishing the paper work for today's court appearance.

Lorna and I sit at a long table while John Rea feeds us the paper work, hot off the Xerox machine. "Read it and make sure it's correct," he says. "And please check spelling and things like that."

"Here you told me to take vacation time, and now you want me to edit," I grin.

We proof the papers.

I'm thinking, "I may never go back to the Press again. Yesterday may have been my last day there." And a kind of peace fills me. I half hope I will never have to go back.

We all head for court.

San Francisco is bright and windy. This city is always windy. I like the wind because it makes my hair fly around like it's wild. No one can maintain much dignity in the wind, struggling to keep topcoats closed, skirts down, hats or toupees on, papers together. The wind has a way of equalizing everyone.

The courthouse rises tall and glassy in the winter sunlight.

As we wait for our elevator, Joan explains that temporary restraining orders are almost never granted. "We'll do our best," John says to Lorna and me.

"We all will," Joan adds; "but I just want you to know, in case Renfrew refuses."

I search the attorneys' faces and they don't look hopeful.

Dungan and Quirk, their briefcases bulging, are already in the courtroom when we enter.

The hearing starts late, only thirty minutes before sundown.

Since Adventists honor the Sabbath hours from Friday sunset until Saturday sunset, Lorna and I cannot stay in the courtroom after the Sabbath begins; and knowing that there are a lot of arguments, I realize we won't hear them all. We'll have to leave before everything is said.

We tell Joan that we'll go into one of the side rooms off the main hall, pray, and wait until the proceeding is over; and she can then tell us what happened.

Dungan speaks first. His deep voice clothes his words with immense authority, and he overdresses to his utmost dramatic advantage. Approaching the bench with the look of Final Authority, he begins, "Your Honor, we are here today to discuss the religious discipline a church has seen fit to administer to its erring ministers."

My eyes roll heavenward. His pompous religiosity nauseates me. What does he know about the spiritual attributes of our church? Or of any of us involved in this case?

"The termination of Lorna Tobler and Merikay Silver is religious discipline against two very schismatic ministers of the church," his foghorn voice booms. "If the court grants the requested TRO, the court will find itself interfering with the religious liberty of the Seventh-day Adventist church, a position I am sure the court does not wish to place itself in."

Renfrew sits high overlooking the courtroom, robed in black, pale face looking bored.

Eventually Lorna and I leave. We wait in a side room, reading our Bibles and praying. I don't know if I'm in shock from all the excitement and lack of sleep, or what, but I don't feel afraid or panicky.

I feel peaceful, as though I'm being protected.

"Please, God, move the hearts of everyone in the courtroom," I pray. "Please cause the very best possible thing to happen."

I'm thinking how God sees over the long run what is best, while I can only see what I want right now. "God, please control things according to Your perspective, not mine. Please work on all our hearts; draw us close to You as the Sabbath begins."

It seems like forever before Joan and John join us. Joan beams. John looks amused. Sadly he says, "Well, I hate to break it to you this way, especially on your Sabbath, but . . ." he pauses for effect, "you have to go back to work Tuesday. Judge's orders."

I laugh. Lorna is her usual composed self. She wants to know about the arguments, the judge's comments, the logic, the strategy. All I care about is that I'm not fired. I'm still employed, which means I can still represent the other women at the Press.

Dungan went on and on about the court interfering in the business of the church; and finally Renfrew interrupted and said, "Pacific Press has interfered with the court's decision-making ability by taking upon itself the decision to change the status quo and fire these women."

Lorna nodded. "They tweaked Renfrew's nose and he took a dim view of it."

John said, "When Renfrew granted our TRO, Dungan rose and said, 'We'll ask for a stay, your honor.' And Renfrew replied, 'You won't get it from me.'"

We're all jubilant. The Press can't fire us. I feel like laughing and crying and singing and dancing. The Press can't fire me! I'm thrilled!

I have to go back to work at the Press. I'm depressed!

Extremes. I live in a world of extremes. Jubilation and despair. Always on the edge, on the painful, excruciating edge.

As I drive home I think what a great day the third Friday in February is. Last year I spent the day with Neal Wilson and enjoyed it. This year I spent the day in court making his order to fire me of no effect.

## Sabbath, February 22, 1975

At church this morning I discover that Elder Mills is no longer pastor. A parent whose children attend the church day-care center filed child-molesting charges against him, and the Conference asked him to step aside. I am shocked. Mills is a gentle, humor-filled, good man, and I can't believe he would hurt anyone. My paranoia springs to the surface, and I wonder how this all relates to the fact that I'm a member of his church. How have the leaders worked this one?

I assume they'll remove Elder Mills, who would never allow me to be disfellowshipped; and then they'll put in one of their men, and then they'll start in on my church membership. It seems clear. I don't know all the "hows," but I can imagine the "whys."

The Neal Wilson letter asking that we be fired also mentioned that our churches would be asked to administer spiritual discipline (disfellowshipping). All through church service my stomach churns; but as I drive home through the beautifully clear sunshine and crisp, clean wind, my upset vanishes. I suddenly feel good because of the weather and because Neal didn't succeed in firing me.

I decide to call him. As soon as I reach home, I dial his number in Washington, D.C.

"Hello," he answers.

"Oh it's good to hear your voice again," I say.

Silence, and then he says in a cold voice, "It is, huh?" and I can tell he doesn't know who I am.

As warm and friendly as I can sound I say, "It sure is."

Silence. Then, "Who is this?"

"An old friend of yours."

"You are, huh?" He's still cold, trying to recognize my voice.

"Do you remember what happened a year ago yesterday?"

"This sounds like Merikay."

I laugh because he sounds so relieved now that he recognizes me.

"You know," he says. "I've been thinking about you."

"Yes, I know you have. I've been the recipient of some of your thoughts."

"Roland Hegstad and I were just talking about you

the other day," he says. "We were saying that one of us ought to contact you in Christian brotherly love . . . you know, as friends, and just have a good conversation. But you know, everyone's afraid that if they talk to you, you'll slap them with a lawsuit."

I laugh. "Do you know how foolish that fear is? I can't believe you really think that."

He laughs too. We both know it's a smoke screen and no one really believes I'll sue him for talking to me.

"Well see, *I* called *you*; so you don't have to worry."

"That's right. You took the initiative," he laughs with a sound that says I'm always taking the initiative.

"You know, my friend, I saw your letter urging the Press to fire me and my church to disfellowship me," I say.

"Merikay, if you only knew the pressure I'm under. Everywhere people are saying that I talk double, that I have two standards — one for Merikay and one for everyone else.

"I'm in a position where I'm forced to do things, forced to take positions because of my office, that might not be what I'd choose if it weren't for my position."

"I'm disappointed," I say as firmly as I can, then wait; but he doesn't answer. "But I think we both know where we stand. I understand your motives."

"Sometimes, Merikay, you commit your life to a position that must be maintained. Just as in your case. You've committed yourself to a conscientious belief, because I know you are acting from your conscience. Well, so, you have things to do. You say things, make decisions in accordance with what you've committed yourself to." He talks rapidly as though he's afraid he won't get to say it all, as if he's trying to convince himself.

"These are the nitty-gritty, nuts-and-bolts part of life; and this is what we'd be doing in the courtroom if we ended up there. But on a higher level, you and I would realize that our relationship is stable and that we stand together, as a brother and sister in Christ, in the really big things."

"I see, I see," I say. "You have things that you must do because of your political position."

"Yes."

"I realize that. And I know you will do them."

"That's right."

"I just hope that you realize that there are legal things that I must do to protect myself, and I'll surely do them as well."

"Yes I understand that," he says.

We talk for a few minutes about the weather, about the fact that I've moved. He asks if I'll have the same phone number, and I assure him that I'm keeping the same number.

"All right," he says with a lilt of a laugh. "Well, I have your number, Merikay."

His tone is ominous.

"Do you enjoy the congregation at Milpitas?" he asks.

An icy chill creeps up my neck. Milpitas is a tiny little church with fewer than a hundred members, the kind of church he would never have ever heard of. He *knows* I'm a member there.

"It's a great congregation," I say. "Very spiritual, very friendly."

"I understand you and your husband joined by profession of faith. What's the pastor's name there?" he pumps.

"Boy, you sure have good intelligence-gathering ability."

"I know everything, Merikay," he says.

"You sure do. You and the FBI and the CIA."

"I have nothing to do with them," he says quickly.

"Well, I just thought I'd call and say 'hi,' " I say. "It's such a beautiful day. And I just know things are going to improve."

"You do?"

"Yes. The trial is coming up March 13 and 14, and I think that will settle a lot of things. Maybe after that we can start working toward alleviating the problems of sex discrimination at Pacific Press."

"The 13th and 14th?" I can hear him checking his calendar.

"Aren't you coming for the trial?"

"They haven't asked me."

"I thought you were their star witness," I say. "It's going to be pretty confusing to have you the star witness for one side and me the star witness for the other, and we're supposed to be friends."

He begins explaining that his position in the church requires him to do unpleasant things, but that I shouldn't take it personally.

Then I mention disfellowshipping.

"Do you really think that will happen?" he asks.

"How should I know? After your letter, nothing much would surprise me."

Again he goes into self-defense. He is so smooth, so polished. Even with three thousand miles between us, he charms me.

As I get ready to hang up, he says, "Merikay, I really want you to know how much your phone call has meant. I really appreciate it."

The rest of the day I spend walking in the park. Neal is so "mafioso." Everytime I review our conversation I feel depressed. He's saying, "When I kill you, please don't take it personally. It's only business. I have to do this because of my position."

Whenever I think of him I shudder.

## Tuesday, February 25, 1975

Back to the lion's den.

Richard doesn't come out of his office all day. I only leave mine when I have to use the bathroom.

In the middle of the morning, an envelope is slipped under my door. Inside is this note:

Dear Merikay:

We love you and most wonderful of all, Jesus loves you. I am sure that He is deeply grieved over the trap Satan has placed in your path.

Don't be dazzled by the prospects that he offers, but remember the life of sacrifice that Jesus lived and how He bids us walk in His steps.

The happiness you are seeking will not last long. Only treasure laid up in Heaven will endure. So don't grab the steering wheel, but let God stay in the driver's seat.

Whatever your past experiences have been, or how discouraging your present circumstances are, come back to Jesus who will "meet you a great way off" and throw His arms of love around you. He will exchange your "poverty" for the riches of His grace. Don't go to puny worldly people for help with your problems, when, as a child of God, you can have Heaven's resources at your command.

We are praying every day that the Holy Spirit will touch your heart and that you will catch the loveliness of Jesus. Then instead of frustrations, dissatisfactions and discontent, you will have the wonderful peace of Jesus in your heart.

How I would love to have peace. Right now I'm contemplating what it's going to be like to go to committee meetings and sit with the very men who last week voted to fire me.

My stomach is in constant knots. My eyes hurt all the time. I know Jesus loves me. What I need is a few people to assure me I'm not as hated as I feel.

In the middle of the afternoon, one little gray-haired lady looks in my door and says, "Welcome back." That was the crumb I needed. My spirits rise a little. Before the day ends, I have visits from several people, a call from Bob Ruskjer in southern California, and a visit from Lorna.

I guess Bob Ruskjer is preparing an abundance of material for Joan and John. He also says that Neal Wilson has made a lot of errors in his dealings with Loma Linda University and he's in hot water. According to Bob, Neal is desperate for some political success since General Conference elections are coming up and he wants to gain the presidency. So he's putting everything he's got into winning this Press battle.

That is a terribly reassuring bit of information, especially after my discussion with Neal on Sabbath.

Artist and sculptor Glenn Heath stops by just at quitting time. He teaches art and biology at Mountain View Academy, the Adventist high school three blocks from the Press. He's been a friend of Kim's and mine ever since we moved to Mountain View. Now he stops by to say that he's going to fight Lorna's disfellowshipping.

"She's done nothing to merit disfellowshipping," he says. "And I'll do anything and everything I can to make sure she's not disfellowshipped. But I bet I'll lose my job over it."

Walking out to my car, I feel that Pacific Press is in a frenzy. Maybe the entire Adventist community in Mountain View is too.

## February 26, 1975

Margie, the mail girl, went to lunch with me today.

"You look like the Press is really getting to you," she says as we start to eat. "Lorna never looks fazed by anything, but you do."

"I feel fazed," I say, and start a half-hearted laugh. "*Very* fazed. Almost fazed out."

"You can't look that way," she says, her dark eyes sincere. "You've got to perk up and look more confident."

"Margie, just thinking about perking up tires me."

"You can't look like you're suffering. That's just what they want. The more beat down you look, the more pressure they're going to put on you."

She's probably right. But it's very hard to look perky and confident when you're a shambles inside.

This afternoon I have the privilege of attending Book Publishing Committee. A large number of the men on this committee are also on the Executive Committee, which voted last week to fire me. I'm sure they're going to be thrilled to have me sitting with them deciding the fate of various manuscripts.

## February 27, 1975

The Press is buzzing.

Last night, after the Mountain View Church prayer meeting, there was a secret unannounced meeting in the board room. Lorna is worried that they're in the process of disfellowshipping her. If they disfellowship her, they'll come after me next.

In the late afternoon I stop by Louis Schutter's office. He edits the children's papers for the denomination. He is responsible for printing meaningful stories of Christian principle to children aged five through twelve years.

He's a blond-haired man in his late forties, friendly and good hearted. I like him because he seems moved by principle rather than political considerations.

Today he says that I should not have sued. "I agree with your goals, but I disagree with your method," he says. His words are sincere and kind. I wish everyone was as honest as he. "You may win the battle, the suit, and lose the war. You are so talented, Merikay. I'd hate to see you lose your career within the denomination."

"I'd hate it too," I say. "Because this is where my heart is."

I don't have the nerve to tell him that my heart has already been broken beyond repair.

He's probably right about my career. But I can't help thinking how selfish it would be for me to say that because my career might be hurt, I won't do what's right; I won't try to help others.

It seems to me that sacrificing one career to open the way for many, many others to make careers for themselves is a very small sacrifice.

And then, too, there's no sure way to tell if my career is ruined. Only time will reveal that.

☙

## March 1975

This is the month.

We'll find out this month if the Press can continue their harassing, intimidating, hateful practices. We'll find out if we can be fired.

Bob Ruskjer calls Lorna on the weekend to say that Neal Wilson and the other GC men are angry that we were granted our temporary restraining order.

I can see why they would be. If Neal believes the government has no right telling the Press what to do, he's going to be even more furious when the court says the GC can't make the Press fire us.

The rumor is that the Press will settle two days before trial. I nearly cry for joy, thinking that maybe the whole nightmare is near an end.

But there are so many rumors, and most of them have turned out to be nothing more than hot air.

Joan called to say that Bob Ruskjer had records of more than one hundred lawsuits that the church and Neal Wilson have taken part in.

## March 4, 1975

The Press is buzzing with whispered reports about last night's board of elders meeting at Mountain View Church. The church community and the Press have been heading for a showdown. We've all felt it. Lorna's been certain that the final stroke would be the move to disfellowship her; and as we near trial, she has been sure the move would be soon. The climax came last night, according to the bits and pieces of whispered information.

"Louis Schutter pulled a Gamaliel," Max said.

Louis said it was a joint effort between himself and the pastor of the Mountain View church.

PPPA general manager Jack Blacker is also conveniently on the board of elders at Mountain View church. At last night's meeting he made a motion to have Lorna Tobler disfellowshipped.

"This meeting was the turning point in the growing tension [between the Press and] the church," Louis Schutter said. "There was quite a discussion during which the pastor and I supported each other. We were like pitcher and catcher in a ball game. I said, 'It's unfair to split a church for a pastor, and this issue will surely split our church congregation.' "

According to Louis, there was a break in the meeting, a kind of intermission, for tempers and minds to cool. During the break one of the men took Blacker aside and told him that my attorney had a photocopy of the letter he wrote while president of the Pacific Union, a letter in which he encouraged Dr. Brenneise to sue the Union.

"If you institute disfellowship action against Lorna, that letter will surely surface; and you may face disfellowship procedures yourself," Blacker was told.

When the men resumed the meeting, the pastor did not ask for a vote on Blacker's motion; he simply moved to the next point on the agenda "without any objections from the rest of us," Louis said.

❧

## March 10, 1975

Today starts the big week. I wonder how it will all turn out. The tension is intense but akin to excitement.

My eyes have been really bothering me lately. The problem with the kind of work I do is if my eyes go out, I can't work. It's not that I'm going blind or anything as serious as that; it's just that my body seems to react to stress by getting migraines, which make my vision disappear. My doctor says my eyes will stop hurting, stop getting infected, stop losing their sight when I stop being under so much pressure. I hope my eyes will start improving after this week.

Max looks totally cowed. He told Joan he would not testify unless he was subpoenaed. He fears being fired; and he thinks if it appears he was forced to testify, rather than testifying voluntarily, that he will appear more loyal to the Press. He's very discouraged about the church and the corruption ingrained in the structure. I've never seen him so shaken. He's always been the reformer, the activist, the strong believer in the church and the church's message. Now he's just a discouraged, frightened friend.

## March 11, 1975

Tonight we rehearse. We practice how to respond to the questions Dungan may ask. Rehearsal helps us keep facts straight and maintain control even while under the pressure of trial.

I arrive at Joan's office at 9:00 p.m. Bob Ruskjer and Lorna are already there. John Rea arrives shortly after I do. The information Bob Ruskjer has brought Joan and John is invaluable. Even after I meet Bob face-to-face I can't remember going to Andrews University with him. But I thank him for all the help he's giving my case.

"I'm just really tired of the brethren pretending they're so holy and pure, when this whole thing is political," he says. "They just don't want someone else telling them to obey the law. They don't like being bossed around. They want to do the bossing, all of it, without interference from anyone else. And then they act so sanctimonious."

We rehearse until midnight. I've never been a late-night person. Come ten o'clock and I start fading. Now as we rehearse I get worse and worse.

Lorna is perfect — very dignified, very logical with her answers.

Joan says, "Now, Ms. Tobler, did you ever ask the minister of your local church if participation in the Silver lawsuit or the EEOC lawsuit would affect your membership in the local church?"

Lorna answers, "Yes."

Joan has stressed the importance of saying no more than the answer to any one question. Don't explain or enlarge upon the answer until asked to do so.

Lorna waits for the next question.

"And what did your minister say to you?"

"He told me that my participation in these legal matters had nothing to do with my church membership."

"Was that all he said?"

"He said litigation is not a test of fellowship; and that if it were, it would be necessary to disfellowship the Central California Conference."

Joan and John smile. They've practiced those questions and that last answer several times. They want to get the statement about the Central California Conference into the court record. Then later they'll introduce Bob

Ruskjer's evidence of all the Central California Conference lawsuits.

Although exhausted, Lorna performs beautifully. She
answers their questions efficiently and doesn't forget any
of the details she must include in each answer.

I, on the other hand, am little better than a buffoon.
They ask me a question and I either go on and on explaining, until Joan says, "Stop. Let's try again, and here's how
to answer."

Or I give a nice laconic yes or no when I should say
more.

There are certain facts Joan and John must get into the
court record. And we have to couch those facts in our
answers so that they can build our case on those answers.

I'm so tired I keep forgetting what I'm supposed to say.

We go over and over the kind of questions we expect
Dungan to ask and the kind of responses we must give. We
go over the questions John and Joan will ask and how we
must answer those.

It is 1:00 a.m. and they're still rehearsing me. I talk too
much or not enough, and we're all getting giddy.

"Just give me hand signals," I finally say to Joan. "I'll
watch you. If I should talk less, put your fingers really
close together like this," I hold my two index fingers
about an inch from each other. "And if you want me to
elaborate, just hold your hands far apart."

Everybody snorts.

"Oh, sure," Joan says. "I can just see us doing that with
Renfrew watching from his perch."

John stands, taps his pencil on the desk like an orches-
tra conductor, and begins to "direct" me. With his right
hand he makes great rolling movements toward me, saying in effect, "More. Give me more." Or he brings both
hands down gently, fingers spread, to say, "Tone down;
wind up your testimony."

We roar at the symphony he and I will produce once I'm
on the stand. I can just imagine Renfrew's pale, serious
face if we ever had the nerve to act out such a scenario in
his courtroom.

"Now Dungan is going to try and make it look like
everything you edit is vital theology," John says. He and
Joan rehearse how I should answer Dungan.

John plays Dungan, walking around, his hands behind

his back, his face solemn and important.

"Isn't everything you write and edit religious?" He asks me, pretending to pop pills from his suit pocket.

"Could you be more specific as to what you mean by 'religious?'" I ask, just as I've been directed.

John grabs a book, pretending it's one I've edited. Flipping through the pages he says, "I quote from your book. Pray, pray, pray. Heaven, heaven. Worship, worship, worship. Now is that not doctrinal?"

I giggle. Would anyone believe that we're all here, doing this, at 1:30 a.m. the day before trial?

"Whenever you're asked that kind of question, you say that the topics on which you edit and write would fall into the category of human relationships and moral values," Joan says. "But that you do not deal with specific unique Adventist doctrines."

I nod, trying to etch her words on my brain. They're true, but I might get mixed up and say it wrong on the stand.

"And ask to see the table of contents, because then you can elaborate by quoting nonreligious items," Joan instructs.

The table of contents will refresh my memory; and I can point out that much of my work is plain, old, ordinary book editing, with very little religion mixed in.

When we're all so punch-drunk that we not only forget the answers but can't remember the questions, we head for home.

## March 13, 1975

The big day!

Kim has flown in to be with me during trial. It is so good to be together again. He looks rested, handsome, wonderful!

Artist Glenn Heath drives to San Francisco with us. He and Kim take turns reading me my affidavit so that I can remember dates and order of events. I don't want to be confused on the stand, and after last night's rehearsal I'm concerned that I might be.

The horrible wind and rain are like mid-December instead of March. I hope the rotten weather is no indication of how the trial will go.

We step out of the elevator on the seventeenth floor, into a people-packed hall. I see Bob Ruskjer and Joan and Neal Wilson. Neal walks over to me, smiling, and shakes my hand.

"So you did come," I grin.

He looks tired, rolling a document between his palms.

"Well, you know, Merikay," he smiles down at me, "we go where we think we're needed."

We talk for a few minutes, then drift apart.

I know it seems strange to people that I can continue liking a person and behaving in a friendly way toward him, even when I know he is plotting against me. But I hold an ideal about the type of person I wish to be. I want to be kind and loving and courageous no matter how I am treated.

While Jesus never wavered from His mission, he was kind and loving to those who crossed His path, always assuring them of His concern yet urging them to do what is right and just.

I hope my behavior never mirrors people's negative treatment of me. To maintain my self-respect, I must behave in a way that represents the type of person I wish to be. Nothing would make me feel more defeated than that I begin to respond to viciousness and deceit with a viciousness all my own. While I don't always conform to my ideal, in the case of Neal Wilson I do fairly well.

The crowd in the hall grows. It is like campmeeting, like a family reunion — except that the tension is thicker ... with a tinge of hostility in the air. Elder Mills, my pastor, is there. Kim's twin brother, Marc, and a friend who flew down from Seattle, join us. Friends from Sacramento and Napa arrive.

Many of the men from Washington, D.C., stand in a tight cluster of business-suited, briefcase-toting official-dom. Bietz, Richard, Blacker, and Muir talk together.

I enter the empty courtroom and notice that Roland Hegstad (the General Conference religious liberty leader) is sitting all alone in one of the pews. Walking over to him, I touch his shoulder and say, "Hello. I wasn't expecting to see you here." I'm smiling, happy to see him.

"Well, I'm here," he says in a flat, cold voice. His eyes glance angrily at me. "And you're going to be seeing a lot more of me."

I hesitate, and then try again to be friendly. I ask if he'll be here all week. He does not reply. I ask where he's staying. He does not reply. I mention how bad the weather is. He does not reply. He does not even look my way. Stung, I walk back to the hallway.

The whole place is full of people: officials from the church, from the Northern California Conference; workers from the Press; friends of Kim's and mine.

Elder Mills walks up. "I'm here because the judge requested me," he says. "He wants to question me about your church membership."

"What will you say?"

He smiles as if I should already know what he'll say. "I'll tell him the truth. I always tell the truth. You are a member in good standing. You have done nothing to merit disfellowshipping."

"And how is your case coming?" I ask, wondering what is happening with the charges raised against him.

"It will all work out," he says gently. "The police told me the mother has a history of making such charges about people." He pauses, as though thinking. "I don't think there'll be any lasting effects. The Lord will see us through."

I wonder if there is any connection with my lawsuit and the sudden charges which removed him from his position as my pastor. I wonder, but I know he'd deny it if I asked; so I don't. But I wonder if those charges would have been raised if I was not a member of his congregation.

Eventually the crowd moves into the courtroom. In

ones and twos we stream, like ants, through the doors and
file into the pews.

Kim, Glenn, and I sit directly behind Neal Wilson.

John Rea comes to our pew and hands me a copy of the
Press' opening arguments. Glancing at the list of attorneys who filed the document, I see the name Warren
Johns. Tears fill my eyes. So, he not only accepted the call
to Washington, but he is now actively working against
justice in the Press' case. My chest aches. Just one more
disappointment in a long line of heartaches. I point to his
name for Kim.

"I can't believe it," Kim shakes his head disgustedly. "I
thought he had more brains than that."

When Judge Renfrew enters, his black robes billowing
behind him, we all stand. I feel that next we should bow
our heads for prayer. It's suddenly "church" — all of us
here sitting in pews, all of us religious, all used to standing for prayer at the beginning of every meeting. But we
all sit back down and the trial starts.

Each side makes its opening arguments. Dungan starts
out objecting to the trial and the introduction of any
evidence whatsoever.

"...the first and fundamental objection that the defendants have is to the introduction of any evidence
whatsoever on the part of the government," he says,
"upon the ground that such introduction of evidence in
the circumstances of this case constitutes religious-polit-
ical strife and intrusion of the government into the affairs
of religious organizations, it is all in violation of the
establishment clause of the First Amendment ...."

Then Dungan launches into a description of the history
of the Seventh-day Adventist church, who Mrs. White was
and how Adventists view her writings, how she had visions about the importance of the publishing work, how
she and James her husband founded the Pacific Press
Publishing Association.

As he relates the lengthy history of the Press, Renfrew
finally interrupts to say that he, the judge, is familiar with
much of what Dungan is saying since he's read all the
affidavits and pleadings.

So Dungan grinds to a stop and says, "The Pacific Press
Publishing Association is owned and operated by the
General Conference of the Seventh-day Adventists, which

is the Seventh-day Adventist Church...."

A gasp goes up from many of the people in the courtroom. Glenn leans over and whispers, "The GC is not the church." Kim agrees. I see shock on many faces in the courtroom. But Neal Wilson is nodding.

And Dungan is talking about the church's mission being to preach the everlasting gospel of "... our Lord and Savior, Jesus Christ and the commandments of God, that's what the Pacific Press is and that's all that it is."

His voice drones on and on. He says that the whole case should be dismissed because everything the Press has done to Lorna and me is "religious discipline."

"... we say that every one of those acts had a religious foundation," he says, "a religious purpose grounded in a religious belief which Seventh-day Adventists hold."

John Rea makes the opening statement for the EEOC. His statement is much more like a dialogue because Judge Renfrew keeps interrupting to ask questions.

They discuss at length whether Title VII protection would extend to Lorna and me if we were not members in good standing of our respective congregations. If we were disfellowshipped, we would then be ineligible to work at Pacific Press; and then Title VII could not be used to get us rehired.

The judge and John discuss many similar cases, talking about whether the rulings in those cases pertain to my case, whether the findings are appropriate for our case, and so on.

Renfrew asks what the EEOC wants from the court, and John says he wants an order restraining the Press from firing us and guaranteeing that the status quo will be maintained until the Silver case can come to trial.

The discussion between Renfrew and John goes on and on. John points out that Pacific Press is not a church.

"We submit that Pacific Press can really only raise an entanglement argument [the contention that there is government "entanglement" with religion or religious practices — something prohibited by the First Amendment] if it can show itself to be a church, and that the true test of that is not the individual affiliation of the members .... [if] all the [workers] are Catholics or if it is controlled by Catholics, the hospital does not, therefore, become a Catholic church."

Then Judge Renfrew starts asking about Lorna's and my standing with our congregations. It is clear that Renfrew is concerned about our church memberships. He keeps talking about our being "at variance" and that "variance" might affect our church memberships; and if we aren't members of the church, then we are not qualified to work at PPPA.

After about twenty minutes of discussion, Renfrew decides to call Elder Mills to the stand to see if I am in danger of being disfellowshipped. But Mills is not in the courtroom; so Renfrew recesses for lunch. We're to come back at 1:45 p.m.

People stand and discuss the morning's proceedings. The Press management gathers together in a tiny black knot at one end of their pew.

People file out, talking together or quietly thinking. Kim and I and Marc and Glenn and several of our friends take the elevator to the basement cafeteria.

Standing at the end of the line, we talk about the morning. Kim thinks Renfrew is against me. "All he does is interrupt and argue with attorney Rea," Kim says.

I'm also disturbed by the judge's questions. He seems to believe that the GC is the church. Of course, Renfrew is Episcopalian; and his church structure is different from ours. He may be confusing the two. In any event, Kim is right and his point bothers me.

We move through line, choosing salads and sandwiches, putting the different dishes on our orange plastic trays, moving closer to the cash register. I see where the coffee and coke are, but I can't find the milk. Just then I notice Dungan with two cartons of milk on his tray.

"Where did you get your milk?" I ask, but he doesn't seem to hear.

I walk over to him. "Excuse me, Mr. Dungan. Where did you find the milk?"

He looks past me and walks to a table on the far side of the cafeteria.

I go back to search for the milk on my own.

As we head for a table, I notice Elder Mills sitting with some other men. Walking over I say, "The judge tried to call you to the stand; so you might want to be in the courtroom when things start again."

He looks up at me and nods.

"We're supposed to be back at 1:45," I say, then join Kim and our friends for lunch.

After eating and talking about the attorneys and the issues, I head back for the courtroom. Kim and Marc and our friends are going to visit the government book store; then they'll join me.

When I step out of the elevator, I nearly bump into Joan and John. Joan is crying and saying, "I have never been so horrified!" and John is drained of color.

"What's wrong?" Fear grips me.

"Come here, come here," Joan pulls me into one of the little side rooms off the main hall. "My husband was in the cafeteria, and he overheard Neal Wilson threatening your minister," she says.

I look at her in disbelief. "Wilson said, 'If you testify in Merikay's behalf *you'll* be disfellowshipped; and you'll lose your job and your retirement!' "

My mind reels. I look at the walls of the room, at the ceiling. My mind is as blank as the ceiling. I am empty, shocked hollow.

Kim comes in. "What's wrong?" he asks.

"Elder Mills has been threatened if he testifies in my behalf," I say, my voice machinelike as it speaks.

Kim looks at Joan, and she repeats what she's told me. "Is he going to testify?" Kim wants to know.

"I've asked him," Joan says. "And he said to me, 'I have so much to lose.' " Her voice breaks and tears start to flow.

Kim's and my eyes lock in abhorrence.

"I've got to find him," I say, walking into the hall.

The hall is full now as everyone returns for the afternoon session. Elder Mills stands alone near the elevators. I hurry to him.

"I've just heard about your lunch," I say. His eyes are red, as if he's been crying. "Look," I say — and I can't search his eyes, so I stare at his hands, then his tie, then his hands again — "I won't hold anything against you if you don't give a good report of me. There's no reason you should be hurt because of this."

"But you'll keep being a part of my congregation, won't you?" he asks. His voice is very soft, very pained. "I may not be the minister, but I'll be there sitting in the congregation. You won't leave us?"

Even now I hear his concern for me, for my soul; and I

love this gentle, sweet man.

"I'll never reject Jesus Christ," I say. "I could never do that."

We stand there together silently a few minutes. Then Kim emerges with Joan and John and they motion us back to court.

The courtroom is packed. More people have come to listen and take part in the proceedings. Renfrew enters and we start again.

Elder Mills is called to the stand. As he sits in the witness chair he looks calm, totally relaxed.

Dungan points out that Elder Mills is presently suspended from ministerial duties. That angers me, and I am more certain that the charges against Mills connect in some way with my lawsuit.

Joan questions Elder Mills. She establishes that he has known me for about ten years, that I joined his congregation through a vote of the congregation, and that I was at the time involved in a lawsuit against the Press.

At every step of this process Dungan objects, saying that because Mills is under suspension he cannot speak with authority; but the judge overrules all objections.

Mills details the procedure for disfellowshipping: A special church trial is held. Both sides are heard. Then the congregation votes whether or not to disfellowship. He discusses the grounds for disfellowshipping — such things as breaking the Sabbath, drinking alcohol, [failing] other "tests of fellowship," or disregarding fundamental doctrines of the church.

Then Joan asks if during his twenty years as an SDA pastor he has ever known of a person being disfellowshipped for engaging in civil court litigation.

He says he hasn't.

"During the course of your membership in the Seventh-day Adventist Church, have you ever known an organization such as a publishing house, an institutional organization, taking ability to disfellowship or censure?" Joan asks.

"No; I have not."

The courtroom is like a tomb. The silent tension is almost unbearable. All eyes focus on Elder Mills. Yet he seems so relaxed. There isn't a wrinkle or a stress line on his face.

"We're going outside to pray," Kim whispers to me as he and Marc slip out of the pew.

"Have you ever known of any such an organization making a recommendation to the local church for disfellowship?" Joan asks.

"I have not known of such action."

"During the period that you have known Mary Kay [sic] Silver, up to the present date, ... have you observed anything with regard to her conduct that would lead you to believe that she was a candidate for disfellowship?"

"I have not." The words are spoken clearly and gently. Tears fill my eyes.

"... Have you ever known of an incident in which a member's disfellowship has been recommended because of engaging in litigation with another Adventist; have you ever heard of that? ..." Joan asks.

"I have not heard of it. It may have been done, but I have not heard of it."

Dungan asks a few perfunctory questions; and then, before Elder Mills is dismissed, Judge Renfrew asks him: "Would you believe it's a serious matter if the General Conference Committee recommended to the Pacific Press Publishing Association that an employee be discontinued in his or her employment and canceled, would that be a serious matter ..."

"I don't know why they would recommend it, sir." Elder Mills replies. "It would be serious in that the person would be out of employment, it would be serious for their livelihood."

After a few more questions from Joan, Elder Mills steps down and walks back to his seat.

John Rea addresses Renfrew for a long time. Then Joan asks to admit an affidavit with several attached documents which are copies of lawsuits filed between Adventists, filed by Adventists against SDA institutions, and filed by SDA institutions against Adventist members.

The whole afternoon is filled with Dungan trying to prove that the court has no jurisdiction in this case, while Joan and John try to prove that the General Conference has no jurisdiction over the local congregation. On and on and on.

Joan points out that we aren't asking for much. We merely ask that the status quo be maintained (that Lorna and I continue in our jobs) until the Silver trial.

"... if a preliminary injunction is not granted, the people who are employees at Pacific Press and the people who are employees at another Adventist institution and other religiously-affiliated institutions would see that the law which safeguards other employees does not safeguard them, ...." Joan says. "There is no reason to believe that employees of a religious corporation or religious organization are any less in need of the protection of a law such as this ...."

Finally Renfrew recesses until Friday.

I hurry out to find Elder Mills and thank him; and there is Neal Wilson with his arm around Mills' shoulders, walking him down the hall. I shiver. The two of them walk slowly down the long, gray, marble hall. Then they stop and Wilson, one of his long, skinny arms stretched out, leans up against the wall and talks to Mills. Wilson talks to Mills for several minutes. Then he walks away and Elder Mills comes to me.

He's nervous, restless, and says he's going home.

"Thank you," I say. "Your testimony was beautiful. Thank you."

"In times like these we've all got to be strong," he says.

---

Note:   All testimony quoted in this book can be read complete and in court-
        room context in the trial transcripts of case C-74-2025 CBR, Volume I.
        Specific quotes contained in the last few pages are documented as
        follows:

| Betrayal Page | | Court Transcript Page |
|---|---|---|
| 292 | — Dungan's statements | 4: 18-25 |
| | | 11: 25-12: 2 |
| 293 | — Dungan's statements | 12: 5-7 |
| 293 | — Dungan's speech | 14: 4-6 |
| 293 | — John Rea's statements | 40: 6-12 |
| 296-97 | — Elder Leonard Mill's testimony | 59: 7-11 |
| | | 59: 12-19 |
| | | 61: 5-10 |
| | | 61: 15-22 |
| 298 | — Joan Bradford's closing statements | 116: 11-19 |

## Friday, March 14, 1975

Today's court session will be short. We don't even get started until 4:00 in the afternoon, and Sabbath starts around 6:00 or 6:30. No Adventists will be able to stay after the Sabbath begins.

Dungan has been asserting that our church structure is hierarchical. Consequently, someone like Neal Wilson or the General Conference Committee would have the power and authority to order Lorna and me fired or disfellowshipped. The judge professes not to understand our church structure, and so Joan is attempting to establish that it is not a hierarchy. She calls Floyd O. Rittenhouse, a retired Adventist college president, to discuss the structure of the church.

The entire time is spent establishing, once again, the procedure for disfellowshipping and the fact that a lawsuit does not constitute grounds for disfellowshipping.

As the Sabbath nears, we all leave. Kim will return to Seattle. We walk to my car, holding hands. It is so good to be with him again. I am pleased that he's happy and well. I thank him for coming.

"I just wish I could stay for the whole trial," he says. "As soon as you know something, call me right away."

I promise I will.

All weekend I think about the trial.

Lorna calls. Joan calls. John calls. I phone Lorna. We talk and talk and talk. None of us think Renfrew wants to rule in our favor. I just hope he will not let his emotions get in the way. He's supposed to be impartial. And that's all I want him to be. Simple justice, that's all I want. I wonder if I'll get it.

Sabbath afternoon Elder Mills phones. He admits that Neal Wilson threatened him. "But I don't know if he will carry through on his threat," he says. His voice sounds stronger, more confident than it did last week.

I pray that he will not suffer because of his friendship with me.

When I'm not talking about the trial, I'm reviewing my affidavit to try and ensure that I won't flub up when I'm put on the stand.

## Monday, Tuesday, Wednesday
## March 17, 18, & 19, 1975

Arriving at the courtroom I notice a much smaller group. Most of the General Conference men are gone. But Neal Wilson is still here. He says "Good morning," as he shakes my hand.

"Hi. You're still here!"

He nods sadly, as if being here is a great burden. "I'm afraid I'll be here until the bitter end, Merikay."

Bob Ruskjer is on the stand today, followed by a worker from the Press. Then Bob is called back again.

Everybody seems to be on the stand forever because there are so many attorneys asking so many questions. Dungan asks questions and then Joan and/or John; and then Dungan may have some more questions. Then maybe Joan or John has a few more, and then Judge Renfrew might ask a few . . . and it just goes on and on. All those Perry Mason TV shows, where a few sharp questions settled the whole case, were a far cry from reality.

Bob Ruskjer is good on the stand. It's obvious that he's done trials before. He is relaxed. His answers are clear and well-stated, and most of the information he imparts strengthens our side.

Lorna takes the stand. She isn't on for long. She just says that she had asked her pastor if her involvement in my lawsuit would endanger her church membership, and he assured her it wouldn't.

Dungan doesn't cross-examine her, and I can tell she is disappointed about that.

Then I am sworn in.

Joan begins asking about my salary, and I answer two or three questions before I am told I'm speaking too softly. The court reporter can't hear me. We begin again.

I am embarrassed, and try to speak louder.

Joan asks if I was ever counseled by my congregation, my pastor, or the board of my church to cease litigation.

"No," I say. That ends Joan's questions.

Then Dungan walks over, looking like a movie villian. He hands me a photocopy of a book-manuscript report. Reading and evaluating manuscripts is part of my job; and for each manuscript I read, I fill out a report.

He asks me questions about the report he has handed

me and enters the report as evidence. He repeats this
procedure two or three times and then has no more questions. He has just used me to enter evidence detrimental to
my side.

When Dungan says he has no more questions, I stand
up to leave. Judge Renfrew tells me to sit back down, that
I'm not through yet.

Embarrassed, I sit down again.

The rest of the questions come from John Rea concerning book reports on such manuscripts as *The Brown Dog*
and *The Great White Wolf*. I sit in the stand while John
and Renfrew dialogue.

From my witness seat I can look at the back side of the
judge's bench. From the front, the side you see while
you're in the pews, the bench or the judge's seat is tall,
beautifully polished wood, very impressive.

It's certainly a different view from here.

The back side isn't even finished — rough, raw wood,
with carpeting that doesn't quite reach. Wires run along
the unfinished bare boards, giving the whole thing a
stage-prop appearance.

I wonder if the judge feels more like this is all make
believe because he's on the stage-prop side.

From the pews the facade looks solemn and authoritative, almost as if the voice of God is going to descend from
the judge's chair.

From here it looks like it might fall over if you bumped
it by mistake.

I'm asked a few more questions, then dismissed.

The rest of the day is spent with each side arguing for its
viewpoint. Dungan still wants the judge to throw the
whole case out of court because the government can't tell
the church what to do. Joan and John ask for a preliminary injunction until the Silver case can go to trial.

Joan's final words are: "Other employers must abide by
Title VII. These people who are here before the Court as
plaintiff interveners, and their fellow and sister employees who work for Pacific Press, are wage earners in an
employer-employee position. There is nothing before this
Court to show that the doors of this Court should be
closed to employees simply because they are employees of
a religious organization."

Silence fills the court. We wait to see if Renfrew will

grant the Press its motion of summary judgment, which will effectively throw the case out of court and seal Lorna's and my terminations.

He glances at his desk, then at Joan, then says, "Well, I'm going to deny the motion."

Tension drains from me. Thank You, God! The trial will continue, and perhaps we'll get our preliminary injunction.

---

The quotes on this page are taken from Court transcript of case C-74-2025 CBR, Volume I, page 308: 1-8.

## Thursday, March 20, 1975

Unlike last Thursday, with its wind and soggy gray clouds, today is clear and shining. As I drive to San Francisco I can't help feeling happy. The bay is deep blue as I drive along The Bayshore Freeway. Whitecaps spill over the rocks and soak into the sand. It's one of those crystal, sparkling days that makes me feel in love with life.

As I turn toward the city parking lot I notice Neal Wilson, Jack Blacker, and R.R. Bietz standing on the corner, waiting to cross. I feel so good, so happy to be alive on such a fabulous day, that I just can't ignore them. Rolling down my window, I honk and wave as I go past.

"Good morning!" Neal Wilson calls out cheerily.

Later, in the courthouse hall, I see Neal and walk over to him. "You three looked so handsome out there in the morning sunlight," I say. "I just couldn't resist waving."

"Well, we didn't know who that young lady was," he sort of blushes.

"Oh, come on; you knew me. Who else would do that?"

We both laugh and enter the courtroom.

Neal Clayton Wilson is the second witness of the day. He walks slowly, deliberately to the stand. His whole body exudes confidence, authority, power.

The first order of business is entering a lot of documents for exhibits and evidence. Then Dungan questions Wilson about how people join our church and how important our church structure is. I keep my eyes on Wilson's face, trying to look like his friend. Whenever he makes a fair and genuine point for his side, I nod, acknowledging it.

But I do not get friendly looks back. In fact, whenever his eyes touch my face they chill me. He can be a very frightening man. I feel it half way across the courtroom.

Dungan asks, "Would you describe the organization of the Seventh-day Adventist church as being congregational or hierarchical or something else?"

Trying to establish our church organization as hierarchical has been the goal of Dungan's team. We are not a hierarchy, and Adventist theologians and lawyers all over the nation who have seen the arguments implying that we are have been up in arms. Yet the Press wants

Judge Renfrew to think we are; because then they can argue that their actions against Lorna and me are religious actions, taken at the request of our religious leaders.

Wilson's voice booms with authority. "It is definitely not congregational ....

"Words sometimes ... mean one thing to one person and something else to another. Hierarchical, to some, would indicate that the authority emanates from the top and flows through. That is the reason why Seventh-day Adventists have chosen to term their particular type of church government representative where the authority flows from the church level by delegated responsibility and authority to various levels of the church, but, in fact, considering that there are levels of authority, it could well be stated that it ... has a definite hierarchical framework with the clear understanding that we have chosen several other types of government which are included in the representative structure such as the Episcopal Church has, where the Bishop does have authority; and the Methodist church, the Presbyterian and so on.

"But it is a representative type of government where the authority flows from the church's delegated authority and responsibility and then those appointed in that way are required to act for the whole church."

I know that Neal used the example of the Episcopal church's bishop to get Judge Renfrew to identify *his* church's structure as our church's structure. I hope the judge doesn't fall for it.

I notice Renfrew is blowing under the collar of his gown. Sitting there, all scrunched down in his chair, blowing under his collar, his eyes scanning the courtroom, then resting on Wilson's face. Renfrew seems bored or strained by the proceedings.

Dungan asks Neal to describe the organizational structure of our church and the relationship between the General Conference Committee and the Press.

"The General Conference Committee is the highest authority in the Seventh-day Adventist Church," he says. He drags out the "s" sounds at the ends of his words. "General Conferencccccce" "highessssst authority." He also draws out the word "Chuuuurch." It sounds as though he's preaching rather than testifying.

But in the midst of his testimony Judge Renfrew interrupts to say he must attend to a criminal calendar. We break for lunch.

I wonder if Neal Wilson is convincing the judge that our church is hierarchical, and that therefore this is *not* an employment problem but rather a religious problem. I hope not. But who knows what goes on behind that pale face with the strawberry blond eyebrows?

After lunch Neal Wilson returns to the stand. He sits tall and thin, his dark hair and royal blue suit standing out against the blond wood and light gray marble of the room.

From the letter Neal sent to the Press asking that we be fired, Dungan reads, "Referring to Ms. Silver and Ms. Tobler, the General Conference Committee recommends that their local church boards be apprised of this action."

Wilson then explains the significance of the letter.

"Obviously the General Conference Committee felt that this discipline was necessary . . . ," Neal says. "However, I think normally the church is very long suffering and patient . . . .

". . . in this particular instance, the Church felt that inasmuch as these ladies were at variance with the Church, the local church . . . where they hold membership should be informed of that. No action was suggested but it was a matter of information."

I'm angry that he keeps saying that the church felt this or that. *He* felt it, or the General Conference Committee, or some board, but *not the church*. The church is all of us, every member of my congregation, the whole body of Christ.

He is trying to instill in Judge Renfrew's mind the idea that the General Conference Committee is analogous to the Pope in the Catholic church — that they're the church, and they're not! I am angered by his testimony because I know he's misinforming Renfrew and, possibly, successfully.

Then Dungan asks Wilson to explain the phrase "at variance."

Neal launches into a dissertation about how, when we join the church, we agree to give up our individual rights for the good of the whole; how, when we join the church, we agree to live in harmony with the spiritual family. When we are no longer in harmony with these principles

— "... whether doctrinally, organizationally, relationship-wise with his brother or his sister in the faith, one is considered to be at variance with the Church," he says.

Dungan asks Wilson to explain the phrase in his letter that says Lorna and I are "unresponsive to spiritual counsel."

Wilson looks very tall and thin and very dark on the stand. He speaks slowly and with great emphasis.

"Seldom does the Church take action of a disciplinary nature, whether with an organization, Pacific Press, or a church congregation or with an employee of the Church or a member of the Church without first having made every effort to try and counsel and to appeal and to show a better way and to indicate that the present course ... could lead them into serious conflict and could well result in harm to the Church...," he says.

"... the General Conference Committee felt that, in this particular case, recognizing the facts that a number of individuals had tried to give counsel to the ladies in question, there seemed to be no responsiveness to that spiritual counseling or a lack of reception of it."

"Elder Wilson, did you, yourself, give any spiritual counsel to either Ms. Silver or Ms. Tobler relating to the matters now before the Court?"

"Yes, I did."

I shake my head back and forth. "No you didn't," I mouth to him; but his eyes register nothing.

"Under what circumstances?" Dungan asks.

"Even though not required, because of my particular responsibilities, to do so, I did take the initiative to spend some time with Merikay Silver and Ms. Tobler also was present for a portion of the time on my first encounter...."

"... we had quite a lengthy discussion about the whole problem and I tried, in a very tactful, a very earnest and a very personal way, to point out that this certainly was no way to resolve this particular kind of problem, in which I totally concur with the opinion stated by His Honor, Judge Renfrew," Neal looks at the judge, "this is really no way to solve this kind of problem and probably it will never be resolved fully in this manner."

I marvel at Neal Wilson's skill. He has given a misleading impression of our church's structure to the judge by comparing it to the judge's own church, and now he appeals to the judge's vanity by quoting him and saying loud and clear for all to hear that he agrees with Renfrew.

Dungan's next question implies that a church "doctrine" and a church "teaching" are interchangeable.

Neal says that it is definitely a teaching of the church that members are not supposed to litigate.

For about half an hour Dungan and Wilson talk about Bob Ruskjer, about all the litigation that our side has introduced as evidence, and that kind of thing. Rather dry from my viewpoint, but important to their side of the case.

Dungan then tries to show that my working for the Press is not a typical employer-employee relationship. He asks Neal what kind of relationship exists between church members in the employ of a church-related institution.

"All of the employees of the Church, and specifically the Pacific Press, are in either a minister or missionary relationship with the Church," Neal says.

I look at the ceiling. "They're not going to try saying I'm a minister," I shake my head. I can't believe this. It's all so misleading. And I'm sure the judge is buying it all. He seems *so* impressed, *so* awed, by Wilson.

Neal goes on and on about how we're all missionaries or ministers and that we have this special commitment, spiritual and heartfelt; and that we forego high wages because of our love of the work and our commitment to try to further the cause of the church.

That ends Dungan's questions. But before Joan can cross-examine, Judge Renfrew says, "I would like to see counsel in chambers, and I would like the plaintiff interveners and Elder Wilson and any other representatives of the defendants to wait in my outer room. I'd like to talk to all of you."

So we all walk back to the judge's chambers and outer room.

Wilson, Blacker, Bietz, Lorna, and I sit in the outer room together. There's a comfortable, overstuffed couch and a couple of chairs. A huge window looks out over San Francisco, sparkling in the sunlight.

On the wall, in a frame, hangs Judge Renfrew's official appointment to the federal bench. It is signed by President Richard Nixon and Attorney General John Mitchell.

I think that considering recent political history, I

wouldn't have that appointment with those signatures hanging on *my* wall.

Everyone is stiff with silence.

Neal sighs, "When I think of all the other important things awaiting my attention."

"This has been waiting a hundred years," Lorna says.

Silence chills the room.

I walk to the window, smiling at Lorna's words. I look at the dome of city hall, the green of Civic Center Plaza.

When I turn back, Neal motions for me to sit beside him. I do. We talk about parachuting and mountain climbing.

"You did quite a job on the stand," I say.

"Are you trying to console me, Merikay?"

"No, no, you speak very well," I say, "clear and loud. Yesterday everyone said they couldn't even hear me. It's pretty embarrassing, you know."

Then I ask if his sermons are like his testimony. "Do you preach with a warm or an authoritative air?" I ask.

"Elder Wilson is a brilliant speaker," Blacker says, his voice glowing. "Why, I've heard him take a Bible verse and speak for forty minutes on it, extemporaneously; and the whole talk was filled with original, brilliant concepts."

I start to giggle over the grossly obvious bootlicking, but I can see that Neal is eating it up. It's so transparent, but the men appear to take this kind of compliment seriously.

We talk for a few more minutes. Neal's relaxed, but both Bietz and Blacker are so stiff and quiet I wonder if they're breathing.

"Well, if I ever get on the stand again, I'm going to copy you," I say to Neal. "I'm going to talk clear and loud."

"Next time let's be on the same side," he says.

I nod. "Remember what you told me about the different levels of life?" I say. He doesn't respond. I touch his arm, "This nitty-gritty level is a real bummer, isn't it?" He does not respond.

The door opens; the attorneys emerge. We all head back to the courtroom.

"The judge was trying to get us to say we would not cross-examine Wilson," Joan tells me. "And of course we would not agree to that."

Just one more thing that rocks me. There are so many shocking surprises. I never thought a judge would try to orchestrate the trial he's supposed to be ruling on. All I can do is shake my head.

Cross-examination starts with Joan getting Wilson to once again review the steps required for disfellowshipping. Then she reads a quote from his deposition, where he says that I am not a "heretic" theologically or philosophically, and should not be a candidate for disfellowshipping.

Then she reads from Dungan's brief, where Dungan writes, "Neither of the intervener plaintiffs is in good standing with the Church. Neither is eligible for employment at Pacific Press, and each is a prime candidate for early disfellowshipping."

She then asks Wilson if he authorized that statement.

"We placed our case in the hands of our counsel and he made his reply," Wilson says.

"Is it your answer that neither of the intervenor plaintiffs is in good standing with the Church, and each is a prime candidate for early disfellowship?"

"I would say that the first [statement] is correct," he says. "The second might be modified somewhat ...."

They talk again about where the authority to disfellowship is based — in the local congregation rather than the General Conference.

There are questions and answers about church-related employment. Joan asks if I would be a candidate for disfellowshipping or for firing if I had not filed the class action lawsuit. Wilson says that I would not.

Joan then points out that it is my filing the suit which makes me a candidate for being fired from my job and disfellowshipped from my church.

Wilson says it wasn't the filing of the suit, but my *persistence* in following that path despite people counseling me against it.

Joan asks Neal if he counseled me to drop the lawsuit.

"Yes, I urged her not to continue in the lawsuit," he answers.

I shake my head no. My mouth is dry, my heart is beating hard. He never counseled me to stop the lawsuit.

"Was that on the date of your visit with her in February of 1974?" Joan asks.

"That would have been the date, right."

Joan then refers to his deposition testimony which is filed in this case. Reading from his deposition, she says, "Question: Can you recall any discussions you had in that meeting with her, what you said to her and what she said to you?"

" 'Answer: But I would have to honestly state that specific points are very vague in my memory at this point, and I have not reviewed that document since that time . . . .

" 'I entered into conversation with her in trying to help her understand other points of view that should be taken into consideration; and while there was probably *no attempt to persuade* each other, we had a fair exchange of concepts.' "

Joan stares at Neal for a long moment of silence. He stares right back. I'm amazed at his nerve.

"I have no further questions," she says.

Wilson steps down.

Richard Utt is the next person called to the stand. He looks very uncomfortable and keeps licking his lips and grinning.

Attorney Quirk examines Richard. They introduce a long list of books, which they mark for identification. Among the list is *Coco the Range Pony, Elo the Eagle, Rudo the Reckless Russian*, and others.

They discuss Richard's work history. He was a pastor and then a missionary in Panama and Costa Rica. He has a master of divinity degree. He is now head PPPA English language book editor.

They discuss Adventist publishing philosophy.

Richard gives very long answers. Of course he's never been known for brevity, but I wonder if anyone rehearsed him for this. It doesn't seem so. He goes on and on and on with his answers.

Judge Renfrew chews on the collar of his gown.

Being a judge must be very boring at times. At least Renfrew looks bored. As long as Richard continues, Renfrew chews.

Richard and Quirk go through every single book on the list so Richard can explain the "spiritual story behind each."

It seems as though the point of it is to show that the Press publishes only religious books; and therefore the court has no right forcing them to keep me employed, editing such spiritually sensitive work as these books.

Then Joan begins cross-examination. She shows Richard a procession of Adventist magazines — *Life and Health, El Centinela, Review and Herald,* and others, asking him to scan certain articles in each, to see if they are appropriate for publication in Adventist magazines.

Then she and Richard discuss the articles and their authors.

Dungan and Quirk look at each other in confusion as this exercise goes on and on. Joan's list of articles is almost as long as Quirk's list of books.

Quirk asks, "Can we have some indication of where we are going with this?"

Joan says that she will make it clear after just a couple more questions.

Richard doesn't know what's happening, and neither does anyone else. Renfrew seems to listen intently for a change.

Quirk writes notes on a yellow legal pad, listening to Joan and Richard and writing.

Joan asks Richard to examine two last articles and state if they are the kind suitable for SDA publications. He says, "Yes, it appears so."

Then Joan says to Judge Renfrew, "I would like to introduce all of these into evidence. All of these articles have been written by Adventists who sued Adventist institutions."

The lead in Quirk's pencil breaks and shoots across the table. He stands and objects on the grounds of irrelevancy.

Judge Renfrew overrules and asks Joan what her collection of articles shows.

"It shows, Your Honor, that the writing of articles for Adventist publications has been taking place by persons who entered into litigation with Adventist organizations . . . .

"Even more significant, the Richard T. Walden who has written all of the Walden articles that I have put in and who apparently is still on the faculty at Loma Linda University, was the plaintiff, he and his wife were plaintiffs in an action against Loma Linda University in 1964 which went on to trial and on to judgment and he is still working in an Adventist institution and he is still writing for Adventists."

Judge Renfrew argues with her. He says he would have to know the nature of the cases to see if these other authors' lawsuits were similar to mine.

Then he would have to know if those other plaintiffs had been counseled not to sue, and in spite of counsel had continued suing, before he could determine if there was a parallel here.

Joan Bradford says that I was never counseled against litigation, and the judge says that Wilson testified I *was* counseled.

Joan says, "She requested an opportunity to speak with him in February of 1974 and he did meet with her at her home; and his deposition, which is closer in time than today, states that there was no attempt by anyone to influence the other, that they had a pleasant exchange of views and there was no attempt to persuade."

Renfrew says, "Well, the problem with that is that in the cross-examination, you see, we have the direct unequivocal testimony that he did counsel her not to persist in the lawsuit. Now we have some ambiguous paper in his deposition and no question was put to him asking him to reconcile it. As a matter of fact, there was no question put to him. You just read that into the record."

Joan asks to recall Wilson to the stand, and once again Neal takes the stand.

Joan reads Wilson the passage from his deposition where he said there was no attempt to persuade each other. She asks him if that statement, made under oath, is true.

"That is correct," he says. "And I think you will notice the sentence, it says, 'I entered into conversation with her in trying to help her . . . understand other points of view that should be taken into consideration.' And I spent considerable time. She asked me the question, 'What have I done wrong? Why is everybody unhappy with me?' "

Neal C. Wilson, SDA world leader, is fabricating lies. Right there on the stand. He is making up a conversation that never happened. His characterization doesn't even sound like me. I am shaking my head no. I can barely sit still.

"And did you counsel?" Joan Bradford asks.

". . . I urged her and told her that she was taking the wrong route . . . ."

"Did you *counsel* her?"

No one stirs in the courtroom. Wilson stares at Joan, a half smile on his face, one hand laying casually on top of the other. He lifts his top hand up about three inches, and then drops it back, just looking at Joan.

He never counseled me. I know that and he knows that, and he knows that I know that. I wonder what he's thinking in this long silence.

Then in a loud voice, he says, "I did tell her that she ought to submit this to the General Conference if she felt that she wanted to. She said that if she trusted the General Conference of the Church, she would, but at that point, she didn't trust the Church."

I nearly jump off my pew. I can't believe the dialogue he is inventing. I can't believe what I'm hearing, what's coming out of his mouth. My face burns. That man, probably the most powerful individual in my denomination, is lying. And he thought about the lie for a long moment before he uttered it. And he knows that I know he's lying.

I have never felt so angry, so hurt, so betrayed.

He is betting that I like him so much that I will refuse to counter his words on the stand. He is probably certain that I will not hurt him.

(Isn't that the way oppressors always think about those they oppress? Haven't oppressors always thought the people they "ruled over" would passively take it? That's why they're always so shaken when the revolution comes. They never expect the victim to protest victimhood.)

Well, Neal, I love you; but you aren't going to get away with this one!

Joan ends her questions. Dungan has no questions. Joan asks for a two-minute recess.

We walk out into the hall and I know what she'll say before she utters the words. "I'm putting you back on the stand."

I nod, heart racing. "I know."

I can feel adrenalin charging through my veins. Another man I trusted and had hoped would help, another Christian brother whom I loved and cherished. My heart aches at what I must do.

From the stand I gaze at Neal Wilson — sitting in his

pew, his face expressionless, his eyes dark and hidden behind his tinted glasses.

The room is silent.

"Do you recall a visit with Elder Wilson of General Conference," Joan Bradford asks, "in February of 1974?"

"Yes."

"Where did that conference with Elder Wilson take place?"

"In my home ... in San Jose."

"... how did that visit or conference come about?"

"I had written to him and asked him if we could get together. I had heard from a number of friends that he was making statements about my position in the Silver lawsuit and my attitudes in the Silver lawsuit at public meetings around the country, and I [had] never met him. He didn't know my position and he didn't know my attitude, and I thought it would be kind of important for him to know me and my attitudes ...

"I wrote and asked him to meet with me so that when he ... said things about me he would know me. He would be, you know, more accurate."

Joan asks, "Then *you* wrote to *him*?"

"Yes."

"And *he* responded to *your* letter?"

"He phoned me and we set up a time when we could get together."

"And you met together at your home, then, as a result of your contacting him?"

"Yes."

She asks how long he was there and whether anyone else was present. Then she asks me the contents of what was said during that day.

I review our discussion of parachuting and mountain climbing. I tell how I gave him the document I'd prepared, how he read it and asked me questions like: "What do you mean here?" "What do you think we could do there?"

Then Joan asks the big question: "Did he state to you that you should not be in litigation, that you should not be in a lawsuit?"

"I don't believe he ever said those words," I say. "I don't believe he ever said, 'You should not sue,' but he said things like, 'What, specifically would you like here?' and then I would say something and he would say, 'Well, how could we do that? Could we do this or could we do that?' He would make specific suggestions or [ask] questions and, you know, it made me very happy because this was the first person that had ever listened to me, . . . and asked me questions about how we could . . . settle it . . . .

". . . it made me extremely excited and happy that maybe . . . something could be done."

"Did you ask Mr. Wilson to participate any further in attempting to settle the matter?" Joan asks.

"I don't remember my exact words, but since this was the first person that would respond and I knew that management listened to him also and he listened to management, . . . I said something to the effect of, 'Oh, you're the only one that listens to anybody. . . . do you think you could help us? Would you be . . . like a mediator between us . . .?' "

"What was his response?"

". . . I don't remember any specific words. I got the impression that he might be interested in it; but I don't remember him saying 'Yes, I would' or 'No, I wouldn't.' "

We then talk about the number of conversations I've had with Neal Wilson and the kind of relationship we have, trying to point out that we have a friendship, a friendly person-to-person relationship — not a great spiritual leader-humble follower relationship.

"Has anyone at General Conference ever counseled you not to engage in litigation?" Joan asks.

"No."

"Has anyone at General Conference ever told you to go see somebody else to get advice with regard to the problems at Pacific Press?"

"I don't believe so."

"Has anyone at Pacific Press or otherwise in the Adventist denomination told you where you could go to seek advice and help as an alternative to pursuing litigation?"

"No," I say. ". . . I suppose the closest thing to counsel that I've had is to be told over and over again to be patient, the brethren will take care of me. . . . But no one said, 'Do not sue or stop suing.' "

After Joan, John Rea questions me. As we speak, I look out at all the men in business suits — all the men from the Press staring at me, their ties straight, their faces blank.

I look at Neal Wilson and see no expression as he gazes back. Nothing.

I feel destroyed. There is no truth or integrity in this room full of church men. They are all hoping that the court will allow them to fire us and treat the other women workers any way they please.

They will go to any lengths to protect their right to discriminate, misuse, abuse, cheat, and steal from their workers.

John asks about the Wickwire letter, then asks if Richard Utt or anyone else ever explained the steps I was supposed to take to find relief for my complaint.

"No."

Now, like a tank, Dungan approaches. He wants to know if I knew Wilson's General Conference position when I wrote to him. I didn't know his title.

Then Dungan refers to the letter Bietz wrote me.

". . . He refers to the instruction of Christ as outlined in Matthew 18:15-20," Dungan says. "Does that mean anything to you?"

"Well, could I see it?"

"Yes. I show you your affidavit, Exhibit C, paragraph two, the instruction of Christ as outlined in Matthew 18:15-20."

I look at what he's handed me — a copy of Bietz's letter to me.

"Does it mean anything to you? . . . Do you know what's in Matthew 18:15-20?"

"I would have to look at it," I say.

"I beg your pardon?" He appears surprised that I don't have that section of the Bible memorized.

"I would have to look at it to see."

"When you received Bietz's letter in August of 1972, did you go look?"

"I'm sure I did."

"On the first page he says, 'The problem here, Mrs. Silver, is that you should have contacted the Chairman of the Board about the matter before going to the outside.' " Dungan looks up at me, his eyes chastising me as so many men's eyes have for the past two years.

" 'If the Chairman of the Board would not pay any attention to your request, then you should have gotten in contact with Elder Pierson, the President of the General

Conference,' " Dungan reads on. "What did you understand that to mean?" he asks.

"I had not known that. No one had told me that. When
I was told to contact the Chairman of the Board, I did and
it was then that he said I should have done that first, but I
hadn't known that."

"All right. But when he wrote this on August 17, 1972,
did you understand then that it was a requirement of the
Church," Dungan says, "that if you failed to receive
satisfaction at one level, you go to the next level?"

"No I didn't," I say. I am reminded that I don't like
Dungan. He is rude, pushy, and vulgar. "I don't think I
understood that . . . I should have gone to him first and I
didn't; and he was . . . saying, 'Shame on you. You should
have come to me.' "

Dungan continues, trying to make me say that I understood Bietz was outlining the steps I was supposed to use
to resolve my problem at Pacific Press; but that was not
my understanding, ever, and I fail to say what he wants.

Then he starts in on my February visit with Neal
Wilson.

"Did you understand . . . when you met with Elder
Wilson in 1974, that he was giving you any different
counsel than Elder Bietz had given you in August, 1972?"

"Well, I don't believe that Elder Wilson and I got together for counsel so much as to see what it was that I
wanted. . . . He more or less came to see what my ideas on
the case were because nobody had asked me.

"Any counsel that came out in our discussion was very
informal such as, . . . 'Would you be willing to mediate for
us at a settlement conference?' That sort of thing . . . .

"He didn't come with a purpose to counsel me because
when he came in . . . he said, 'Well, I gave you today,
Merikay.' You know, 'I want to hear what you have to
say.' And he took my document and read it. He didn't
bring me a document or anything like that."

". . . when you wrote to Elder Bietz and he replied, . . .
did you know that he was . . . not only the Chairman of the
Board of Pacific Press, but also a Vice President of the
General Conference?" Dungan makes all this sound so
impressive, so important, as if these jobs with their titles
had been handed down from heaven on tablets of clay. It's
almost silly the mock reverence he puts into his voice.

"No I don't believe I knew that. I knew he was Chairman of the Board."

"Did you know he was an official of the General Conference?"

"I don't know all the officials at the General Conference."

He asks me a few more questions and then sits down.

John Rea rises to ask me more questions. My eyes follow the grain pattern in the wood in front of me. Over and over again they follow the swirling pattern. Little by little the horror of this day, of all that's taken place in this building, starts to seep into my consciousness.

I answer John's questions; but I'm beginning to feel crippled, raw, and dying inside.

John reviews the story of the Department of Labor's investigation. Once again I tell how the information given to the investigator was inaccurate, how I gave him photocopies of Max's and my W-2 forms, how shocked the investigator was at the discrepancy between our W2s and the figures supplied him by management.

As I concentrate on my words, I remember what I felt when the investigator told me he'd been kicked off Press grounds. I realize how devastated, how totally wiped out I am.

In answer to John's question I say, "Bohner had said [to the investigator], 'I'll see you in court.'... If they wouldn't even tell the truth to the government inspector and then they are saying to me, 'Be patient, ... we love you, be patient,' and they won't even tell the truth," my voice breaks.

In my head the words are roaring, "And they're still not telling the truth. Even now, even in court they lie. They'll never tell the truth. Never."

I start to sob and finish my answer saying, "If they won't even tell the truth, I felt, you know, where can I put my trust and my hope?"

I'm weeping in loud, sniffling sobs.

I'm crying and there's no tissues. And my nose always runs when I cry. And I never cry in public. And the whole courtroom is silent while I'm sniffling and sobbing and wishing I could fall through the floor and disappear.

"No further questions," John says softly.

I look at Dungan, sure that he'll come in for the kill now. I'm trying desperately to compose myself; but the more I think about it all, the more devastated I feel.

Dungan has no questions.

I look at the judge. He's all scrunched back in his chair, his eyes red as if he, too, is about to cry. He just looks at me. It seems forever in the silent courtroom, and I'm sniffling and trying to brush away my tears.

"You may step down," he says gently.

I sit down long enough to see Lorna recalled to the stand, but am too upset to remain. I go to the women's room and weep. I weep for all the lies that have been poured out in an unending attempt to legitimize discrimination. I weep for all the ladies at the Press and throughout the denomination who believe that these leaders have their best interest at heart. I weep for my childhood and youth, when I worshipfully admired the men in leadership positions and longed to have their dedication and commitment. Great hacking sobs fill the bathroom as I weep for my lost innocence.

I weep for all the devout Adventists who pour their tithes and offerings into church coffers, and with blind affection embrace and love and trust and cherish and obey the leaders of this denomination.

I weep for the end of an era — the era when I loved and believed in "the organization and the men leading it," when I longed with every fiber of my being to labor in "the work," for that special feeling of being "part of the family of God."

I cry until I am exhausted. Until I vomit. Until there are no more tears. And then, feeling totally spent, depleted, wasted, I go back to the courtroom. By then the session is over. People are leaving. Neal Wilson is shaking hands with everyone and saying good-bye. I want to take him aside for a moment to talk, but he has no time. He's on his way to pressing problems at Loma Linda University.

Joan and her husband and Lorna and I go to the lobby to discuss the day. Lorna says that the courtroom was filled with shame when I broke down.

I can't tell her that I was also filled with shame — and despair. That more than just my heart had broken this week. That Merikay Silver, as she had always been, full of hope and Adventism, is no more.

Note:   All testimony quoted here can be read complete and in courtroom-context in the trial transcripts of case: C-74-2025 CBR, Volume I.

## Friday, March 21, 1975

Today is closing argument time.

Unlike the first day with dozens of dignitaries from Washington, D.C., the local conference, and the Press — as well as all my friends and Kim and Marc and everyone — there are maybe ten people in the courtroom this morning.

No one from the Press or GC is here, except for the three attorneys — Dungan, Quirk, and Noland.

Judge Renfrew enters and proceedings begin.

During John Rea's closing arguments, he asks for preliminary injunction, as he has been asking throughout the trial. In part he says:

"... Defendants have conceded that the underlying policies which we seek to enforce in Title VII are the same as the doctrine which they describe in their terms as description of or on the basis of race, sex, color and national origin.

"On that point I believe we have no dispute.

"The question, then, is for an Adventist citizen: who is going to be her court, who is going to decide whether or not discrimination has occurred, what the class is, what the remedies are, what is the standard? ...

"It is easier to resolve this thing with the immediate question, which is ... that two people have come to this court seeking relief. They incurred the displeasure of their supervisors and displeasure at certain points turned into retaliation.

"... they are at the moment employees and are until further order of the court. We ask that having come to the court, and on behalf of their sister employees, that the questions of exemption be resolved in the Silver case and Tobler case informally, not by retaliation.

"What Defendants ask the court for is permission to walk out of the courtroom and fire Merikay Silver and Lorna Tobler.

"They would have been fired if they couldn't have come here for relief.

"Thank you, Your Honor."

Next it's Joan Bradford's turn. She reviews the Press' constantly shifting defense.

"The Defendant employer seems to be saying, 'We can

dismiss you from your employment because you persisted in litigation.' At one time they were saying, 'Because you commenced litigation,' but now it seems they say it is all right to commence but not to persist.

"What that really means is that you have no protection whatsoever under Title VII."

She reminds Renfrew that she placed into evidence 124 lawsuits between Adventists and Adventist institutions in San Bernardino Superior Court alone. And that ninety-eight of those cases were filed against Adventist institutions, and that all the plaintiffs in all those cases are still employees of the denomination, many still writing for denominational publications.

Then she talks about what would happen if Renfrew ruled in favor of the Press.

". . . if this court were to rule as Defendants are ascerting [sic], then the door of this court would be closed not only to appeals under Title VII, it would be closed to those employees who have the risk of moving into the EEOC, trying to find out if they have a right under Title VII, because the employee could then be terminated without the employer having to do anything but know that the court had closed its doors.

"I don't think that this court or any other court is going to close its doors to wage earners who make their livelihood out of their employment with an institution because that institution is a religious organization.

"Thank you, Your Honor."

Dungan makes his final argument:

". . . the whole case is about the fact that one who is a candidate for baptism in the Seventh-day Adventist church must be instructed concerning the organization of the church.

"One who is to be baptized in the baptismal vows must say that he recognizes the organization of the church. The official publication of the church which regulates church membership speaks of the organization of the church and, the necessity for following the five steps from the individual believer to the world wide organization. That's the church manual."

And then he goes over documents he handed Renfrew, which list the Press' contentions.

He makes the point that the Press is operated only for

denominational work, that all of its publications are intended to express and convey some facet of the Adventist organization.

That employees of Pacific Press have to be Adventists in good standing.

That I ignored years of patient, spiritual counsel, and determined to pursue litigation.

That the Adventist church structure is hierarchical.

That this is a case about church employment.

"The only thing left for me to comment upon is the hypotheticals which were posed by counsel for the intervenor Plaintiffs.

"The kind of wax-work parade of horrors of what is going to happen and that the doors of the Court would be closed to people if a First Amendment defense is recognized here.

"Of course, that is true. The rhetorical question was asked. Who is going to be her Court? The answer is, she has a choice. She can have this Court or the church. She can't have both.

". . . and what the First Amendment allows the Court to do is to look at the literature, doctrine, discipline of the church. Find out where, under the church's organization, authority lies. Find out what that authority says and that is the end of the matter.

"And, therefore, we should submit that the Motion for Preliminary Injunction should be denied."

Dungan goes back to his table.

Renfrew says, "There will be a brief recess, after which I will announce my ruling."

Joan rushes over, her face bleak and white. "If he's already made his decision, it's probably against us," she says.

I walk out into the hall with her and John and Lorna. Everybody concurs. They're all standing around with long faces, trying to figure out how they could have done better, what they could have said to convince Renfrew.

I feel crushed.

I go to the women's room and pray. I'm sure that God will let justice triumph. I can't believe that the judge will rule in favor of the Press' argument.

When we return to the courtroom, I keep praying.

Eventually Renfrew and his staff of clerks enter, and we're back in session.

Tension runs through me like an electrical current, from my feet through my skull.

Renfrew reads: "All right, Plaintiffs, and Plaintiffs-intervenors, this court orders to Defendant Pacific Press Publishing Association, its successors, agents, assignees, principals, assignors, and persons acting in concert with them, are: Temporarily restrained from terminating the employment of Lorna Tobler and Merikay Silver through March 6th, 1975, thereby causing immediate and irreparable injury to Equal Employment Opportunity Commission; temporarily restrained from failing to continue the employment of Lorna Tobler upon the same terms and conditions of employment, including but not limited to her pay, responsibility, job functions and participation in employee activities, as she enjoyed in the two weeks of employment preceding February 14, 1975; and temporarily restrained from failing to continue the employment of Merikay Silver upon the same terms and conditions of employment, including but not limited to her pay, responsibilities, job functions and participation in employee activities as she enjoyed in the two weeks of employment preceding February 14, 1975.

"Okay, that is all. Are there any questions?"

There are none.

He leaves the courtroom.

Everyone on our side is hugging and kissing.

The attorneys go back to the judge's chambers to set the trial date for Silver v. Pacific Press.

Joan returns to say that trial is set for October.

---

Note:   All testimony quoted here can be read complete and in courtroom context in the trial transcripts of case: C-74-2025 CBR, Volume I.

Closing arguments can be found on transcript pages 421-445.

## Good Friday, March 28, 1975

Joan calls while I'm at work. She says that the General Conference appealed Renfrew's decision the day after it was given. I am not surprised. All I'm doing now is trying to hang on until the trial is over. Just come to work each day and hold on.

Richard no longer speaks to me. Max is no longer available. I come here, do my work, go home, and hope October and the trial get here as quickly as possible.

It's Friday night, the hours of the Sabbath.

I didn't watch the sun go down tonight. The house isn't cleaned, and I don't feel calm and full of peace.

I'm mixed up — chaotic. Many emotions and ideas rush through me. I battle between the familiar traditions and beliefs of my past, and the new philosophies that will compose my future.

I think of other Friday nights — the vacuuming and dusting finished, the apartment fresh and expectant, my body bathed, my mind relaxed. I think of the quiet Friday nights spent listening to religious music or reading the Bible or some inspiring book by Ellen White.

The rest of the world was outside in the dark, honking its horn angrily at some old person who didn't move fast enough when the light turned green.

But tonight it's different for me.

Not because I don't believe in the Sabbath any more. I do. But something's different. I'm changing. For months I've been in the process of being rejected by those I thought loved me, those I thought were my family, my friends.

And in my own way, I suppose, I am also rejecting them. Not because I dislike them as people, but because I can no longer bear to be part of a corrupt and corrupting system — a system that destroys in the name of God, that grasps greedily instead of giving, that is profit-oriented rather than people-oriented.

A system that takes the name of Jesus, who freely gave love and healing to all, and uses that name to crush and break the weak.

I can't bear to be part of a system claiming such high standards yet practicing such extreme mistreatment of people.

Here it is, Friday night, the Sabbath. The time God set aside so I could meditate and study His word and be drawn close to Him.

Friday night. And the place is a mess with unfinished class assignments, and I don't even have any hymns on the stereo.

Tonight I'm lonely.

Instead of being intimately involved with "the church," growing close to the editors of its publishing houses and magazines, forming deep relationships with its ministers

and evangelists, sharing the ups and downs of life with
fellow church members, I feel empty — I no longer belong.

It's Sabbath, and I'm not out there honking at the old
person, for I have known the closeness of fellowship, the
secure warmth of community and a shared heritage, the
peace of knowing my group had "The Truth."

But I no longer know any of that, and I don't belong
anywhere any more.

The past, with its calm assurances, doesn't exist for me
now.

The future, with whatever changes will have solidified
me into a more complete person, has not yet arrived.

And the overwhelming fact that fills me tonight . . . is
loneliness.

## Thursday, April 3, 1975

Last night Elder Mills called. He said that his case was thrown out of court and all charges dropped because the little girl who supposedly told her mother he molested her won't repeat the charges to anyone. The mother says the little one told her, but the little girl doesn't say anything to anybody.

Elder Mills said he went to the police station and saw the records in his case. It appears that the president of his local, employing conference, the Northern California Conference, told the police that the conference and he would cooperate in any way necessary to secure Mills' conviction.

"They wanted to put me in prison," he says, his gentle voice shaking. "They *really wanted* to put me away!"

I asked if he would be resuming pastorship at Milpitas, and he said he didn't think he'd be allowed to.

Today I sit, editing manuscripts and thinking about Elder Mills — and Neal Wilson chilling the hallway of the courthouse. Every time I remember them walking down that long marble hall, Wilson's arm around Mills' shoulders, I shiver.

In the mail this morning I receive a letter from Jack Blacker.

April 3, 1975

Mrs. Merikay Silver
English Editorial Department

Dear Mrs. Silver:

On February 14, 1975, the General Conference Committee recorded an action recommending to the Pacific Press that you be terminated from employment. On February 19, 1975, the Executive Committee of the Pacific Press recorded an action that we support and implement the General Conference recommendation. On March 25, 1975, the United States District Court issued an order that the Pacific Press refrain from failing to continue your employment. The order included the statement that "nothing in this order shall be construed to limit Pacific Press Publishing Association in the exercise of its discretion in assigning editorial responsibilities."

Accordingly, the Executive Committee of the Pacific Press has exercised its discretion and recorded an action that removes you from membership on all of the publishing committees in which you have held membership heretofore. This action is effective immediately.

Very Sincerely yours,

W.J. Blacker
General Manager

I just finish Blacker's letter when there is a knock at my office door. Tulio Peverini, an editor from the Spanish Department, enters.

Tulio is young, maybe thirty-eight or thirty-nine years old. He's a handsome man with earnest brown eyes. I know he's come to counsel me.

He sits down and says he wants to talk about the lawsuit.

I don't know if he's been sent by management so that when we go to trial in October they can say I was counseled, or if he's here out of genuine personal concern; but I take a deep breath and try to relax. I can tell it's going to be a long afternoon.

"I am afraid you are in danger of losing your soul," he says.

I thank him for his concern and tell him that I sincerely hope I won't lose my soul, that I'm trusting Jesus Christ to hold me close.

"Drop the suit," he says. "You should drop this whole lawsuit. You should rather suffer injustice than go to court and bring shame to Christ's name."

"Tulio, it's not going to court that brings the shame," I say. "It's the illegal practices of the Press and the Press' insistence that we don't have to obey the law because we're religious that is shaming."

I can see my words pain him. And I am sorry for that.

"The leaders are ordained of God," he says to me.

"That doesn't mean all their actions are ordained of God," I say.

He shakes his head and his eyes fill with tears. I can see he is sincere, and I appreciate that. But he does not listen to me. Nor does he appear to consider what I say. He only stresses over and over again that I should let the good brethren decide what to do and how to do it.

For two hours he "reasons" with me. For two hours I feel the same frustration I've felt for years here at the Press — the frustration of ears closed to my experience, my reasoning, my facts.

Before he leaves, we kneel for prayer. I bow as he spends long minutes praying for my soul, praying that the Lord will soften my hard and stubborn heart, praying that before it is forever too late God will open my eyes to the terrible sin I am committing.

Shortly after Tulio leaves Richard enters.

He is in his yelling mode again. He only operates in two modes toward me any more — the silent and the yelling. He tells me I am wicked, disloyal, despicable, selfish. I am asking for things that are totally unreasonable and I will never win.

When I go home at the end of the day, my only regret is that this is Thursday, and I have to come back tomorrow.

## Thursday, April 10, 1975

I have nothing to do.

Richard has removed all my manuscripts and is giving me no new work.

He has told the art department to consult with him on all the books I've been guiding through to completion. From now on they won't discuss cover design, type faces, or anything else with me. He is taking over everything I've been working on.

I sit here in my office, reading books I've checked out from the Press library.

I sit here, writing my own free-lance stories and articles.

I sit here, thinking about the trial, about all the months of struggle, about all that has happened, all that has been said, all that has changed in my life.

## Monday, May 26, 1975

The ringing phone tears me from sleep. I turn on the light and see that it's almost midnight.

When I answer Lorna says, "I'm sorry to wake you up; but I just heard from Joan, and I thought you should know that the appeals court has granted Pacific Press a stay of injunction relief."

I rub my eyes, trying to wake up, wondering what that means. "Uh huh," I say. I sit up in bed and breathe deeply, trying to wake up. "Now what does that mean, 'a stay of injunction relief?' " I yawn.

"It means we're fired."

Suddenly I am wide-awake. "We're what? After that whole trial, we're what?"

"Joan said the appeals court stayed Renfrew's relief until after the Silver case. So we're out. It's just a matter of time until we get our notices."

Suddenly it's funny. "You don't think they'd keep us on, out of the goodness of their Christian, brotherly-loving hearts, do you?" I ask, starting to laugh. We both giggle. The tension is too strong not to laugh. We talk a few more minutes, and then hang up.

I call Kim in Seattle, waking him up, to break the news. I ask that he call Bob Ruskjer and tell him. We hang up.

Kim calls Lorna. Then he calls Bob Ruskjer. Bob calls Lorna, then me — at 1:00 a.m. He cracks one joke after another. I'm hooting with laughter. I need that release. We laugh and talk until 3:30 a.m.

When we hang up I am so relaxed and exhausted from all the laughing that I go right to sleep.

## Tuesday, May 27, 1975

It is hard coming to work today.

It is hard because I know I'm going to be fired. Difficult because I had so little sleep last night.

I spend the morning cleaning out my desk and files and cabinets.

I return the books I've been reading to the Press library. I gaze at the three-volume set of Paul Tillich's *Systematic Theology* that Max suggested I read. What a marvelous, inspiring set of books they are! How my mind soared while reading them.

Now I will not have the opportunity to read any more books from PPPA's library.

I return to my office and wait.

I wait all day but nothing happens.

It's confusing, frustrating, empty ... waiting to be fired.

## Wednesday, May 28, 1975

Nothing happens.

All day I sit in my empty office with nothing to do, waiting to be fired. And nothing happens.

Kim calls during the evening to see if we've been fired yet. He wants Lorna and me to come to Seattle for a visit as soon as we are fired.

Lorna is going to Germany to be with Gus.

I don't know what I'm going to do. Take a nap, probably — a *very* long nap.

## Thursday, May 29

Today I am axed.

Midmorning a young man from the Treasury Department brings my termination notice, effective immediately.

Along with the notice I receive a number of checks for vacation time, severence pay, etc. Altogether I have a little more than $2,000 to live on for a while.

I sit at my desk staring at the letter and the checks.

I came here forty-seven months ago with such glorious dreams, bursting with hope and joy, thrilled to be "in the work."

I think about those days of heady happiness.

The fun I used to have with Max and Richard, talking about upgrading PPPA books and getting them out to the public.

I think about how innocent I was when I asked Bohner for head-of-household allowance, how certain I was that he'd give it to me.

As I pack up the last scraps of personal belongings and take my keys over to Richard, I think about the decision I made so many months ago to fight for the principle of equality here — to "stand for right though the heavens fall."

Kim and I had talked about the possibility of losing my writing career.

Now as I walk to my car I think about the career I've lost, the job I've lost, the "friends" I've lost, the feeling of church-family unity I've lost, the trusting admiration of the leaders I've lost, the marriage I've lost.

Neither Kim nor I had any idea of all we would lose.

I've lost everything. Everything except my health and my life. Everything else is gone.

As I drive home I shake as though I'm freezing. I am shaking with feelings I cannot describe. I can't cry. I can't laugh.

I am relieved to be free of the Press.

I am enraged that I've been fired for insisting that Press management do what is morally and legally right.

Forty-seven months of hopes and dreams and excitement and disappointment and anger and triumph and failure and disillusionment.

Forty-seven months.

| | |
|---|---|
| July 1975 | Judge Charles Renfrew decertifies the class. Since I am no longer employed by Pacific Press, I cannot represent the other women working there. He says that individual women can sue for their rights or can choose to join the Silver case as plaintiff interveners. |
| May 1976 | Ninth Circuit Court of Appeals reverses Renfrew's decision for EEOC on technical, procedural grounds. The case is remanded to Renfrew who dismisses it. |
| August 1977 | EEOC files suit on behalf of Lorna Tobler. Suit is filed on retaliation and to recover head-of-household benefits for Tobler. |
| April 1978 | The Silver case settles out of court on the morning of trial. I settled for $60,000 (half went to the attorneys), a letter of recommendation which I could use when applying for work, and the guarantee of a clean slate at PPPA (all references to the suit, all derogatory remarks, etc., removed from personnel file). |
| May 1978 | EEOC files class action lawsuit against PPPA, based on the evidence accumulated during Silver case. |
| June 1978 | Lorna Tobler's trial takes place. Judge Renfrew hears final oral arguments. |
| December 1979 | Judge Renfrew is appointed to a post within the Justice Department by President Jimmy Carter. In light of his appointment, he must "clean up" his calendar in San Francisco and so hands down his ruling in the EEOC (Tobler) case. Renfrew rejects Press' claim that the government has no right to interfere with their employment practices. Judge rules against PPPA. |
| April 1980 | Pacific Press appeals Renfrew's ruling. |
| August 1981 | Judge Spencer Williams (who replaces Renfrew on this case) issues an opinion in favor of the EEOC's class action litigation. His ruling sweeps away the last procedural and technical |

barriers to restoration of wages, medical benefits, and special allowances to PPPA's women workers.

May 1982    Appeals court upholds Judge Renfrew's ruling in the Lorna Tobler (EEOC) case.

September 1982    After years of working in a hostile environment, being threatened again and again with dismissal, Max is phoned during the PPPA Board Meeting. The caller is PPPA general manager. "We've had a difficult day," the GM sighs, "We just had twenty-two names which we had to cut from the payroll."

Max asks, "Was my name on that list?"

"Yes, Max, I'm afraid it was," the general manager says. "Come to my office this evening and we'll meet together with the brethren to discuss your termination settlement."

PPPA paid Max six months' salary, and Max never returned to his office.

December 1982    The Ninth Circuit Court of Appeals orders the Northern California District Court to issue an order to Pacific Press to pay the judgment in the Tobler (EEOC) case.

February 1983    Lorna Tobler receives $77,000 from PPPA as back pay, front pay, fringe benefit differential, plus interest.

October 1983    Judge Spencer Williams enters his judgment, which requires PPPA to deposit more than $600,000 in a bank, to be disbursed in nontraceable checks to the women workers of the Press.

December 1983    More than $600,000 is distributed to eligible women workers and former workers of Pacific Press Publishing Association. The end, the successful end, of the case.

# After

*None should consent to be mere machines,*
*run by another man's mind.*
*God has given us ability to think and to act....*
*Stand in your God-given personality.*
*Be no other person's shadow.*

Ellen G. White
*Ministry of Healing*

THE PACIFIC PRESS TRAUMA MARKS THE GREAT DIVIDE OF MY life. Before the Press I was someone else, living in a different world, accepting norms and truths which diverge from the reality I experience today.

For years I tried to write this story and couldn't. The pain still rippled through me in waves of grief and sorrow and the words would not come. Then I met poet James Kavanaugh, a man who grew up in the same Kalamazoo, Michigan, as I. A man who also suffered enlightenment in a rigid religious system, and because of that, experienced rejection and expulsion from his world just as I had from mine.

Meeting him, reading his work, and realizing that his creative spirit had not been crushed, sparked renewal of my own creativity.

Thank you, Jim, for showing me that life continues even through death. Thank you for your gentleness, your humor, your patient ear.

## Change

Change and loss are pain-filled, shocking reminders that we are still alive. That we exist. They produce a quality of understanding that can be grasped in no other way, and in that fact they justify themselves.

If we do not permit the possibility of change — if we do not allow ourselves to question, to doubt, to challenge cherished assumptions, to consider a variety of viewpoints — we refuse the possibility for growth, courage, and the magic intensity of becoming.

I no longer belong to the church. I have been expelled through the wrenching birth of knowledge . . . knowledge I did not seek, but can never forget. I have emerged from the shattering experience a new person, with a renewed sense of purpose and hope.

After nearly two years of separation, Kim and I were divorced in July 1976; and I resumed my birth name: Merikay McLeod. I shall always be grateful for his initial support and encouragement. While the Press struggle tensions eventually destroyed our marriage, we are united in the belief that sex discrimination has no place in a society or organization which claims justice and morality as distinguishing characteristics.

We were young. We were idealistic. We fought the best fight we were capable of, and we paid dearly for our struggle.

**Freedom**

"Freedom's just another word for nothing left to lose," wrote Kris Kristofferson.

Today I am free, having been released suddenly and violently into a world that did not ask for me. Freedom can be very lonely, very frightening. But freedom also brings all possibilities within its reach. It opens all the doors, and life in its abundant variety rushes in.

Viktor E. Frankl writes in *Man's Search for Meaning*, ". . . everything can be taken from a man but one thing: the last of the human freedoms — to choose one's attitude in any given set of circumstances, to choose one's own way" (p. 104).

The Spirit of Christ and the spirit of church (as I have been forced to know it) are contradictory. Christ's spirit is free and giving, serving, creating, loving with no limits and no fears. That spirit is the one I choose and seek to emulate.

I am no longer the girl who wrote the story *NOW!* She is gone. In her place is a woman walking through life as wide-awake as possible. I welcome all that comes my way — the pain as well as the pleasure, the sorrow as well as the joy. For I know that life blends both, and to truly live I must experience it all. I choose to live as fully, as abundantly, as I can.

## Thinking

While an academy student, I heard a statement of Ellen White's quoted again and again. It was: "Be thinkers, not mere reflectors of other men's thoughts."

If we do not allow ourselves to think, to compare rhetoric with actions, if we do not contemplate truth, do not notice the reality between stated ideals and institutionalized policy, then we trap ourselves in a world of someone else's making.

Loren Eiseley, in his book *The Immense Journey*, talks about the difference between the brain structures of humans and insects.

"There is a mystery about those thickenings which culminate in the so-called solid brain," he writes. "It is the brain of insects, of the modern fishes, of some reptiles and all birds. Always it marks the appearance of elaborate patterns of instinct and the end of thought" (p. 53).

Failing to think, to reason, to examine, and draw our own conclusions, dooms us to the same instinctive reactions as solid-brained insects. Moral strength and nobility spring from thoughtful determination. Integrity has no meaning for robots, for the easily programmed automaton who will support whatever is "in" with the "men at the top."

## Apologies

I think of those who used to admire me and look to me as an example, and I apologize for any confusion my growth may cause you. But I cannot be your example. Only your friend. You must find your example within yourself and the heart of your Creator. Live your own life as only you can. May God draw close as you discover your own uniqueness, your own values.

I think of the teachers, the ministers and their wives who prayed for me through my childhood and youth, who cared for me, and who may now feel as though they somehow failed because I walk a different path from theirs.

May I assure you that your loving guidance was just what I needed at the time. Thank you. It is people like you who make this world a little easier to take.

I apologize for any pain this book may cause my family, although they have assured me they understand my growth. My parents, brother, and sister have been a continuing source of comfort and encouragement to me.

## Thank you

I could not have survived the Press years without the exquisite friendship and reinforcement of Lorna Tobler and Max Phillips.

Thank you, Lorna and Max. Your love, your mutual vision of a better world where both men and women are treated as equally-valued human beings, kept me alive. You will always flourish in my heart. I owe you more than I can express.

## And, with reservations . . .

And I suppose I should acknowledge Len Bohner, R.R. Bietz, Jack Blacker, and Neal C. Wilson, without whose unflagging persistence and iron clad determination this whole situation would not have gone on and on and on and on and on and on and on.

## What I have learned

People need tenderness more than they need challenge. We need love and understanding more than we need leadership or authority. Most of the time our needs go unacknowledged and unmet, within as well as outside the church.

I know what it feels like to be hated. I know rejection. I know pain and loneliness. But I also know the joy of discovery, the ecstasy of new beginnings.

I no longer have all the answers; but I revel in the questions, letting them stretch my mind beyond all limits. And I thrill at my momentary glimpses of reality.

A year or so after the Press fired me, my sixth grade church-school teacher phoned my mother and asked her to relay a message to me. She said that after nearly thirty-five years of teaching within the denominational school system, she was finally receiving a pay increase that would raise her income to equal that of men teachers.

"Tell Merikay that I know my raise is a direct result of her actions, and I want to thank her."

The sweetness of that "thank you" fills me still.

If I can leave you with anything, may I leave you with the joy of growth, with the hope of a better world in our lifetime, with the continual unfolding of a woman in the process of being created, with the courage to think for yourself and to act on your convictions. Never let anyone, any organization deny you your personhood, your equality, your integrity.

Change is inevitable. We will always exist in the midst of it. It is our choice whether we will be its victim or its architect.

# INDEX